Geir Lundestad

The American "Empire"

OTHER TITLES BY THE SAME AUTHOR:

The American Non-Policy Towards Eastern Europe 1943–1947: Universalism in an Area Not of Essential Interest to the United States (1978)

America, Scandinavia, and the Cold War, 1945–1949 (1980)

East, West, North, South: Major Developments in International Politics 1945–1986 (1986)

Geir Lundestad

The American "Empire"

and Other Studies of
US Foreign Policy in a
Comparative Perspective

Oxford
University Press

Norwegian
University Press

Norwegian University Press (Universitetsforlaget AS), 0608 Oslo 6
Distributed world-wide excluding Scandinavia by
Oxford University Press, Walton Street, Oxford OX2 6DP

London New York Toronto
Delhi Bombay Calcutta Madras Karachi
Kuala Lumpur Singapore Hong Kong Tokyo
Nairobi Dar es Salaam Cape Town
Melbourne Auckland

and associated companies in
Beirut Berlin Ibadam Mexico City Nicosia

British Library Cataloguing in Publishing Data
Lundestad, Geir *1945–*
    The American "empire" and other studies of US foreign policy in a comparative
perspective.
    1. United States. Foreign relations. Policies of government
    I. Title
    327.73

    ISBN 82-00-21093-6
    ISBN 82-00-21092-8 pbk

Cover: Ellen Larsen
Cover illustration: Tron Jensen

Printed in Norway
by A.s Verbum, Stavanger

Contents

Preface

In 1975 I published my first book on American foreign policy, *The American Non-Policy Towards Eastern Europe 1943–1947*. It was generally well received and on the whole I look back upon that first effort with considerable satisfaction. As the title indicates, the book focused on the American side. The relevant American source material seemed overwhelming to a newcomer in the field of American diplomatic history and I made little effort to put the American policy into a broader perspective. I did try to include something about local Eastern European inputs into Washington's policy, but too little was said about British policy and Soviet policy was for the most part relegated to a separate chapter at the very end of the book.

In my second book, *America, Scandinavia and the Cold War, 1945–1949* I was more concerned with the Scandinavian side than I had been with the Eastern European one in my first effort. I had begun to react against the one-dimensional picture presented by many US diplomatic historians, who tended to see not only American foreign policy as determined in and by the United States, but also the policies of many other countries. I felt a need to analyze the local input into Washington's policies and also to show the extent to which local factors determined the policy choices of the Scandinavian countries. My main regret now is that I did not go even further in this direction.

Yet, at the same time there could be no doubt that the two superpowers did exercise considerable influence on international events and developments. My first attempt to look at the overall influence of the superpowers in some depth and to balance superpower, regional, and local aspects was made in my third book, *East, West, North, South: Major Developments in International Politics 1945–1986*.

In the last few years I have been trying to analyze US foreign policy in a comparative perspective. This effort has resulted in several articles, some of which are included in this book. The first one—"Moralism, Presentism, Exceptionalism, Provincialism, and Other Extravagances in American Writings on the Early Cold War Years"—provides much of the justification, if there is any, for the book as a whole. "Uniqueness and Pendulum Swings in US Foreign Policy" is an attempt to deal explicitly with one of the most important characteristics of American foreign policy, the pendulum swings. In "The United States, Great Britain and the Origins of the Cold War in Eastern Europe" I have looked at *The American Non-Policy Towards Eastern Europe* again, and this time I have paid more attention to the British side than I did the first time around. This was done to provide at least some comparative background for the American policy.

"The American 'Empire' 1945–1990" is by far the longest piece in the book. The roots of this study go back some time. In April 1983 I presented a paper at a conference in Salzburg. The topic of the conference was "Reconstruction and the Restoration of Democracy: US–European Relations 1945–1952" and the title of my paper was "Empire by Invitation? The United States and Western Europe, 1945–1952." In September 1984 the somewhat revised conference paper was published in *The Society for Historians of American Foreign Relations Newsletter* and two years later another revised version, with the same title, was published in the *Journal of Peace Research*. I received many reactions to the two articles and in 1988–89, during my sabbatical from the University of Tromsø, I decided to revise the original study completely and to expand it substantially (and at least indirectly respond to the many points various critics of the articles had raised). A major part of this revision consisted of putting American policies into a more comparative perspective. As in the other pieces, the emphasis was to remain on the United States, but some basis of comparison was at least to be provided. The American "Empire" was the outcome of this process.

The Woodrow Wilson International Center in Washington, DC provided a most hospitable environment for my work on the American "Empire". At the Center, I am most grateful for the assistance provided particularly by its assistant director Sam Wells, by Robert Littwak of the International Security Program and by my research assistant Elizabeth W. Hofheinz. Among the fellows, I benefited especially from conversations with David French, Tim Lamperis, Charles Maier, William McNeill, Geoffrey Smith, and Akio Watanabe.

John Gaddis has provided inspiration and support throughout the years and I am pleased to recognize that fact on this occasion as well. I am also indebted to Michael Hogan and Melvyn Leffler for both intellectual and social reasons.

I am grateful to Teis Daniel Kjelling for having prepared the index so quickly and so cheerfully.

As always my warmest thanks go to my wife, Aase, and to our two boys, Erik and Helge. They accompanied me on some of my many trips across the Atlantic and they picked up the slack when I went alone (and there have been many other absences as well). Thanks, again.

1

Moralism, Presentism, Exceptionalism, Provincialism, and Other Extravagances in American Writings on the Early Cold War Years*

Americans traditionally have seen themselves as a unique people with a special mission in the world. While other states had interests, the United States had responsibilities. This idea has been expressed with rather striking force by presidents of different political persuasions. Just to mention some recent examples, John F. Kennedy referred to "our right to the moral leadership of this planet." Jimmy Carter came out strongly against *Realpolitik:* "a nation's domestic and foreign policies should be derived from the same standards of ethics, honesty and morality which are characteristic of the individual citizens of the nation . . . There is only one nation in the world which is capable of true leadership among the community of nations and that is the Unites States of America." Finally, the master of nationalist rhetoric, Ronald Reagan, again and again reaffirmed his basic creed, the "undeniable truth that America remains the greatest force for peace anywhere in the world today . . . The American dream lives—not only in the hearts and minds of our countrymen but in the hearts and minds of millions of the world's people in both free and oppressed societies who look to us for leadership. As long as that dream lives, as long

* This essay was originally prepared for a conference of the European Association for American Studies in West Berlin, 28–31 March 1988. For the changes I have since made, I acknowledge the assistance of Michael J. Hogan and the copy editor of *Diplomatic History*. I also thank the Woodrow Wilson Center in Washington, DC, for its technical and economic support and my research assistant there, Elizabeth W. Hofheinz, for her tireless efforts at the word processor. The essay was published in *Diplomatic History*, Fall 1989, Vol. 13, No. 4. It is published here in a slightly altered form.

as we continue to defend it, America has a future, and all mankind has a reason to hope."[1]

Such moralism and the belief in US exceptionalism constitute staples of American political rhetoric. In this essay I am going to argue that these two characteristics and their close relatives, presentism and provincialism, as well as some further extravagances, are found all too frequently in American *scholarly* writings, albeit in more diluted form. My examples will be drawn from the debate about the origins of the Cold War, although I fear that my charges also may hold true for other areas of scholarly interest. Of course, these points are not all entirely new. In fact, in recent issues of *Diplomatic History* Sally Marks referred to the "Europeanist" charge that "the practice of American diplomatic history is fundamentally isolationist" and Christopher Thorne accused American diplomatic historians of "ethnocentrism."[2]

I Moralism

"The more one broods about the Cold War, the more irrelevant the assessment of blame seems."[3] That line from Arthur M. Schlesinger, Jr., may seem rather self-evident, but nevertheless it is still true that *exactly* such a moral assessment of blame is a most important criterion in categorizing the various interpretations of the Cold War. Very few historians put all the blame on one side, but it is painfully clear where most of the blame goes.[4]

On the so-called traditionalist side, Schlesinger himself first analyzes the Cold War "as if it were the result of disagreements among national states," but then adds a few pages to show that it "could have been avoided only if the Soviet Union had not been possessed by convictions both of the infallibility of the communist word and the inevitability of the communist world . . . The most rational of American policies could hardly have averted the Cold War."[5] Most of the other traditionalists are equally emphatic that Stalin, the Soviet Union, or communism were primarily to blame.[6]

On the other side, among the rather diverse group of historians labeled revisionists, near unanimity prevails that the opposite is really true: Truman, possibly Roosevelt, at least the United States, or—this has been the preferred version—capitalism are guilty of having caused the Cold War. Among "hard" revisionists Gabriel Kolko combines determinism with moralism, a fairly normal if somewhat paradoxical position. He lashes out against the very term Cold War because "it minimizes the nature and causes of mankind's fate today, leading us to believe that conflict and violence are accidental rather than inevitable consequences of the objectives of American foreign policy and the imperatives it has imposed on movements of social transformation throughout the world."[7] The more moderate Lloyd Gardner, concurring with a view first put forward by that spiritual father of Cold War revisionism, William Appleman Williams, places the blame on the United States because, as the strongest power, it ought to have shown more understanding for Moscow's interests. "Responsibility for the way in which the Cold War developed, at least, belongs more to the United States," Gardner argues, because "at the end of the war it had much greater opportunity and far more options to influence the course of events than the Soviet Union, whose situation in victory was worse in some ways than that of the defeated countries."[8]

Since the early 1970s the initiative in the Cold War debate has been with a group of historians often called postrevisionists. The interaction between the United States and the Soviet Union is clearer with them than with the other two schools, but even they apparently feel that the guilty one—normally in the singular—has to be pointed out for all to see. In his pathbreaking *The United States and the Origins of the Cold War, 1941–1947*, John Lewis Gaddis is able to hold out against explicit blame-throwing until the two very last pages. Then even he succumbs. In a long paragraph beginning "if one must assign responsibility for the Cold War," and apparently one must, he ends by reversing Gardner's conclusion: Stalin's "absolute powers did give him more chances to surmount the internal restraints on his policy than were available to his democratic counterparts in the West."[9] In Daniel Yergin's version of postrevisionism the reader is left with the rather strong impression that if only the United States had adhered to his so-called Yalta axioms [seeing the Soviet Union as a "traditional Great Power"] and had not given in to the wicked ways of Riga [seeing it as a "world revolutionary state"], the Cold War might well have been averted, at least in the way we came to know it.[10]

Even the group of realist historians, which so strongly denounces the moralistic-legalistic tradition in American foreign policy, does not avoid at least indirect blame-throwing. Louis Halle,

who added so much to our understanding by stressing the importance of vacuums in creating international tension, quite clearly
did not see the two superpowers as equally bound by the laws of
physics. Vacuums had to be filled, but his combination of physics
and morality is evident even from one of his chapter headings:
"The creation, in 1945, of the power vacuums on either side of
Russia into which *it* tended to expand."[11] The Soviet Union expanded, not the United States. Only with the Truman Doctrine
and the Marshall Plan did the United States develop a response to
this Soviet expansion. On this point, then, the realists actually represent a special version of traditionalism.

II Presentism

British historian D.C. Watt has argued that "American historiography of the Cold War tells us very little of the Cold War, much of
intellectual history in the 1960s and 1970s."[12] Although Watt's
statement is an exaggeration, there is still sufficient truth in it to
raise some disturbing questions about the quality of historical
scholarship. Presentism, that is, history reflecting present political
purposes, is closely related to moralism. As with moralism, moreover, presentism has clearly been a strain in American writings on
the early Cold War years.

   Some of the leading traditionalist historians actually had been
involved in shaping the policies they analyzed. Herbert Feis held
jobs with the State Department and the War Department for
many years. The paradoxical side of this is that Feis was an economic expert who paid very little attention to the role of economic
factors in American foreign policy. The more obvious side is that
his positions within the Roosevelt and Truman administrations
probably strengthened his identification with the policies he analyzed. Traditionalists Martin F. Herz and Joseph M. Jones also
held policy positions.[13] Among the realists both Halle and George
Kennan had worked with the State Department. Schlesinger's
identification with the Roosevelt-Truman-Kennedy tradition
within the Democratic party has rarely been in doubt, although he
was not directly tied to the policies of the 1940s in the way these
others were. But presentism is not primarily a question of formal
ties. In the East-West atmosphere of the 1940s and 1950s it is easy
to see why not only official America but also most American

scholars regarded the Cold War as, in Schlesinger's words, "the brave and essential response of free men to communist aggression."[14]

Some scholars will break with the overall climate of the times; so also in this period. In *American-Russian Relations, 1781–1947* and much more fully in *The Tragedy of American Diplomacy*, William Appleman Williams attacked the scholarly consensus by arguing that an American Open Door policy had in fact threatened Soviet security interests.[15] But Williams's long remained an isolated voice.

There can be little doubt that the changing climate internationally and in the United States itself constituted the basis for the spread of Cold War revisionism on America's campuses. Consensus was out in the study of US history, as it was in American politics. Conflict was in. As Barton Bernstein argued in his 1969 introduction to the revisionist anthology *Politics and Policies of the Truman Administration*, "the breakdown of liberalism and the disastrous war in Vietnam compelled many Americans to reexamine the Cold War. Under the impact of these events, scholars and others are questioning anticommunism, the uses of national power, and the belief in national innocence."[16] If America was wrong about Vietnam, maybe it also had been wrong about the Cold War. So, from 1965 to the early 1970s a virtual flood of revisionist writings appeared. In late 1968, Walter LaFeber predicted that this time revisionism would stick. Not only that, "for the foreseeable future it now seems very likely that throughout the American diplomatic history profession such questions will be increasingly revisionist and radical in tone, and will construct a picture of American history that will move so far away from the Liberals that the present revisionists will be revised."[17]

The revisionists were indeed revised, but not in the direction LaFeber had predicted. The center held in politics as in American historical writings. While Gaddis in his *The United States and the Origins of the Cold War* undoubtedly had been influenced by revisionist writings, for instance in his analysis of the various instruments or levers Washington used to strengthen its position, the book is also an attack on Cold War revisionism. Gaddis in a way heralded an intellectual transition, away from revisionism but still attempting some sort of synthesis.

In Yergin's *Shattered Peace* we see more immediate political influences at work. The book is a defense of the détente of the 1970s. As Yergin himself writes: "History is shaped by the time in which it is written. This work was researched and executed during the latter years of the Vietnam War and the period of what might be called tentative détente." Yergin's conclusion was that "détente is not possible with a world revolutionary state, but it is with a more conventional imperialistic and somewhat cautions nation interested as much in protecting what it has as in extending its influence."[18] Adhering to the Riga axioms led to the Cold War and Vietnam; the Yalta axioms led to the cooperation of FDR and Nixon, to tentative détente.

A swing away from the more extreme forms of revisionism could be noticed within revisionists ranks. Although Diane Clemens's conclusion was standard revisionism, the main body of her book on Yalta represented a stimulating multinational analysis of the conference itself. Barton Bernstein moved from a relatively hard to a more moderate version of revisionism.[19] Thomas Paterson's development was perhaps most symptomatic of the changing balance in the scholarly debate on the origins of the Cold War. In his PhD dissertation of 1968 he wrote that "the wielding of American economic power in Eastern Europe, accompanied with repeated calls for political change, further aroused Soviet security fears, and served to encourage the formation of a Soviet bloc, which in 1945–46 Russia may not have planned or even desired."[20] Paterson toned down this kind of strong revisionism in *Soviet-American Confrontation* (1973), and in *On Every Front* (1979) he would appear to have placed himself at absolute dead center of the debate with practically all rough edges removed.[21]

A less dramatic movement toward the center could be noticed also on the traditionalist side. Schlesinger moved from spirited antirevisionism to condemnation of blame-throwing, although he had some difficulties in sticking to the latter position.[22] In Gaddis Smith's biography of Dean Acheson, published in 1972, there was a curious discrepancy between the rather middle-of-the-road main part of the book and the revisionist-inspired conclusion.[23] New names among the traditionalists were Lisle A. Rose, Lynn E. Davis, and, most strongly antirevisionist of these, Robert James Maddox.[24]

In a way the 1980s broke with earlier periods in that historical writings did not reflect the changing political climate in the same way that scholarship from earlier periods had done. Reaganism was difficult to detect among Cold War historians. David Horowitz provided the exception. In 1965 he had written a rather popular revisionist book. In 1986 he wrote a ringing defense for the contras in his "Nicaragua: A Speech to My Former Comrades on the Left."[25] Part of the explanation may be found in the (temporary) synthesis which postrevisionism represented, but the fact that scholarly interest now moved somewhat away from the early Cold War years probably contributed as well. The swing toward conservatism could be seen in the many reappraisals of President Eisenhower and in the attack on liberal and leftist writings on the Vietnam War. Here, in fact, the usual interpretive pattern of writings on World War I, World War II, and the Cold War was reversed. As Robert A. Divine has recently observed, "nearly all the early writers of Vietnam were highly critical of American intervention. As a result, when revisionism began in the later 1970s and early 1980s it came in the form of a belated justification for US policy, rather than the usual critique."[26]

III Exceptionalism

Politicians have provided the best examples of the belief in American exceptionalism. Again, most explicit of them all was Ronald Reagan when he argued that "I have always believed that this anointed land was set apart in an uncommon way, that a divine plan placed this great continent here between the oceans to be found by people from every corner of the earth who have a special love of faith and freedom."[27] Scholars rarely use such language. In fact, prominent American historians have repeatedly warned against the confines of a nationalist perspective. Yet, as Warren F. Kuehl argued in his SHAFR presidential address in 1985: "What seems to be lacking, despite repeated admonitions of the scholars we honor by electing them to presidential posts, is a conscious attempt to break the mental lockstep, to recognize the complexity of history, and to rise above self-imposed and limiting national perspectives."[28]

Most traditionalists, realists, revisionists, and postrevisionists do indeed tend to see America as unique. Some do this rather explicitly, others more implicitly. On the traditionalist side, Feis summed up Roosevelt's main concern in the words "the nations needed moral law and freedom."[29] We are led to believe that this rather unique attitude continued unchanged during Truman's administration. Traditionalists often see the United States as the moderator of British and Soviet policies, as trying to protect world cooperation and self-determination against the balance of power schemes of older and, presumably, more evil powers. William McNeill writes that Americans "felt no direct responsibility for European affairs except in Germany, and if their offer [to act as compromisers] failed to satisfy the Powers most directly concerned, there was little an honest broker could do but retire gracefully."[30]

Realists agreed that legalism-moralism had dominated Washington's policies, although they made it perfectly clear that they disliked this domination. As George Kennan wrote, "I see the most serious fault of our past policy formulation to lie in something that I might call the legalistic-moralistic approach to international problems. This approach runs like a red skein through our foreign policy of the last fifty years."[31]

Obviously, the revisionist approach is different. American foreign policy was not only misguided, as the realists thought, but some revisionists even appear to argue that in historical perspective it was evil. At one point Kolko writes that "there was nothing qualitatively unique" about the goals and tools of the United States, but he then goes on to state that "what was new was the vastly more destructive technology which now accompanied the expansion of states—of which the United States was both the most powerful and first after 1943—and the human consequences of international conflicts."[32] So, again, perhaps the United States becomes unique after all.

At least some of the revisionists, like the traditionalists, evidently think that under different circumstances the United States would have a mission to perform. The problem was that America's true values were corrupted by certain evil influences. These influences may have been a flawed president (Truman was certainly the favorite here, as the writings of D.F. Fleming and Gar Alperovitz demonstrate);[33] or some version of the military-industrial complex (as in the writings of Richard J. Barnet);[34] or, more frequently, the needs of the capitalist system.

In *The Tragedy of American Diplomacy,* Williams wrote that the main tragedy was the way in which sincere idealism had been subverted by ulterior forces, primarily the greed of capitalism and an overvaluation of power. America wanted to create a world in its own image. Although Williams states that this feeling may not have been "peculiar to Americans," the "scope and intensity" of the feeling probably was. Certain contradictions existed in American foreign policy, but Williams, who some have described as a determinist, then concludes that "if that aspect of the problem can be resolved, perhaps then it will be possible to evolve a program for helping other people that is closer to American ideals and also more effective in practice."[35]

As we have seen, postrevisionists are generally somewhat less moralistic than traditionalists and revisionists. Probably in part as a result of this, they also tend to see the United States as more of an ordinary power than do the other schools. Yet, Gaddis's emphasis on "the narrow range of alternatives open to American leaders" is the single theme which runs through his book. This limited range is the result of the democratic nature of the American political system: "The Russian dictator was immune from pressures of Congress, public opinion, or the press. Even ideology did not restrict him."[36] Yergin comes to a somewhat different conclusion in that he sees the "national security state" as the crucial factor in the development of the Cold War. But "as embedded as the national security state may be in our political and economic system, a national security state is even more firmly entrenched in the Soviet Union."[37] Thus, the United States could be more flexible than the Soviet Union, not less as Gaddis argued.

Although the works of American Cold War historians, no matter which school they represent, reveal explicit examples of a belief in US exceptionalism, the root of the problem can be traced to the methodology that dominates the profession in the United States. In their research and writing American diplomatic historians tend to analyze only US policies. They may make superficial references to the policies of other countries, particularly those of the Soviet Union, but they make few efforts to really compare American policies to those of other countries, and thus fail to explain what was so unique about them. In the universities, meanwhile, many history departments offer US diplomatic history as a separate field with rather limited regard for the policies of other powers. This sense of separateness was institutionalized on a national scale in the mid-1970s when members of SHAFR decisively rejected the idea of opening their association to all scholars of foreign policy.[38]

Christopher Thorne recently argued for changing SHAFR into the Society for United States Historians of International Relations and *Diplomatic History* into the *Review of International History*. In fact, he concluded his article by asking American diplomatic historians the provocative questions: "would you have anything to lose but your national, cultural, and disciplinary provincialism?"[39] There are more high-quality specialists on more topics in the United States than anywhere else, but it sometimes appears that the American specialist, the Soviet specialist, and the Europeanist on the same campus actually live in worlds largely isolated from each other.

The twin facts of American historians being so numerous and the material first made available being so overwhelmingly American are important explanations for the concentration on the United States even in the international debate on the origins of the Cold War. With archives in Western Europe also being opened up, we have already seen some signs of a change in emphasis. In fact, some have gone overboard in promoting new material and new interpretations, a sort of sensationalism often found in American writings, including those on the Cold War. Thus, John Gimbel, one of those who cannot easily be fitted into any of the schools mentioned and impressively knowledgeable in certain German developments, dramatically oversold his fine study of US-French-German relations in 1946–47 by calling it *The Origins of the Marshall Plan,* a much wider topic of which his story constitutes only one part.[40] When Fraser J. Harbutt, a traditionalist in sympathies, argued in *The Iron Curtain* that "Churchill was the pivot on which the whole process turned, acting successively on . . . Truman, American public opinion, and Stalin," this again was too much of a good thing.[41]

IV Provincialism

British political scientist Denis W. Brogan has pointed to the historical American "illusion of omnipotence" and defined it as "the illusion that any situation which distresses or endangers the United States can only exist because some Americans have been fools or knaves."[42] The classic example is McCarthy's accusation that China was lost because of the presence in the State Department of certain Communist sympathizers, as if America somehow could dictate events in the most populous country in the world. A somewhat less dramatic example, but from a different end of the political spectrum, can be found in works by Warren Cohen and Nancy Tucker. Even more clear-cut was William H. Chafe's conclusion in his textbook, *Unfinished Journey,* that "American officials rejected the opportunity to turn China into an independent Tito-like state."[43] If only Washington had chosen another course, Mao would have become another Tito.

Sally Marks has referred to the charge that American diplomatic historians see "American foreign policy as exclusively determined in and by the United States."[44] My point would rather be that American historians frequently see not only American foreign policy as determined in and by the United States but also the policies of other countries. The belief in the capacity of the United States to determine events in different parts of the world can be called American provincialism. Again, stronger or weaker versions of such provincialism can be found in the writings of all the Cold War schools.

Thus, on the traditionalist side, the Truman Doctrine and the Marshall Plan are often seen as American initiatives which practically single-handedly saved Western Europe from communism. In *The Fifteen Weeks,* Joseph M. Jones writes that the period from 21 February to 5 June 1947 suggests "not the limits but the infinite possibilities of influencing the policies, attitudes and actions of other countries by statesmanship in Washington." The United States stopped the advance of communism and brought about Western European integration and Atlantic defense cooperation.[45] Harry Bayard Price is almost equally ebullient in his analysis of the Marshall Plan, while realist Halle and traditionalist Feis provide more moderate variations on the same theme.[46]

Revisionist analyses of the origins of the North Atlantic Treaty Organization (NATO) probably provide the best example of provincialism. With some exceptions, as in most of the cases I deal with, the revisionist perspective is generally one of Washington thrusting itself into Europe to extend its influence. Little or nothing is said even by "soft" revisionists about the extent to which the Western Europeans actively encouraged the Americans to take a more active interest in their affairs. In sweeping terms LaFeber states that "now that the Marshall Plan was reviving Europe economically, the United States, in the full splendor of its postwar power, was attempting to strengthen its ties with, and influence over, Europe by creating military institutions which could provide fresh channels for American aid and policies."[47] On this point Gabriel Kolko is in fact more attuned to the policies of the Western Europeans, although he sees their desire for American military support as related to the danger of a resurgent Germany, while the United States desired to "strengthen Western Europe's ability to cope with internal revolt as well as to sustain a psychological mood of anti-Soviet tension that the administration thought functional."[48]

A postrevisionist interpretation of a more peculiar provincialist kind appears in Stephen E. Ambrose's *Rise to Globalism*. On the one hand, Ambrose apparently agrees both that the Soviets posed a threat to Western Europe and that the Europeans actively sought to involve Washington in their affairs. On the other hand, he appears to go even further than many revisionists when he argues that the objective of the United States in entering the NATO alliance was that "Europe would become, for the American businessman, soldier, and foreign policy maker, another Latin America."[49] Presumably Western Europe would now be as firmly subjected to Washington's domination as Latin America had been.

Daniel Yergin's version of provincialism is most evident in his apparent belief that if only the United States had stuck to the Yalta axioms, the Cold War could have been avoided.[50] Postrevisionist helmsman John Gaddis is much too good a historian to believe in single-factor explanations, yet he too focuses on the domestic scene. He argues that revisionists were right to emphasize the importance of internal constraints, but "they have defined them too narrowly: by focusing so heavily on economics, they neglect the profound impact of the domestic political system on the conduct of American foreign policy."[51]

There were certainly important domestic constraints, but an equally valid criticism of the revisionists would have been that they also underestimate the external constraints and influences. In my book, *America, Scandinavia, and the Cold War, 1945–1949,* I tried to show that in their very few comments on US-Scandinavian relations, American historians of various persuasions in fact agreed that the United States determined the alliance choice of the Scandinavians in 1948–49. My own findings, however, led me to the conclusion that while American influence was important, many different "local" factors were more crucial.[52]

Provincialism is not limited to the Cold War debate. It is found in many other fields of both scholarly and political debate. In *Inevitable Revolutions: The United States in Central America,* Walter LaFeber shows that it is possible to exaggerate American influence even where Washington undoubtedly did count for more than in most other regions.[53] The American literature on the Vietnam War is dominated by the American experience, while all kinds of local factors have not received anything like their due attention.[54] In the political debate the left probably exaggerates Washington's ability to determine events in Israel and South Africa, while on the right Ronald Reagan provided examples of provincialism when he made his predecessor responsible for the overthrow of the shah in Iran and of Somoza in Nicaragua.

V Comments on Some European Contributions

So, most American Cold War historians will probably have to be found guilty of the cardinal sins of moralism, presentism, exceptionalism, and provincialism. But the harshness of the sentence must depend in part on the extent to which these sins are uniquely American. On this point I shall do no more than to start the process of comparison and offer a few comments on Western European writings on the Cold War, however broad the term "Western European."

It is a simple task to demonstrate that many European historians have followed their American counterparts in being preoccupied with the moralist problem of who was to blame for the Cold War. A whole string of prominent Europeans has written in a traditionalist spirit at least as pronounced as on the American side. In France, André Fontaine and Raymond Aron could be mentioned as examples; in Britain, Desmond Donnelly, Wilfrid Knapp, John Wheeler-Bennett and Anthony Nicholls, Roy Douglas, Victor Rothwell, and even Alan Bullock.[55] The British tradition has been particularly obvious on this point. To provide only the most recent example, Hugh Thomas argues in *Armed Truce* that "the prime cause of conflict" was the "ideology of the Soviet leaders." The second cause, in his opinion, was "the Soviet desire for security against a third German invasion, which could be obtained only at the cost of insecurity, and lack of independence for their scarcely disposable neighbours."[56] Evidently the Russians were to blame for the Cold War.

One difference between the debates in the United States and in Western Europe on the origins of the Cold War would seem to be the weak impact of revisionism on scholars in Europe. Revisionists certainly exist in Europe too. Claude Julien provided one prominent example with *L'empire américain*.[57] But most European Cold War historians clearly continued to think that the Soviets were primarily to blame and probably saw revisionism as just another example of American moralistic self-flagellation, or as another swing of the pendulum so characteristic both of American foreign policy and of American scholarship. Postrevisionism developed adherents in Europe, but this would seem to be an even more mixed group in Europe than in America. Here we could possibly include Germans Wilfried Loth (although leaning toward revisionism) and even Ernst Nolte (leaning toward traditionalism). I also count myself among the postrevisionists.[58]

Thus, while moralism has been strong in Europe too, presentism has taken a different and less pronounced form. A closer study of various national scenes could reveal interesting differences of which I am at present unaware. But certainly in Norway and Sweden, the countries with which I am most familiar, traditionalism dominated historical writings at least until the early 1970s. Revisionism never really caught on.[59]

Europeans have tended to be skeptical about American claims to uniqueness. To many Europeans, what was unique about America was its uncanny ability to make the most inspiring idealism coincide almost perfectly with rather ordinary national objectives. As that great friend of the United States, Winston Churchill, put it in 1945 after listening to yet another American sermon on the evils of international power politics: "Is having a Navy twice as strong as any other 'power politics'? Is having an overwhelming Air Force, with bases all over the world, 'power politics'? Is having all the gold in the world buried in a cavern 'power politics'? If not, what is 'power politics'?"[60]

Most Europeans reacted rather negatively when events in Europe, as in other parts of the world, were seen as primarily determined in Washington. Locals tend to insist on the importance of the local scene, unless, of course, the outcome is unfavorable.

Then it is convenient to blame outsiders; the CIA is a particular favorite in many different parts of the world.

In correcting the emphasis on America's role, the pendulum could swing far out in Europe too. After all, America often did exercise considerable influence. British historian Alan Milward's stimulating *The Reconstruction of Western Europe, 1945–51* could be seen as an example of this kind of excessive swing. On the economic side Milward argued that the problem in Western Europe in 1947 was simply a payments crisis brought about by the success of European recovery. On the political side he sees the Payments Union and the Coal and Steel Community as independent, even anti-American initiatives.[61] I would argue that a payments crisis was no small thing and that the fitting of Germany first into a Western economic framework and then into a military alliance was premised upon an American leadership role in Western Europe.[62]

Instances of European provincialism abound. The British dwell on the famous Roman-Greek comparison, with the Americans providing the money and the British allegedly the brains within the Atlantic Alliance.[63] The French are incessantly preoccupied with the grandeur of France. Even small countries frequently have vastly exaggerated views of the role they can play. The Netherlands, Greece, and Norway are not even *moral* superpowers.

VI A Note of Admiration

There are many reasons why American historians have dominated the debate on the origins of the Cold War. The United States is a vast country with many excellent universities. The United States was, with the Soviet Union, the most important actor on the international scene. The sources were first and most abundantly made available in America. But, just to correct any misunderstandings, also the best analyses of the Cold War have generally been made there. The European debate to a large extent has simply reflected views often originating and being most persuasively argued in the United States.

I must express my particular admiration for William McNeill. In 1953 he published *America, Britain & Russia: Their Cooperation and Conflict, 1941–1946,* which, although moderately traditionalist in tone, is even by today's standards a rich, wise, and balanced book. McNeill is not preoccupied with the question of who was to blame for the Cold War; he pays more attention not only to Soviet but also to British policies than most later American historians have done; he often sees the importance of the local scene; and he weighs the influence of military, political, and economic factors. All this becomes the more impressive when one keeps in mind that the book was actually written in London during the Korean War and was based on much more limited sources than those available to the scholars of the 1970s and 1980s. Perhaps McNeill himself captures a major reason for his achievement when he explains how he avoided much of the partisanship so characteristic of Cold War writings: "An American, living in a foreign land, isolated in large degree from currents of feeling running strong in the United States, but unable all at once to share the concerns and perturbations of British public life was, therefore, in a position to rework the immediate past without being much affected by the postwar passions and fears that were, and are, so strong."[64]

Only in 1972, with the publication of Gaddis's monograph on the origins of the Cold War, did a book appear which could rival McNeill's. Gaddis's sources were much richer than McNeill's; Gaddis was able to draw upon the vast literature, however unsatisfactory, of the two decades between McNeill's and his own work. Yet, Gaddis's perspective was also more America-oriented than McNeill's. I fear that one reason McNeill's book has not received even more attention is that it would be rather depressing for later historians to admit that they have been able to add relatively little to a work of the early 1950s.

VII What is to Be Done?

Enter Norwegian moralism: How, then, can we avoid the cardinal sins I have tried to outline in somewhat exaggerated form in this essay? Most likely, they can never be eradicated, but we should manage to be less extravagant in our transgressions. Historians are trained, or at least I happen to think that they ought to be trained, primarily to analyze what happened and why certain developments took place. Although it is impossible to refrain entirely from moral judgments in performing these tasks, the search for the "guilty" person, country, or system turns our attention away from both the crucial and the most interesting questions of history, questions which we, if we have the right qualities, can answer with some degree of accuracy. In short, we should still follow Ranke and ask "What happened?" and try to stay away from Acton's "What went wrong?"

Nor can presentism be rooted out. As Arthur Schlesinger, Jr., has argued, "the historian, like everyone else, is forever trapped in the egocentric predicament, and presentism is his original sin." History without any sort of reference to present concerns may even lead us into irrelevance. But, as Schlesinger also writes, very sensibly, although the historian can never quite succeed, "his professional obligation is to strive to transcend the present."[65] Some have succeeded better than others; some interpretations last longer than others. As McNeill has argued, "a work that achieves a modicum of detachment is likely to age better than others, since it does not necessarily become naive or antiquated at the moment when a particular cause fades from current relevance."[66]

In a study of American writings on the emergence of the United States as a great power in the 1890s and the American interventions in the two world wars, Ernest R. May concluded that "those historians who concerned themselves exclusively with American events tended also to be those who were on the hunt for villains. Those viewing occurrences from more than one perspective were less interested in alleging mistakes and apportioning blame." In other words, in these three cases May found a linkage between exceptionalism/provincialism—he called it parochialism—and Actonism.[67] This linkage would seem to hold true also for American writings on the Cold War, with the addition that here, to a greater or lesser extent, practically all the historians succumbed to an America-dominated perspective and to blame-throwing.

We understand through comparison. For instance, we should not take it for granted that America was "special" or that it was not special, for that matter. We need to know much more about the concrete ways in which America was special, and the ways in which it was not. We only know after we have made certain comparisons with other countries. A better grasp of how and why other states pursued the policies they did adds to our understanding also of what characterized American policies. Just to mention the obvious example of Vietnam, Secretary of Defense Robert McNamara was right: The United States had many more helicopters than the French. And the Joint Chiefs of Staff representative was right: "The French also tried to build the Panama Canal."[68] In other respects the French and American experiences were to prove similar.

Such comparisons are difficult. They may lead to high levels of abstraction. One example is provided in the writings of Charles S. Maier, a historian who is more familiar than most with the histories both of America and of several European countries. In his celebrated article, "The Two Postwar Eras and the Conditions for Stability in Twentieth-Century Western Europe," he refers to "elites superintending Western society" over half a century—a concept that boggles my mind, at least.[69] There were many different elites in many different societies. To compare means to study differences as well as similarities.

Although parts of Michael J. Hogan's *The Marshall Plan* elaborate corporative ideas similar to those in the works by Maier and other "New School" historians, Hogan, like Maier, nevertheless represents a stimulating comparative approach.[70] Bruce R. Kuniholm's *The Origins of the Cold War in the Near East* and James Edward Miller's *The United States and Italy* could also be mentioned in this context. Kuniholm and Miller are more traditionalist than Hogan; they are also less ambitious. But all three try in varying degrees to balance American, British, and even "local" perspectives.[71] Further removed from the origins of the Cold War, interesting American-British comparative studies have been done by Christopher Thorne, William Roger Louis, D.C. Watt, and Tony Smith, among others.[72] In my own articles, "Empire by Invitation? The United States and Western Europe, 1945–1952" and "Uniqueness and Pendulum Swings in U.S. Foreign Policy," I tried to relate the American experience to that of other countries, but again the problems involved in using a term such as "empire" are obvious.[73]

As far as provincialism is concerned, the main problem lies in striking the right balance between the many cases where the United States did exert great influence (for instance, the economic and political reconstruction of Germany and Japan and their integration into wider economic and military systems) and the many cases where the limits of America's power were so clearly illustrated (Eastern Europe and China; later Vietnam, Iran, Nicaragua, and Lebanon). My pleas, then, are for less moralism and presentism and for more comparison and attention to the interplay between international and local factors. These points ought really to be largely self-evident for scholars of international relations. Nevertheless, as we have seen, we still have quite some distance to go.

In fact, I think it is high time for scholars even of the American domestic scene, or any other domestic scene for that matter, to become much more interested in comparisons. What elements in a national history are to be analyzed? How are they to be analyzed? Such questions can be answered on the basis of a comparison with earlier periods in that country's national history, but in many cases it would be even more fruitful to make the comparison with the relevant period in the history of another country.[74] The benefits already derived from the comparative study of slavery could be mentioned in this context. Those who lay claim to uniqueness should be particularly eager to test their views against the histories of other countries.

To use a paradox, the study of American foreign policy should focus less on America. Instead, more attention should be paid to the many complex "local" factors which in different ways influenced Washington's policies and/or helped determine the outcome of the events we are studying. Foreign policy is policy toward some other country. We, the non-Americans, can, as a minimum, be the experts on the "receiving end." Even more important, we can help in making relevant comparisons between America's policies and the policies of other countries to find out exactly what, if anything, was so special about Washington's actions and attitudes. Perhaps it is impossible for Americans to do all this. That would in a way be rather comforting for us moralist, presentist, nationalist, and provincialist foreigners. At least our nationalism and provincialism may provide a counterweight to American exceptionalism and provincialism.

Thus, foreigners may have something to contribute to the study of US foreign relations, perhaps not so much by aping the Americans, but more by insisting on our separateness. There would seem to be not only room but also a great need for non-American contributions. If the study of America's foreign relations is to be made more international, Americans and non-Americans have to work together toward the common goal of greater understanding.

2

The American "Empire" 1945–1990*

1945 – Early 1960s:
The Heyday of the American "Empire"

I Introduction

In the vast literature on American diplomacy after 1945 studies
abound of various aspects of American diplomacy in rather short
periods and toward specific countries; quite a few can be found
also of American diplomacy in general. Few efforts have been
made to bring together the American and various "local" experiences in a comprehensive way. This is such an effort.

I shall deal with two basic questions. First, what were the main
characteristics of the overall American role after the Second
World War? Second, more particularly, what was the nature of
the relationship between the United States and the countries
within its "empire"? So, this study will focus upon America's military, political, and economic position and on certain international
responses to this position. I shall not deal explicitly with either the
motives of American foreign policy or the political process inside
the United States.

In brief, I shall argue two main points. First, in absolute and
clearly also in relative terms, the United States emerged in 1945 as
the strongest power in centuries. Its tremendous lead over other
Great Powers provided the basis for an expansion which was more
comprehensive than that of the Soviet Union and in important respects also more comprehensive than that of Britain in the 19th
century. It can in fact be argued that the United States created its

* Much of the work for this study was done during the academic year 1988–89
when I stayed at the Woodrow Wilson Center in Washington, DC. I thank the
Center for its intellectual, economic, and technical support. I also thank my research assistant there, Elizabeth W. Hofheinz, for the many duties she performed.

own version of "empire." One distinguishing characteristic of this "empire" was that it was informal; it resembled the informal parts of the British Empire. In key areas one could talk of the United States actually being invited to play the role it did. This is what I have earlier called "empire by invitation."[1]

Second, starting in the 1960s it became obvious that America's relative strength was declining and its influence receding somewhat. In its heyday (1945–early 1960s) the United States had suffered defeats in Eastern Europe—the Soviet backyard—and China—the world's most populous country. Now it suffered an increasing number of setbacks and outright defeats in many different regions. In part this reflected the fact that the balance between superpower and "local" force was changing in favor of the latter. In America's relations with its allies the emphasis shifted somewhat away from invitational and cooperative arrangements against the Soviet enemy to trilateral economic disputes among the more troubled America, an increasingly integrated Western Europe, and a Japan which now had probably the second largest economy in the world. Yet, even in 1990 the United States was still clearly number one among the world's countries, with no clear successor state in sight.

If this study attempts anything, then it is to try to draw together elements which are generally analyzed separately. First, despite being an historian, I have benefited greatly from readings in political economy and political science. My analyses will draw upon insights from these fields. In the social science tradition, my analysis will focus on broad long-term developments. One of my hopes is that this study will further stimulate the dialogue across discipline boundaries. Second, I shall attempt to integrate security, political, and economic aspects. Top policymakers dealt with them as an integrated whole and developments in one area certainly impinged on developments in the others. Academics cannot pretend otherwise if they want to develop any sort of synthesis of the post-war years. (Cultural aspects also belong here, but unfortunately that is a vast and treacherous area of its own.) Third, although my emphasis is certainly on the American role, I believe in the importance of comparative research. Too much of American Cold War research has been rather exclusively America-oriented.[2] To some extent this study will compare characteristics in American foreign policy with the Soviet position, also after the Second World War, and with the British role in the 19th century. And, as already mentioned, the American experience has to be related to "local" experiences within the American "empire."

II The Debate about America's Rise

The debate about America's rise in the world after the Second World War has been carried out within two different scholarly communities. The historians have been concerned primarily with the origins of the Cold War, while the political economists have focused on what they have called American "hegemony." The two communities have had very little contact and within the one it is rare indeed to find anything but the most superficial references to works from the other. This may reflect the difference in perspectives, including chronological ones, between historians and social scientists, with the historians analyzing the first few years after the Second World War and the social scientists broader structural developments. In addition, many, but not all, of the historians deal almost exclusively with military and political issues, while the political economists are similarly single-minded in their pursuit of economic ones. Thus, Cold War traditionalists barely mention economic interests in discussing the motive powers of US foreign policy while political economists almost entirely leave out even the existence of organizations like NATO and the implications security considerations had on economic developments.[3]

In the Cold War debate traditionalists emphasize Soviet expansion. In Herbert Feis's words, during the Second World War the Russians under Stalin "were trying not only to extend their boundaries and their control over neighboring states but also beginning to revert to their revolutionary effort throughout the world. Within the next few years this was to break the coalition . . ." To the extent this phenomenon is dealt with at all, traditionalists tend to see America's rise largely as a response to the Soviet/Communist challenge. Their writings project an image of American slowness in responding to this challenge. They tend to focus on America's weaknesses, such as the comprehensive demobilization after the war, and on Washington's unwillingness to use whatever strength it possessed. Little is said about the organization of the "free world." America's leadership is taken for granted and this leadership is exercised to defend common security interests. Thus, in a somewhat extreme traditionalist version, under the Marshall Plan economic instruments are "employed solely in support of mutually agreed principles and objectives."[4]

Cold War revisionists, on the other hand, like to point to America's expansion and to its comprehensive economic objectives. These collided not only with Soviet, but also with British objectives and those of the political left in general. In mirror-imaging the traditionalists they tend to blame primarily the United States for the Cold War, because, in Lloyd Gardner's words, "At the end of the war it had much greater opportunity and far more options to influence the course of events than did the Soviet Union, whose situation in victory was worse in some ways than that of the defeated countries." Often the Soviet Union is seen as largely responding to very ambitious American objectives. Washington's organization of the "free world" could be rather harsh. In Gabriel Kolko's extreme version, the US "ruled together with England in the West with an iron hand, [while] the United States called for free elections and self-rule in Eastern Europe."[5]

Postrevisionists are found somewhere in the middle of this continuum, but postrevisionist helmsman John Lewis Gaddis tends to lean to the traditionalist side in his emphasis both on Soviet expansion and on the restraints on America's power, however vast. Again, the world is dominated by the two superpowers. American leadership of the West is taken rather for granted. Common interests are more or less assumed on the Western side. Little is said directly about the relationship between the United States and other powers, even Britain.[6]

In some ways the world of the political economists resembles that of the revisionists. They stress both the economic side and American leadership. Most political economists see the period from 1945 and into the 1960s as one of American "hegemony." The United States took over the role Britain had played until 1914, while the interwar years are seen as "the interregnum between British and American leadership." Contrary to the revisionists, however, the political economists tend to focus rather exclusively on relations within the American-dominated Western system and as a consequence even Robert Gilpin, who is more interested in the security dimension than most political economists, writes that "The United States emerged from the Second World War as the dominant or hegemonic economic and military power in the international system. This *unchallenged* [my emphasis] American preeminence was partially due to the wartime destruction of other individual economies."[7] Next to nothing is said about the communist-dominated world, since it played such a limited role in international finance and commerce. There is only one international system, the economic one, and within that system the United States was the undisputed leader.

The writers of the corporatist school provide a bridge between history and political economy in that they are historians focusing on the early Cold War years, but are primarily interested in the organization of the Western side. And indeed the analyses of Charles Maier and Michael Hogan in particular have influenced my own work. Yet, in addition to the often sweeping nature of their overall corporatist framework, they too tend to be rather preoccupied with the economic side at the expense of the security dimension.[8] Historian Paul Kennedy, too, combines many different elements in his magisterial presentation *The Rise and Fall of the Great Powers*, but, as we shall later see, he is really much more concerned with America's relative fall than with the nature of America's expansion and influence in its heyday after 1945.[9]

III The International Environment

Major wars often transfer the mantle of leadership from one country to another. Some powers are defeated; sometimes the winners spend so much of their strength that even victory leads to decline. The wars of Louis XIV (1672–1713) resulted in the partial defeat of France and speeded up the decline of the Netherlands. Britain was the big winner. Britain's rise to power was to lead to the first British Empire, which was considerably strengthened by the outcome of the Seven Years' War (1756–63). The Revolutionary and Napoleonic wars (1792–1815) ended France's attempts at European domination and marked the beginning of the second British Empire. The First World War (1914–18) signalled changes which were brought to fruition in the Second World War (1939–45).[10]

The Second World War was by far the most destructive and violent conflict the modern world had witnessed. The changes in the international system were also dramatic. The surrender of Germany was unconditional. Germany lost more territory now than after the First World War. It was to be (temporarily) divided into four zones of occupation. Japan was permitted to keep the Emperor, but was still to surrender "unconditionally." It lost all its acquisitions since 1854. The defeats of Germany and Japan were to create giant vacuums in Central Europe and in the Western Pacific–East Asia, vacuums of a size the modern world had never seen before. Although politics is not physics, vacuums of such a size in such crucial areas had to be filled.[11]

The old and largely Euro-dominated world of Great Power politics collapsed. In many ways Britain had the most distinguished war record of any power. Yet, it was broke, and the sorry state of the British economy was an important factor behind the British retreat in the early years after the war, from India–Pakistan, from Palestine, from Greece–Turkey. Britain became economically and militarily dependent on the United States. France's prestige had collapsed with its defeat in 1940. It was not even present at Yalta and Potsdam. It was given a zone of occupation in Germany only because Churchill wanted it to have one and Roosevelt and Stalin did not really care. China was given a seat on the UN Security Council largely because Roosevelt insisted. China was the "faggot vote" of the US, as Churchill called it. China had tremendous potential for the future; in the short term it was to be ravaged by civil war.

Japan's victories in the early phase of the Second World War stimulated the independence movements in Asia. Starting with India–Pakistan in 1946–47, colonial rule in Asia was to be almost entirely abandoned within a decade. Few, if any, policymakers thought that Asia's independence would have many consequences in Africa. Within another decade, however, most of Africa was free as well. The end of colonialism was to create new vacuums. As Under-Secretary of State George Ball argued in March 1965, "One cannot dismantle a vast and highly developed power structure such as prewar colonialism in the brief period of a quarter century without creating power vacuums and power dislocations of major dimensions."[12]

The vacuums created first in Central Europe and Western Pacific–East Asia and then in Asia and Africa resulted from vast historical forces far beyond the control of any single power. Nevertheless, the United States may well have contributed more than any other country to their creation. The United States came to bear an important share of the burden of war in Europe and most of the burden in Asia. Among the Allied leaders, Franklin Roosevelt was the most insistent on the unconditional surrender of the main enemy states. The American attitude to colonialism contributed to its downfall, and was, Churchill's rhetoric notwithstanding, frequently taken into account when London and other capitals made colonial decisions during and after the war.[13]

So, the Second World War led to more comprehensive changes in the international power structure than any war before it. The old powers were either defeated or were in decline, even in victory. The mantle of leadership was transferred to the United States. That country was in fact emerging as the most powerful state the modern world had seen. Its main rival was the Soviet Union, also a relative newcomer on the very top of the international scene.

IV Empire—Some Words on the Term

The proper meaning of the term "empire" has long been debated. Many want to reserve the term for its narrow use, referring to the formal political control of one state over another's external and internal policy. In this sense the term will most frequently be applied to the historical period often described as the "age of imperialism" (climaxing in the years from the 1870s to the First World War). Others favor a broader definition, where empire simply means a hierarchical system of political relationships with one power clearly being much stronger than any other. Under such a definition not only the Soviet sphere of influence, but also the wider and looser American one could be called an empire.[14] I shall generally follow this latter usage.

The effectiveness of the outside power's control may be entirely separate from its more formal aspects. First, even within the formal British Empire there was sometimes the form without the reality. For most practical purposes the white dominions had all become independent states well before the Second World War. This was reflected in Balfour's formula from 1926, under which Britain and the dominions were stated to be "autonomous Communities within the British Empire, equal in status, in no way subordinate one to another in any aspect of their domestic or external affairs, though united by a common allegiance to the Crown, and freely associated as members of the British Commonwealth of Nations."

Here it was considerably clearer what the Empire was *not* than what it actually was.[15]

Second, there was the reality of empire without the form. Certain areas were formally outside the British Empire, but Britain was nevertheless as influential here as in many of the formally ruled areas. British influence in parts of China, in parts of the Ottoman Empire, particularly in Egypt, and in Argentina ("the sixth dominion") at times exceeded that in the dominions at least. This is what Robinson and Gallagher have called Britain's "informal empire." British rule in India was quite complex; some areas were under direct British rule, others were ruled indirectly through local rulers. The same was the case in Africa. Although the distinction between direct and indirect rule could be more formal than real, it too underlines the diversity within the British Empire. Similar complexities had existed within other empires, such as for instance the old Athenian and Roman ones.[16] Formal political control thus becomes a rather unsatisfactory criterion for empire.

There can be little doubt that the Soviet Union exerted far more effective control over Eastern Europe, particularly in the years from 1948 to 1953, but also later, than Britain generally did over its most important areas of rule. The non-contiguous parts of the Soviet Empire, such as Vietnam and Cuba, had a freer position. Still, since the Eastern European countries were formally fully independent, even the Soviet Empire could not be called this under the narrow definition of the term.

Robinson has worked out newer and more timeless definitions of "informal empire",[17] but they are probably too vague to be really useful. Yet, the complexity of imperial rule remains. Within the American "empire" some important areas were at least temporarily under direct American occupation (Japan, the American zone in Germany, and so on); there, and in certain Caribbean/ Central American and Pacific states, the American role could be just as striking as in some of the more directly ruled parts of the British Empire. On the whole, however, Britain had a formal empire, but few imperial institutions. The United States had no formal empire, but more developed institutions—in the form of alliances, security treaties and partly also economic arrangements— than the British.

So, when the term "empire" is used about the American role it refers to an informal hierarchical structure. (The quotation marks are to make it clear that the term is used in its wide sense.) The states within this empire were generally politically independent; many, if not most of them, were political democracies, but they were still tied to America through important military, political, and economic arrangements. The American influence was more pronounced in shaping the overall structure (in creating NATO, for instance) than in forcing individual countries to make specific policy choices they would not otherwise have made (compelling them to become members of NATO, for instance). In Charles Maier's terms, the American "empire" generally implied "power to", less often than "power over".[18]

V The American Position of Strength, 1945–Early 1960s

After the Second World War the United States was by far the strongest power. British Foreign Secretary Ernest Bevin argued in June 1947 that ". . . the US was in the position today where Britain was at the end of the Napoleonic wars."[19] Paul Kennedy has also argued that the American position in 1945 resembled that of the British in 1815. Both countries had completed a triumphant war; their technological revolutions had really taken off; their rivals were exhausted, and it seemed that they could both more or less control world markets.[20]

In some important respects, however, the American position after the Second World War was really stronger, also in relative terms, than the British had been at the height of *Pax Britannica*. It was much stronger than the Soviet position after 1945. Harold Laski, British professor of political science, writer, and Labor politician, certainly overdid it, but may still have come closer to the mark when, in November 1947, he wrote that "America bestrides the world like a colossus; neither Rome at the height of its power nor Great Britain in the period of its economic supremacy enjoyed an influence so direct, so profound, or so pervasive . . . Today literally hundreds of millions of Europeans and Asiatics know that both the quality and the rhythm of their lives depend upon decisions made in Washington. On the wisdom of those decisions hangs the fate of the next generation."[21]

America's strength rested on four main pillars: its vast economic superiority, its substantial military lead, the broad domestic base for the policy pursued, and America's strong international-ideo-logical support. The economic base was the most impressive. In constant 1958 prices the American gross national product had grown from USD 209.4 billion in 1939 to USD 355.2 billion in 1945. "Only" 400,000 Americans had lost their lives during the war. In the Soviet Union approximately 20 million had died; steel and agricultural production had been cut in half during the war. Overall Soviet production figures are not known, but a very rough guess is that in 1945 Soviet production may have been only one-quarter of that in the US.[22]

In the 19th century Britain probably had the world's largest GNP only for a very short period around 1860. In 1830 both Russia and France appear to have had higher production, in 1870 the United States and Russia. Throughout much of the century Britain was the industrial leader and remained the mercantile leader, but at no time did it produce more than roughly one-third of the world's total manufactures. In 1945 the United States produced almost as much as the rest of the world together. The US lead tended to be greater the more advanced the technology. In the decade 1940–50 the United States was behind 82 percent of major inventions, discoveries, and innovations. The highest corresponding percentage for Britain had been 47 percent in 1750–75. With 6 percent of the world's population, the United States had 46 percent of the world's electric power and its businesses controlled 59 percent of the world's total oil reserves. America produced 100 times more cars than the Soviet Union and eight times as many as Germany, Britain, and France combined. In 1950 the US held 49.8 percent of the world's monetary gold, reserve currencies, and IMF reserves.[23]

There were areas of economic life where Britain played a more important role in the 19th century than the United States did after the Second World War. Thus, British foreign trade constituted a higher percentage of world trade than American trade was ever to do. In 1870 Britain had 24 percent of world trade; in 1950 the corresponding US percentage was 18.4.[24] But in the trade field it is difficult to know where economic and political leverage ends and vulnerability and dependence begin. The United States traded considerably less; the other side of the coin was that it was more self-sufficient, also in important strategic raw materials and food.[25]

With the reconstruction after the Second World War and the

rapid economic growth in most of the world in the 1950s, the US share of world production was bound to diminish. In 1950 the United States produced about 40 percent of world GNP, in 1960 around 30 percent. Yet, the United States still produced more than twice as much as the Soviet Union and continued to enjoy a lead over its chief rivals that was much bigger than Britain had ever achieved in the 19th century. In 1960 the United States had 59 percent of world foreign investments. That was probably slightly more than Britain had at its highest (although, as for trade, in relation to the size of their economies foreign investments were much more important for Britain than for the United States). In the 1950s the US provided over half of global development assistance, an instrument which barely existed before the Second World War.[26]

The strong economy provided the basis for America's military strength. Until 1949 the United States had a monopoly on the atomic bomb, and until well after the Cuban missile crisis of 1962 it held a commanding lead in the number of nuclear weapons (although Khruschev did his best with his exaggerated claims after the launching of Sputnik in 1957 to neutralize this fact). The bomb was not the decisive card in international relations which many Truman administration policymakers had initially hoped, but it certainly strengthened America's role and many saw it, in Secretary of State Marshall's words, at least as "the main deterrent to Soviet aggression".[27]

The United States had by far the strongest Air Force in the world. In 1944—at its highest—America's production of aircraft—95,000—surpassed that of Japan and Germany combined. Before the Second World War the Royal Navy was still slightly larger than the US Navy. The war changed that, so much so that in December 1947 Admiral Nimitz could argue that the US Navy now had a "control of the sea more absolute than even possessed by the British." The Soviet blue-ocean Navy was quite small until the 1960s. The great American weakness was the number of personnel, particularly on the army side. During the war the US and the Soviets both had about 12 million men under arms. Although the Soviets demobilized more than was recognized at the time and came down to 2.8 million in 1948, the American strength was only about half of that. This number was more than doubled as a result of the outbreak of the Korean War, but the Soviets did remain far ahead on this one point. Yet, the Second World War had given most dramatic evidence of how quickly the United States could shift from a civilian to a military economy. It is difficult to come up with good estimates of Soviet military spending, but there can be little doubt that overall the United States outspent the Soviet Union. In fact, by one estimate as late as 1960 the US stood for 51 percent of total military spending while it had only 13 percent of total personnel.[28]

The domestic political side was the third pillar of America's strength. Since the Civil War the United States had probably had the largest gross national product in the world; its economic lead was vast even before the Second World War. Yet, despite this economic basis, the US had rather limited military strength (in 1940 defense expenditures still came to less than 1 billion dollars). Most important of all, politically the United States had little desire to be a world power. Thus, until the Second World War a vast discrepancy existed between the resources of the US on the one hand and its willingness to use these resources in Great Power politics on the other. (This gap was even wider than the similar gap with regard to Japan in the 1980s.)

The events of the Second World War brought about a revolution in American attitudes. Isolationism in its traditional form was destroyed. It had rested on two main assumptions. The first one was that the United States could not be attacked, the second that the basic dividing line in international politics really lay between the United States and the other Great Powers. Pearl Harbor showed that the United States could be attacked after all and Hitler in particular demonstrated that ideologically the US was much closer to some states than to others.

After 1945 the United States joined the United Nations and took part in the occupations of Japan, Germany, Italy, and Austria. Defense spending, even in the low years from 1946 to 1950, was considerably higher than before the Second World War. In the course of 1946–47 a remarkable consensus developed on the main lines of America's foreign policy, particularly the containment policy toward the Soviet Union. Secretary of Commerce Henry Wallace's alternative on the left, which stressed a greater understanding for Soviet views, was not seriously considered by the Truman administration. Wallace's ouster from the Cabinet in the fall of 1946 confirmed that; his dismal showing in the 1948 pre-

sidential election ratified his defeat. Senator Robert Taft's unilat-
eralist–isolationist alternative on the right had greater support, but
even his partial opposition to the Marshall Plan and his more direct opposition to NATO was of little importance. Taft's failure to
win the Republican nomination in 1952 and his death soon after
signalled the rapid decline of this kind of right-wing criticism of
containment.

The Soviet Union had to be contained; to do this the United
States had to enter into alliances outside the Western Hemisphere,
also in peacetime; defense spending had to be much higher than in
the past, although there was still disagreement as to exactly how
high. Thus, almost all leading Democrats and most Republicans
rallied around an ideology which could possibly be seen, as Franz
Schurman does, as a merger of the old internationalism and the
nationalism which had formed such a strong part of the isolationist
tradition. The isolationists had wanted to protect the uniqueness
of America from the rest of the world. Now the United States had
become so strong that it could not only remain uncontaminated by
the evils of the Old World, but even promote America's values in
the rest of the world.[29]

Institutionally America's policies were drawn up on the basis of
strong executive leadership, but also presidential-congressional bipartisanship. The President and the executive branch had relatively firm control of the foreign policy process. Through the Ton-
kin Gulf Resolution of 1964 Congress largely supported the President and few lawmakers questioned the fact that Congress was
brought in only after the US had already been committed. The
most serious challenge to executive leadership came in the early
part of Eisenhower's presidency in the form of the Bricker amend-
ment, which was really directed more at FDR and Yalta than at
Eisenhower. The Truman–Vandenberg model of bipartisanship
disappeared with the "loss of China" and Senator Vandenberg's
death, but the essence of bipartisanship survived. The continuity
from Truman to Eisenhower was marked. Thus, the extension of
the pact system from Europe to Asia had started under Truman
and met with the overwhelming support of Congress also under
Eisenhower.[30] Even the changes from Eisenhower to Kennedy
were, as we shall see, much smaller than Kennedy's rhetoric indicated.

Ideologically British imperialism had rested upon a sense of superiority. Great Britain stood for Christianity and "Western Civilization," for material benefits and economic advancement. The crucial point was that this belief was held not only by most Englishmen, but for a long time was also shared by most of the peoples subjected to their rule. So self-evident was this belief in fact in the first half of the 19th century that it did not really have to be very actively promoted. Only with what could be seen as Britain's slow decline from the 1870s were these "truths" spelled out in any great detail through exhibitions, jubilees, the press, and the schools. The superiority was closely related to race. The white race was seen as superior to the yellow race which in turn was superior to the black. (Within the white race Anglo-Saxons or Northern Europeans stood above Southern Europeans.) In this sense British colonialism was different from French, in that in theory at least the French came to stress culture over race. If you adopted French culture, you could also achieve the rights of a Frenchman.[31]

In Marxism–Leninism the Soviet Union had an ideology with claims to historical inevitability and global validity. The class struggle could not be held back. The masses would prevail over the ruling classes. The world was bound to move from feudalism to capitalism, socialism, and, the highest stage, communism. Thus, like the British, the Soviets possessed an ideology which could justify many forms of expansion.

Did the United States have an ideology which could not only unify the American people but also justify expansion and serve to attract support abroad? Michael Hunt has argued that ideology has shaped American foreign policy, and that historically this ideology has been based on three elements: a sense of national mission, hostility toward social revolutions, and the racial classification of peoples. It is easy to come up with examples, for instance in the form of quotations from prominent individuals, that indicate that at least the first element has remained strong throughout American history. The second probably has a rather more mixed history than Hunt indicates, but is certainly, as we shall see, relevant to the years after 1945.[32]

As regards Hunt's third point, the Second World War did much to undermine racism, but remnants could still be found in America's foreign and, particularly, its domestic policies. Thus, even Franklin Roosevelt wondered whether the inbreeding of European and Asian races would not produce a less "delinquent" Asian stock. The Truman administration, and Secretary of State Dean Acheson in particular, in Dean Rusk's phrase, generally "overlooked the brown, black, and yellow peoples of the world." The Eisenhower administration was largely passive on the race issue, despite the rapidly growing number of Third World countries. Southerners, from James Byrnes to William Fulbright, generally had to support the racism of their region if they wanted to maintain their political base.[33]

Hunt's three elements were important in the American context. They were less suited to commanding broad international support. A related point, namely America's identification with democracy or, in its almost equally common negative version, opposition to Soviet totalitarianism was really crucial.

In its imperial heyday Britain faced opposition from many local sources, but it was not consistently challenged by any one Great Power. Rivals came and went. France was the primary colonial rival, but was occasionally overshadowed by Russia and in the early 20th century the French threat was replaced by the German one. The United States faced one consistent threat, the Soviet Union. This provided the American people with a unifying anticommunist ideology. As we shall see, the perceived threat probably also provided the single most important reason for the invitations issued to the United States to increase its economic, political, and military role. And the United States could deliver; America's role rested on its tremendous economic and military strength.

Interest, ideology, and concern for others flowed together in a seamless web. As Truman privately expressed it, "We are faced with the most terrible responsibility that any nation ever faced. From Darius I's Persia, Alexander's Greece, Hadrian's Rome, Victoria's Britain, no nation or group of nations has had our responsibilities." It was now America's task "to save the world from totalitarianism."[34] No one could surpass Kennedy's very public inaugural promise that ". . . we shall pay any price, bear any burden, meet any hardship, support any friend, oppose any foe to assure the survival and the success of liberty." Arthur Schlesinger, Jr., one of the President's advisors, wrote of the mood of the early Kennedy administration that "Euphoria reigned; we thought for a moment that the world was plastic and the future unlimited."[35]

America was unique and it was upholding universal values (such as international cooperation, democracy, and freer trade). The possible tension between uniqueness and universalism was rarely explored. Foreigners often supported America's leadership and shared many of its values. In most countries support for the United States far exceeded that for the Soviet Union. This was certainly the case in the democratic countries where public opinion could be most easily measured.

Yet, even friendly foreigners were bound to comment on the extent to which America's idealism coincided with rather ordinary national interests. In 1945 Winston Churchill, as close a friend of America as any, captured this skeptical note almost perfectly when, faced with yet another American lecture on the evils of power politics, he replied: "Is having a Navy twice as strong as any other 'power politics'? Is having an overwhelming Air Force, with bases all over the world, 'power politics'? Is having all the gold in the world buried in a cavern 'power politics'? If not, what is 'power politics'?"[36]

VI The Expansion of the United States until the Early 1960s

The First World War and the October Revolution actually resulted in a contraction of the new Soviet state (the independence of Poland, Finland, and the Baltic States, border changes with Rumania and Turkey.) In the interwar period the only significant expansion took place in Outer Mongolia. In 1944–45 the Soviet Union not only regained most of the territory it had lost after the First World War, but also expanded its rule considerably. The expansion was largely the work of the Red Army. Moscow came to exercise close control over Eastern Europe, looser control over North Korea. The communists won a momentous victory in China. That victory was based on little support from the Soviets, but it certainly strengthened the Soviet position, at least temporarily, i.e. in the 1950s. The communists also won in North Vietnam. Since the Soviet Union by itself constitutes one-sixth of the earth's land area, this could be regarded as the largest empire the world had ever seen. Yet, the Soviet *expansion* was limited to its border areas. In the first ten to fifteen years after the Second World War the Soviet Union was not a global superpower at all.

In that respect the British Empire was different. Before the

First World War Britain's Empire constituted 23 percent of the world's population and 20 percent of its area. (It actually grew somewhat after the First World War, but then the signs of breakdown were nevertheless becoming increasingly clear.) The British Empire was more than four times the size of the Roman and its population did not fall much short of the combined populations of the contemporary French, German, and Russian Empires.[37]

Despite its vast complexities, the Empire basically fell into two categories, both scattered over very diverse areas. One was the white dominions: Canada, Australia, New Zealand, and South Africa, the other the "colored" colonies with India as "the jewel in the crown." Britain also dominated the seas and most of the world's strategic strongpoints: Gibraltar, Cape Town, Suez, and Singapore.

The expansion of Great Britain in the 18th and 19th centuries was the result of Britain's strength and the weakness of the periphery. Manchu China was declining; so were Mogul India and the Ottoman Empire; Africa was "backward" and characterized by a high turnover of regimes. Before the Second World War at least one billion people outside Europe were controlled by a few Western states. As has so often been said, the sun never set on the British Empire and only intermittently on the French one.[38]

Yet, here I shall argue that the American "empire" after the Second World War was in important ways more comprehensive than either the Soviet or even the British Empire. Compared to the Soviet Empire, the American expansion was global, unlike Soviet expansion, which was limited to its border areas, however vast these border areas might be. Compared to the British Empire, the American "empire" came to include units which were much more important strategically, politically, and economically. The British Empire was in most respects a coalition of peripheries. India was celebrated for its importance. In Curzon's words, "as long as we rule India we are the greatest power in the world. If we lose it, we shall drop straight away to a third-rate power." Yet, despite such rhetoric, even India was of relatively limited importance in Great Power politics.[39] Britain's influence was weakest in the very center of Great Power politics, on the European continent.

Like the British Empire, the American one, too, reflected the strength of the mother country. But unlike the British Empire, the American "empire" did not so much spring from the weakness of the periphery, although it did that too, as from the weakness of most of the traditional power centers. The American "empire" was geographically just as comprehensive as the British, and, what was more important, it came to include four of the six power centers of the post-war years: The United States itself, Britain, Western Europe with most of Germany, and Japan. (The remaining two were the Soviet Union and China.) The American "empire" was also most impressive in the sense that it emerged in the course of a ten-year period after the Second World War while the British Empire developed gradually over two to three centuries.

The term "isolationism" as applied to the period up to the Second World War may easily give the wrong impression of America's policies. Yet, there is no doubt that the American role expanded tremendously after the war. The expansion was military, political, and economic. (And certainly also cultural, although I shall have little to say about that part.)

The United States had no allies before the war and no US troops were stationed on territory it did not directly control. After the war Washington entered into numerous alliances, and bases were established in the most different corners of the world. Geographically the post-war expansion was least noticeable in Latin America, because this had traditionally been the US backyard. The Monroe Doctrine had been Washington's unilateral proclamation of its special role in the Western Hemisphere. In 1940–41 FDR extended the Doctrine hundreds of miles out to sea, implied that Canada fell under it, and even broadened it to cover Greenland (1940) and Iceland (1941). Privately, the President believed that the Canaries, the Azores, and even West Africa should be covered because of their strategic importance to the Western Hemisphere.[40]

After the war the special role of the United States was given at least indirect multilateral sanction in the form of the Act of Chapultepec (1945), the Rio treaty (1947), and the Organization of American States (1948). Until the late 1950s American policymakers took Latin America for granted to such an extent that, for instance, all of the Western Hemisphere received less economic assistance than did the Benelux countries alone.[41] This began to change in Eisenhower's last years and was speeded up with Kennedy and the Alliance for Progress, although, as so often happened under Kennedy, the rhetorical change was greater than the practical results. When needed to contain leftist challenges, Washington reinforced its position through interventions (Guatemala, 1954; Cuba, 1961; Dominican Republic, 1965).

The American position in the Pacific had also been strong before the war, with the possession of Hawaii and the Philippines. After the war Ernest Bevin soon complained that the Monroe Doctrine was being extended to the Pacific.[42] The Philippines were given their promised independence, but remained closely tied to the United States economically and militarily. The Japanese Mandated Islands came under American control, with only the thinnest of concessions to the suzerainty of the United Nations. American influence in South Korea remained strong despite the US forces being pulled back in 1948. The Korean War brought the forces back and the American commitment to South Korea's defense was expressed in a long-term security treaty.

The new American role in Japan was the most important change brought about by the war in Asia. The United States was the sole occupier of Japan and the allies from the war had only the most limited influence on the American occupation. After the peace treaty of 1951 Japan was tied to the United States through a security treaty and comprehensive American base rights, under which Japan's defense became an American responsibility and Japan's foreign policy to a large extent an extension of Washington's.

The Second World War had indicated that both Australia and New Zealand would now look primarily to the United States, and not to Britain for their defense. In 1951 this understanding was formalized through the ANZUS Pact. Britain was excluded from taking part, rather pointedly demonstrating the decline of Britain also in this part of the world.[43]

The biggest overall change took place in the American–European relationship. The United States did not withdraw from Europe as it was generally seen to have done after the First World War. The US first extended considerable bilateral aid to many European countries, primarily those in Western Europe; then this aid was given a dramatically new framework through the Marshall Plan, where practically all the Western European countries, including Sweden, Switzerland, and Austria, participated. As early as August 1945 Truman had told General de Gaulle that "the bomb should give pause to countries which might be tempted to commit aggressions",[44] and in September 1946 Secretary of State James Byrnes made it clear that American troops would remain in

Germany for the duration of the occupation. These two American commitments were then given a more lasting and multilateral form through NATO. The United States, Canada, and the ten founding European members were later joined by Greece and Turkey (1952), and West Germany (1955).

The United States was far and away the dominating member of NATO. Indeed the major point of the alliance was to tie the Americans as closely as possible to the defense of Western Europe. The original commitment was expanded in scope through the integrated military command, the increase in the American troop strength, and the military assistance programs, all in turn based on the perception of an enhanced threat largely resulting from the outbreak of the Korean War. The integration of West Germany into a Western framework, just a few years after the war, first economically through the Marshall Plan and then militarily through NATO, was a most dramatic expression of the American role. Thus, Washington's influence was predominant both in (most of) Germany and in Japan, the two main aggressor states of the Second World War. The United States basically filled the vacuums in these two core countries.

The financially strapped British were leaving more and more of their commitments to the Americans. The organization of the Bizone in Germany was an indirect way of relieving the British burden. The Truman Doctrine in March 1947 represented the official proclamation that the United States was replacing Britain in Greece and Turkey. In a historical perspective the United States was not only replacing Great Britain as the organizer of the European opposition to the strongest continental power, but was also playing a much more active role in shaping the continent than Britain had done even in its heyday. Only late and in part as a reflection of its decline had Britain moved closer to France (1904) and Russia (1907). The United States helped form a new Europe through the Marshall Plan and NATO and in many other, both direct and indirect, ways.

In the Middle East the situation was considerably more complex than in Europe. Here too the Western mantle of leadership was being transferred from Britain to the United States, but the transfer was both slower and had stronger elements of conflict than in Europe. The various British withdrawals, starting with Palestine in 1948 and ending with the Persian Gulf in the late 1960s, left considerable bitterness between London and Washington. In American eyes, the British, in some cases, were too slow in leaving (generally in the 1940s and 1950s), in others too quick (in the 1960s). The British frequently felt that they were being undercut by either the Jewish lobby or the big oil companies. The outbursts against Washington could be strong. Thus, in 1954 Foreign Secretary Anthony Eden felt that the Americans were not only trying to replace the French and run Indochina themselves, but that "they want to replace us in Egypt too. They want to run the world." It also proved impossible for policymakers in Washington to put the local situation into the East–West framework which came so naturally in Europe.

The strong American support for Israel did not preclude an expanding role also vis-à-vis the Arabs. Before the Second World War, American oil companies had been operating in Iraq, Bahrein, Kuwait, and Saudi Arabia. At least from 1943 Washington came to pursue an active policy toward Saudi Arabia in particular, and in fact continued Lend-Lease aid after it had been cut to other countries. This made the British minister to Saudi Arabia comment that "it was too bad that an American oil company did not hold oil concessions in the United Kingdom," so that the British too could continue to receive Lend-Lease. The outcome of the American–British oil rivalry was a division of responsibility where American companies would control the fields in Saudi Arabia while British companies would have the lead in Iraq and Iran. The United States also obtained base rights in Saudi Arabia, at first in direct competition with the British. Dhahran became a key base in the Middle East and in return the US provided economic and military support. In 1946 the United States was to take over another British function, namely the role of containing Russian/Soviet influence in Iran. After the overthrow of Mossadeq in 1953 American oil companies even got a 40 percent interest in the oil fields there.[45]

The United States became increasingly involved in extending economic and military assistance to Israel and to most Arab countries. The Truman and particularly the Eisenhower administration favored an extension of the pact system into the Middle East, but when the Baghdad Pact was finally created in 1955 with Britain, Turkey, Pakistan, Iran, and Iraq as members, the US formally remained on the outside, in part because of the Israeli connection, in part because of the conflict between Britain and Egypt.[46]

The Suez intervention came to result in a sharp reduction in the British influence in the Middle East. Not only was the United States the main factor behind the British–French decision to halt the invasion, but, as in Greece in 1947, it also stepped in to try to fill the vacuum which the reduced British role created. This was the intention of the Eisenhower Doctrine of 1957. As Eisenhower himself stated, "the existing vacuum in the Middle East must be filled by the United States before it is filled by Russia." Now the United States took over as the predominant Great Power in the region, although it could still cooperate with Britain, as the joint invasion of Lebanon–Jordan in 1958 demonstrated. Kennedy also tried to improve relations with Nasser's more radical Egypt, but these efforts to broaden the American role largely failed, in part because of the American support for Israel, but probably even more because of rivalry between moderate and radical Arab forces, as revealed in the Saudi-Egyptian conflict in Yemen.[47]

In Asia too the American role expanded dramatically. In South Asia the United States played a role in encouraging the British to give up colonial rule, although Washington increasingly deferred to London as the independence process was speeded up. After having tried to balance India and Pakistan, the United States became exasperated with India's neutrality and Nehru's morality lectures and sided with pro-Western Pakistan. Yet, the alliance with Pakistan and Dulles's denunciations of neutrality should not hide the fact that the Eisenhower administration wanted to maintain fairly close ties with India too and, for instance, came to increase American economic assistance to New Delhi. Kennedy attempted to strengthen these ties further, through military aid against the Chinese and increased economic support, but India's basic neutralist position and the American ties with Pakistan meant that there would be no dramatic change in US–Indian relations.[48]

In Southeast Asia the interests of the United States had traditionally been limited to the Philippines and to rubber and tin imports from Malaya. In the early years after the war the United States largely deferred to the European colonial powers, primarily because of the overriding importance of Europe in the Cold War. Gradually, however, Washington came to play an increasing role, first in Indonesia, where a small European power—Holland— tried to defeat a non-communist nationalist movement, but then also in Indochina where France was struggling to hold on against the Communist-led Vietminh. In Indonesia Washington's threat to suspend economic and military assistance was an important factor in the Dutch decision finally to give up. In Vietnam the United States tried to promote a nationalist alternative at the same time as it financed a rapidly increasing share of France's expenses in fighting the Vietminh.[49] After the French defeat and the Geneva Conference of 1954, the United States took the initiative in creating SEATO, with Pakistan, Thailand, the Philippines, Australia, New Zealand, Britain, France, and the United States as members. In addition came the separate security treaty with Taiwan (and the treaties with Japan and South Korea).

In 1945–46 the Joint Chiefs' lists of essential bases illustrated how dramatically the war had expanded US security requirements. The six most essential ones were found in widely scattered parts of the world: Greenland, Iceland, the Azores, Casablanca, the Galapagos, and Panama.[50] There is no agreed definition of a base, but, by one count, in 1955 the United States had 450 bases in 36 countries. In the late 1960s, at its maximum, the United States had one million men stationed abroad, far more than Britain had had at any time.[51]

The American expansion was in some respects least striking on the economic side. In part this was because here, unlike in military and diplomatic matters, the United States had played an important role even before the Second World War. In absolute figures there was a tremendous increase in American exports and imports. The United States became the world's largest trader, finally surpassing the United Kingdom. In 1943–47 exports were above "normal" as a percentage of GNP, but they soon fell back to their traditional 3–5 percent range of GNP. During and immediately after the war imports remained below 3 percent of GNP, in fact somewhat lower than the historical average. This was extremely low by international standards. In most Western European countries, including Britain, exports and imports regularly constituted 30–40 percent or more of GNP. Only socialist-autarchic countries like the Soviet Union and less developed and geographically isolated countries had lower percentages than the United States.[52] A pronounced increase in America's trading role would only take place in the 1970s.

American investments abroad increased considerably, but well into the 1950s most of the growth was limited to the more traditional areas in the Western Hemisphere, Canada and Latin America. In Europe the growth was so slow in fact that only in 1957 did American investments there surpass European ones in the United States. In the late 1950s, however, American investments in Western Europe started to grow rapidly.[53]

Yet, the overall international economic structure changed dramatically after the Second World War and most of these changes were defined by the United States (see pp. 62–65).

VII "Empire" by Invitation

An empire operates on the basis of some sort of consent from the ruled peoples. Within the Soviet Empire the Communist parties and other pro-Soviet forces enjoyed some hard-core, but otherwise rather limited suppport in Poland, Rumania, and Hungary, clearly more in Bulgaria and Czechoslovakia. Culturally and economically most Eastern Europeans in fact considered the Soviets inferior to themselves, a rather unique situation in imperial contexts. In most of Eastern Europe the basis for the consent of the population, however passive and indirect, was quite simply that they saw no alternative to the Red Army. The Soviet presence was pervasive and the people generally remained calm.[54] When Soviet interests were threatened, Moscow intervened through the Red Army (East Germany, 1953, Hungary, 1956, and Czechoslovakia, 1968). Where the local communists had an independent power base, they soon came to break away from Soviet rule, as in Yugoslavia, Albania, and China.

The British Empire rested on a somewhat different mixture of active support and passive loyalty. In most of the dominions, with their large populations of British descent, the support could be strong, particularly as long as the dominions kept moving toward higher degrees of self-government. In the "colored" parts the situation was much more complex. Examples can be found of the British being explicitly invited to rule over certain areas.[55] In the early phase the extension of British rule more generally rested on the conclusion of treaties with local rulers. This was also the case in Africa, although these were often "unequal" treaties. Later the British tended to "neglect" even such formalities and opposition to British rule increased. Frequently they faced some sort of active resistance. Then the threat and the occasional use of armed force became important both for the introduction and the maintenance of British rule.[56]

Both the British and the local peoples generally believed in the superiority of the white man (and the Anglo-Saxons in particular). With Britain's political ideals and limited resources, imperial control had to be rather "thin." In 1909 the population of the Empire was 7.7 times greater than that of Britain itself, the area ratio was 1:94. In India an administration of 2000–3000, an armed force of 60,000–70,000 (and a slightly higher number of dependents) ruled over 200–300 million people. In Northern Nigeria, during the interwar period more than 10 million people were ruled by some 250 administrative officers. There were areas where white men were hardly seen at all.[57] When the local populations started actively to resist British rule and superiority thinking was largely shattered by the Second World War, British rule was more or less bound to collapse.

After 1945 foreign rule over other peoples was coming to be challenged almost everywhere it existed. It was certainly out of favor in Washington. Yet, America was so strong that it could exert its influence more indirectly. Here the parallel to British informal rule in the 1840s–70s is clear. When Britain was at its peak, informal rule not only sufficed for British objectives, often it flowed more or less naturally from the position of supremacy. Annexation became a sign of weakness, an admission that more direct means had to be used to control the local scene.[58]

With certain exceptions, such as in the post-war occupations, in Vietnam in the 1960s, and in West Germany in general, the direct American military presence was generally rather limited. Occasionally the United States, too, intervened with direct force or through covert activities. Yet, on the whole, intervention was both undesirable and unnecessary. Washington's supremacy was more in accordance with the will of the local populations than was Moscow's and even London's supremacy. Soviet rule was to a large extent imposed; British rule survived as long as it did because it was not opposed. As we shall see, American "rule" was frequently invited. In this sense the American "empire" can be called an empire by invitation.

So, although this study supports the revisionist argument that the American expansion was really even more striking than the Soviet one, it differs from revisionist accounts in that it stresses the invitational aspect of much of this expansion. Occasionally the United States did thrust itself into the affairs of other countries. Yet, the basic pattern, particularly in the early post-war years, was a different one. The rule was that the United States was invited in.

Neither the Europeans nor any other foreigners could determine US foreign policy. That was done in Washington largely on the basis of America's own interests. (A discussion of US motive powers is not part of this study. The debate on this point very much resembles the debate on the origins of 19th century imperialism.[59]) The point, however, in this context of the American-local relationship is that on many occasions various outsiders tried to influence Washington in the direction of greater interest and more assistance. Often they did this with success, and although the basic decision tended to reflect America's own concerns, the foreigners could, as a minimum, influence the scope and timing of the decision.[60]

The invitational aspect was most clearly seen in Western Europe's attitude to the United States. Britain, the old imperial power, offered the best example in this respect. Although London underestimated Britain's fall from Great Power status, the Attlee government, as did the Churchill governments both before and after, clearly favored both financial assistance from America and a strong US military presence in Britain itself and in Europe in general. In line with this, Whitehall expressed disappointment when Lend-Lease was abruptly cancelled, hoped for a credit substantially larger than the USD 3.75 billion it received, and desired to continue wartime cooperation in atomic energy and the existence of at least some of the combined Anglo-American boards, particularly the Combined Chiefs of Staff, to a much larger extent than was actually done.[61] In 1948–52 the number of US bases and military personnel in Britain increased dramatically.

There was a desperate need for economic assistance in most of the Western European countries and the United States was the only major source of such assistance. In fact, in the period from July 1945 through June 1947 Western Europe on a yearly average received larger amounts of assistance than it did under the Marshall Plan; Eastern Europe received very little even in these early years.[62] The Europeans, and particularly the British, played an important role in hammering Marshall's famous initiative at Harvard on 5 June 1947 into what became the European Recovery Program. Under the Marshall Plan the Europeans first requested USD 28 billion from the United States. This was far more than Washington was willing to give. The Truman administration cut the amount to 17 billion and Congress in turn appropriated approximately 13 billion. Thus, on the economic side there can be no doubt that the Europeans were strongly interested in involving the United States closely in Europe's affairs.

The same was true in many countries on the military side as well. After the London meeting of the Council of Foreign Ministers in December 1947, the British under Bevin began to work to commit the Americans as closely as possible to the planned Western European military arrangement. As early as 27 January 1948 Bevin made his thinking perfectly clear: "The [European] treaties that are being proposed cannot be fully effective nor be relied upon when a crisis arises unless there is assurance of American support for the defense of Western Europe. The plain truth is that Western Europe cannot yet stand on its own feet without assurance of support." The Belgians and the Dutch strongly favored these ideas. The French were somewhat divided between a European and an Atlantic approach to defense, but either alternative demanded a stepped-up American contribution.[63]

In mid-March the deterioration in the international situation stimulated Washington to give a positive response to the European pressure. An Atlantic security system would be created, but there was still doubt as to exactly how closely the United States would be tied to this. The Europeans wanted to make the American commitment as automatic as possible, while many in Washington still hoped to maximize the European contribution. All through February 1949 the State Department kept mediating between the Europeans and Congress. The latter disliked anything that smacked of automatic involvement. Norway and Denmark would have preferred a Scandinavian defense treaty with military ties to the Atlantic Pact, ties which would then have been more limited than those under NATO membership. On the other hand, Spain, Greece, and Turkey wanted to join NATO, but were not permitted to do so at this stage.[64]

The pressure for American involvement continued also after NATO had been formed. In the discussions on the regional planning groups to be set up within the alliance, practically all the European states wanted to have the United States as a member of their particular group. After the outbreak of the Korean War, the Europeans worked hard to establish an integrated force in Europe to be commanded by an American, General Eisenhower. Four additional US divisions were sent to Europe; American military assistance increased greatly; and the regional planning groups were transformed into regional commands.

In return the Europeans had to agree to German rearmament, which was a difficult decision for some, particularly the French. The Europeans also agreed to increase their forces and defense budgets considerably. No longer was defense spending a purely national matter; now it had to be coordinated, although rather loosely, within the wider NATO framework. But in this context one element was to trouble Washington: In periods of tension the Europeans had to be reassured and America therefore strengthened its commitment to Europe. Once the Americans had increased their contribution, however, this provided little inducement for the Europeans to do their full part. When the tension abated, the need for any significant increase tended to be seen as small.[65]

In most European countries the respective governments had the support of the voters when they entered into close economic, political, and military arrangements with the United States. This was clearly the case in Britain and in most of the smaller NATO countries. Public opinion polls also revealed that most Europeans (and most Americans for that matter) often saw the Soviet Union as ahead or even winning the Cold War. At least in part this probably reflected the serious way in which the Soviet threat was perceived, a threat which undoubtedly formed the most important part of the background for the invitations issued to Washington.[66] The French, under the combined influence of a strong Communist party and Gaullist nationalism, were the most ambivalent to the US. Yet, even in France majorities supported the American loan of 1946, French participation in the Marshall Plan, and membership in the Atlantic Pact, although the number of uncommitted/uninformed persons was quite high.[67]

In the 1950s and early 1960s, with the probable exception of France from the late 1950s, support for NATO and for the American troop presence remained high in practically all the Western European countries involved. The overall sympathy for the United States was also pronounced, and Presidents Eisenhower and, even more so, Kennedy were perceived in quite favorable terms. Only when the question of dependence on the United States was raised directly did high numbers in all the major Western European countries agree that the dependence was too great.[68]

Although the invitational aspect was nowhere as consistent as in Western Europe, the concept can be applied to some other areas as well, at least in limited time periods. Australia's and New Zealand's security attitudes probably came closest to the European pattern, although the need for military guarantees and assistance was less pronounced here, in part simply because the Soviet threat was more distant and, therefore, more vaguely perceived.

In the discussions in 1945 about how to balance a universal security system with a regional one, the Latin Americans actually pressed hard to emphasize the latter while the United States was more concerned about the impact the regional approach could have on the United Nations. At the San Francisco Conference in the spring of 1945, the Latin Americans in fact put forth a joint statement proclaiming that "If the Security Council is permitted to manage American affairs it would mean the end of the Monroe Doctrine. The Act of Chapultepec meant the perfection of the American system without interference from outside powers. The inter-American system disappears if the Security Council rules."[69]

In this case the United States decided that it could have its cake and eat it too: support for the UN and opposition to blocs in general could after all be reconciled with a regional approach in the Western Hemisphere. Later, in connection with the 1954 crisis in Guatemala, President Eisenhower felt that even the slightly critical British "had no right to stick their nose into matters which concern this hemisphere entirely."[70]

The point in this context, however, is that early on the Latin Americans themselves favored an approach which meant at least an implicit recognition of US supremacy (as could be seen in their reference to the Monroe Doctrine, a unilateral proclamation on the part of Washington). This approach formed the basis for the Rio treaty and the Organization of American States. Frequently the Latin Americans complained that the United States was taking too little interest in their affairs. US economic assistance was paltry. The special relationship with the most populous country in the region, Brazil, faded away, to a large extent because of Washington's neglect.

At the same time, it has to be stressed that most Latins were very sensitive to anything that smacked of "Yankee" interference. Article 15 of the OAS charter thus stated that "No State or group of States has the right to intervene, directly or indirectly, for any reason whatsoever, in the internal or external affairs of any other State." Most Latin leaders rejected anything which was meant to give the US the right to intervene against international communism. The Johnson Doctrine of 1965 was the most explicit statement of this kind, although the intervention force in the Dominican Republic was actually replaced by an OAS force.[71]

Certain other countries also worked quite actively to strengthen the American role. Thus, after its independence Pakistan's leaders conducted a virtual campaign for American economic and military support. The United States held back at first, mainly due to the effect such a policy would have on India, but later came down on Pakistan's side.[72] Most non-democratic countries threatened by external and/or internal communist forces pursued policies similar to those of Pakistan, with similar success. Taiwan, South Korea, South Vietnam after 1954, Greece, and Turkey all worked hard to obtain American military guarantees, all of them ultimately with success, despite a certain initial aloofness on Washington's part, at least on the exact nature of the proposed guarantees. Leaders in Iran and Saudi Arabia invited the United States in, partly for reasons of anticommunism, partly for more local reasons, including a desire to reduce the British role. Even some communist leaders tried to engage the United States. This was probably done largely for tactical purposes as a way of moderating the opposition they faced on their way to power, but possibly also to reduce dependence on the Soviet Union. Ho Chi Minh in Vietnam in 1945–46 and Mao Tse-tung in 1945–48 could be seen as examples of this approach.[73]

The increase in the American influence was nowhere as dramatic as in West Germany and Japan. In both countries comprehensive military, political, and economic reforms were undertaken. The fact that the two countries were occupied naturally placed the whole aspect of invitations in a different light. Washington dominated the local scene anyway; there was no need for invitations. Yet, in a more indirect way the concept can have some relevance even here.

First, in the early 1950s both West Germany and Japan got most

of their legal sovereignty back. In both states the restoration of sovereignty was premised on the acceptance of close ties with the
West. In the German case this was in the form of economic and
military integration, in Japan's in the form of the security treaty
with the US. Yet, in both countries it quickly became evident that
the overall American role was accepted, even popular. In Germany, at the elite level, Chancellor Adenauer's policies were quite
pro-American, particularly in the 1950s, and the rapport between
Adenauer and Secretary of State Dulles was very good, certainly
better than between British Foreign Secretary Eden and Dulles.
At the public opinion level the image of the United States was,
after a surprisingly short period of transition, idealized to an extent witnessed'in few European countries.[74] In Japan the political
situation after the war was simpler than in Germany in that a national government remained intact, more complex in that relations
between and inside parties were quite confusing. Prime Minister
Yoshida was only in part Japan's Adenauer; his internal position
was weaker and so were his ties with the Americans. The close security bond with the United States was fought by the leading opposition parties in both countries. In Germany the SPD abandoned this course in 1959, a clear sign of its unpopularity; in Japan
most of the opposition remained and in 1960 violent demonstra-
tions forced Eisenhower to cancel a planned visit. Still, polls indicated that the United States was far and away the most popular
country in Japan also.[75]

Second, and at a deeper level, Robert Ward has raised the interesting question of why the dramatic changes imposed by the
United States came to be so broadly accepted by the Japanese.
There are, after all, many examples of changes imposed from the
outside being cast off once the period of domination is over. In Japan's case, as in Germany's, the changes have generally lasted.
Just to mention one extreme example, no changes whatsoever
have been made in the constitution which the United States
worked out with very little cooperation from the Japanese.

The answer would in part seem to be that the defeat in the war
shut certain forces out and opened the way for others. The latter
were those promoted by the American occupation authorities, and
the new system was to prove very successful in many ways, certainly economically. Yet, unless the new forces had had something
to latch on to in Japanese history and society, it is difficult to imag-

ine the new arrangement taking hold in the way it did. (The same would apply to Germany, but there it is perhaps somewhat easier to see the continuities from pre-Hitler to post-war Germany.) The Emperor continued, the Diet was already in place, but the American occupation provided a dramatic strengthening of civil rights, including the legalization of the Communist party. The reforms were strongly supported by the radical forces in Japanese society; in that sense the partial reversal in 1947–50 could be seen not only as a reflection of changed Cold War circumstances, but also as a concession to more conservative Japanese forces, the forces which were generally to dominate Japanese politics.[76] In Germany the relationship between Allied, especially American, influence and local forces was well expressed by an official US survey, "The existence of a population that was receptive to reorientation . . . enhanced the Allies' opportunity to help shape German history."[77]

VIII Leader of the "Free World"

The United States was the undisputed leader of the "free world." As such it exerted great influence. The economic arrangements set up after the Second World War, such as the World Bank, the International Monetary Fund, OEEC, and GATT, the military alliances, NATO, ANZUS, SEATO, to a lesser extent CENTO, were all based on Washington's leadership. America's supreme role was most clearly seen in this overall structural influence.

The interwar years had been a period of transition where the United States was beginning to replace Britain as the world's economic leader, but was doing so in a very halfhearted way. As Charles Kindleberger has argued, the lack of an international leader was probably an important factor in the depression of the 1930s.[78] After 1945 the international economic system was dominated by the United States to an even greater extent than Britain had dominated the system before the First World War. As we have seen, the American economy was much larger than the British had ever been, also on a relative basis, although its foreign trade was relatively smaller. Unlike Britain, whose main trading partners had been its political rivals, the United States had the advantage of trading primarily with its political allies. That strengthened the American role.

The United States had rather clear-cut economic objectives.

The most important of these had to do with the strengthening of economic multilateralism and, as a special point under this heading, the promotion of freer trade. The goal was for the market to be the invisible hand which guided international exchange (at least after a period of transition to correct the many imbalances created by the war and with some exceptions, such as for instance those few products where the US itself was not fully competitive). The unstated underlying premise for Britain earlier and for the United States now was that as the strongest economic power it would enjoy great advantages under a regime of freer trade.

The United States really did have all the characteristics of an economic leader.[79] First, through the International Monetary Fund and bilateral diplomacy it helped maintain the international structure of exchange rates. The dollar was tied to gold and all the other international currencies were tied to the dollar, in a way similar to what had been the case under the Classical Gold Standard (1870–1914) under British leadership. Due to the imbalance in trade between the United States and Western Europe full convertibility with the dollar was only introduced in 1958, but the basic structure of the Bretton Woods system lasted from 1945 and until 1971–73 when the dollar was taken off the gold standard and exchange rates were permitted to float.[80]

Second, the United States maintained a flow of capital to borrowers in the same way as the British had done in the 19th century. All in all the United States provided bilateral credits and grants to the tune of slightly more than USD 100 billion in the years from 1945 to 1965. Practically every country in the world received some form of support and in most cases the United States was by far the most important source of outside support. In addition, the United States dominated the World Bank, as it did the IMF, through economically weighted voting arrangements and in other ways.[81]

Third, America served as a lender of last resort in financial and economic crises. The clearest example of that function would be the USD 13 billion provided to Western Europe under the Marshall Plan. Both the regular capital and the crises money would normally come with certain strings attached. The exact nature of the strings varied, but they all tended to strengthen Washington's influence. Under the Marshall Plan, as Theodore H. White wrote from France, the American "expert" "has become . . . as much a stock character as was the British traveler of the nineteenth century, as 2,000 years ago the Roman centurion must have been in conquered Greece."[82]

Fourth, the United States provided a market for distress goods from political friends or supplied such goods itself. The concessions provided to the Japanese in the 1950s were particularly noteworthy. (These will be discussed later.) Even more important, America could increase or share supplies during critical shortages. Thus, the Iranian nationalization of 1951, the Suez crisis of 1956, and the Six-Day War of 1967 caused shortages in the world's oil supply, but they could all be managed by increases in US production and other measures of Western cooperation under American leadership.[83]

Fifth, Washington was the leader in coordinating international macroeconomic policies, particularly trade policies. Under American leadership world trade moved steadily in a more liberal direction. The GATT system based on the Most Favored Nation Principle was a key in this context. In the various trade rounds the United States often made important concessions and for political reasons even promoted regional trading blocs like the European Economic Community. Reciprocity was still the basic principle. The stress on reciprocity probably made the American position somewhat stronger than the British one had been in the 19th century in that Britain tended to believe in free trade as a matter of faith, almost regardless of what others did.[84]

Sixth, the United States dominated the international property regime. In the 19th century Britain had established a property regime strongly biased in favor of the British investor. Expropriations of foreign investments were discouraged and if they nevertheless did take place, full compensation was expected. There were few challenges to this system and those that did arise were generally defeated through a combination of bondholder sanctions and use of the Royal Navy. After 1945 the United States was able to establish a similarly strong regime in the non-communist world biased in favor of (American) multinationals. Until the late 1960s this system worked well, as seen from Washington, partly because US resources were sufficiently strong and concentrated to "punish threats to, absorb the costs of, and bribe medium powers into regime maintenance." Most challenges to the property regime were defeated, in a few cases by covert means (Iran, 1953; Guatemala,

1954). The most significant American concession made in this period was undoubtedly Aramco's decision to accept a 50–50 sharing of profits with the Saudis, a decision which did not cost the company much since the amount could be deducted from US taxes paid, but was still to change dramatically the established international order in oil.[85]

It is important to realize that to some extent the United States pursued policies abroad which were different from those at home. Thus, the economic and social reforms in Japan went far beyond anything that American leaders tried to introduce in the United States itself. The primary reason for this was that the right in Japan had been discredited through its support for the war and that new forces therefore had to be released to prevent a revival of fascist militarism. A similar, but not quite as clear-cut perspective applied to Germany as well. In Western Europe under the Marshall Plan the Truman administration promoted long-term economic planning and, to a lesser extent, Keynesian expansionism beyond anything attempted in the United States. Here the main reason was that Washington wanted to make sure that the economic rehabilitation would be accomplished within the stipulated four-year period, so that no further claims could be made on the American Treasury.[86]

Politically the primary American objective was to contain the Soviet Union and, with exceptions such as Tito's Yugoslavia after the split with Stalin, to isolate communists and those who were seen as their "fellow-travelers." There were also forces on the right which Washington wanted to keep at bay, either because they had been tainted by collaboration during the Second World War or because they were seen as extreme in their nationalism, such as was the case with Gaullism in France.

In Western Europe and a few other places Washington could cooperate with regimes that were democratic, anticommunist, and in favor of freer trade. This was the best of all worlds. Yet, the emphasis on "empire" by invitation and on local support for the American role should not be taken too far. Rarely can a complex world be put on a simple formula. In various ways the United States frequently intervened with armed force of one sort or another. In the period from 1946 to 1965 at least 168 such instances have been counted, with by far the highest frequency occurring in the years from 1956 to 1965. Most of these interventions were in

Third World countries. For the sake of comparison, Moscow intervened only around 10 times in Third World countries in the same period.[87] Most of these interventions were rather small-scale; many received support both locally and internationally. Interventions too could in fact be invited. The American response to the crises over Berlin provided the best example of this.

Still, the United States had Great Power interests which sometimes clashed with its often proclaimed support for democratic rule. There were cases where Washington did not support democracies when they were too far to the left. Thus, in the fall of 1946 the broad-based coalition government in Czechoslovakia, with the communists in a prominent role, still had overwhelming local support. Nevertheless, Secretary of State James Byrnes decided to stop further aid to Prague. The government was out of favor, primarily because it tended to support Moscow on foreign policy issues.[88] About the situation in Indochina in 1954 Eisenhower himself wrote in his memoirs that "I have never talked or corresponded with a person knowledgeable in Indochinese affairs who did not agree that had elections been held at the time of the fighting, possibly 80 per cent of the population would have voted for the Communist Ho Chi Minh as their leader rather than Chief of State Bao Dai." This realization did not stop the Eisenhower administration from taking strong measures to prevent Ho's coming to power.[89]

On the right, particularly in Latin America and in Asia, as we have already seen, many of the invitations to the United States to play a larger role came from non-democratic regimes. Occasionally this was the case even inside Europe. Greece, Turkey, Portugal, and Spain all fell short of normal democratic standards. In Greece the Americans in fact wrote both the Greek application for aid and the thank-you notes in connection with the Truman Doctrine. In Greece and Turkey the administration had broken down to such an extent that under the Marshall Plan Americans were closely involved in running their national bureaucracies.[90] Salazar's Portugal was a founding member of the OEEC and NATO. Franco's Spain was not permitted to take part in the Marshall Plan and NATO, but that was increasingly because of opposition from certain Western European countries. Thus, in 1951–52 the United States entered into bilateral agreements which made Spain an indirect member of the Western Alliance.

Occasionally the United States interfered covertly to influence developments. In Italy in 1947 Washington encouraged the non-communists to throw the Communists out of the government and in 1948 far exceeded normal limits in supporting the Christian Democrats in the election. There, as in several other European countries, Washington encouraged the breakup of unions and parties dominated by communists or "fellow travelers."[91] In 1953 the CIA intervened to help overthrow radical nationalist Mossadeq in Iran, the next year leftist Arbenz in Guatemala. The situation in the Philippines was somewhat different in that a combination of overt and covert means was used there to support the American favorite, Magsaysay, and defeat the Huk rebels.

With the exception of the Philippines, these operations were all rather small-scale; they were still successful from the American point of view. One reason they succeeded was that they could draw upon various local forces, often the army and at least some popular support. Thus, in Iran a few CIA agents and a few hundred thousand dollars brought the Shah back. The CIA–Guatemalan group that started the action against the Arbenz government comprised no more than 150–300 men.

Where the United States tried to overthrow either well-organized governments and/or broadly supported ones, it failed, even in those heyday years of American expansion. That was the case in Albania in 1951–52, in Tibet from the mid-1950s, in Indonesia in 1958, and in Cuba in 1961. In the Cuban case many policymakers had the parallel with Guatemala in 1954 very much in mind. Yet, Cuba, one of the countries where America's influence had historically been the strongest, was to illustrate the limits of Washington's power even on its own doorstep.[92]

The dismantling of colonial empires was one of the most important and dramatic phenomena of the post-war years. It was the result of a complex interaction of forces on the international, metropolitan, and colonial levels. In some instances the United States actually tried to uphold the old order. This was particularly the case when the independence movement was seen as communist-dominated, as in Indochina. In most instances, however, Washington tried to bring about compromises which could provide for political stability and generally stability was identified with liberal advances toward independence.

American anticolonialism helped bring about a change in Britain, the key country in the decolonization process and also the one closest to the US. Various impulses, from Franklin Roosevelt's rhetoric to Washington's very direct pressure on Holland over Indonesia, stimulated the conclusion that the age of the empire was over. And with colonial self-confidence undermined also in this way the transfer of power became a much more rapid process than any had thought likely before and even during most of the Second World War. As Louis and Robinson have argued, "In the shadow of their powerful American ally the British followed certain golden rules more warily than ever: handle the colonies with kid gloves; concede to subjects rather than risk confrontation with them; and above all avoid all dangers of possible uprisings, armed repression, and colonial wars. Only thus could the possibility of American intervention in the African empire be averted."[93] Similar reasoning had of course applied to Asia.

On the security side, whenever NATO had to decide on one policy which simply had to commit all the member states, including the United States itself, the American voice would decide. Thus, NATO strategy became an extension of US strategy. Under Eisenhower massive retaliation was adopted first by Washington, then by NATO. Under Kennedy–Johnson flexible response became the new doctrine both for the US and NATO. Although there was more of a time lag in the latter case, a fact which illustrated both the skepticism and the rising influence of the Europeans, there could be little doubt that American authorities would decide American strategy and thereby indirectly also NATO's strategy.[94]

In many other cases as well, the American domination could be rather striking. Again, it is hard to imagine that, so soon after the war, the Europeans would have agreed to the reconstruction and rearming of West Germany, if it had not been both for American insistence that this be done and an American presence which could provide insurance against a renewed German threat. In East Asia it proved impossible to construct one comprehensive security arrangement, in part because Japan could not be brought together with its former enemies. There a network of separate alliances and security treaties was established. Again, the United States was the linchpin in all this.

When the United States really insisted on a certain course of action, the countries most dependent on it had little choice. This was, once more, best illustrated in the Japanese and German cases. Thus, in 1950, and much to his dislike, Yoshida had to promise to undertake limited rearmament and in 1951–52 he had little choice but to recognize Taiwan and to severely curtail even economic contacts with "Red China." In 1956 the Japanese showed an interest in exploring the conditions under which a peace treaty could be concluded with the Soviet Union based on a compromise solution as far as the disputed Northern islands were concerned. After John Foster Dulles made it clear that the formal cession of Kunashiri and Etorofu to the Soviets would mean that the United States could claim Okinawa, the Japanese reverted to their original position of claiming all the disputed northern islands.[95] In Germany, even after the Bonn Conventions of 1952 and the Paris Agreements of 1954, restraints remained on German sovereignty. In the 1950s German foreign policy was formulated in close cooperation with the United States. In 1962–63 the Kennedy administration was able to stop German exports of oil and gas pipelines to the Soviet Union. Even after the conclusion of the Franco-German treaty of friendship in 1963 the United States clearly remained Bonn's most important reference point.[96]

Naturally the American influence was much smaller in the non-occupied countries. Yet, Washington's attitude became an important element for policymakers in all the countries within the American "empire." This was especially true on the foreign policy side. Thus, even Churchill, the senior Western statesman, was not able to bring about the three-power summit he ached to have after Stalin's death. When the British Prime Minister then suggested that he would go alone to Moscow, Eisenhower responded that if he did so, "the effect on Congress which is this week taking up consideration of our Mutual Defense Program and extension of our Reciprocal Trade Act would be unpredictable."[97] Churchill stayed at home. Frequently allied governments kept an eye on Washington's reaction even when they dealt with economic and social matters. Unless you had a good reason, actions which could be seen as offensive to America were to be avoided.[98]

Suez provided dramatic evidence of the influence the United States *could* have on its two most important allies, Britain and France. The Eisenhower administration was unable to prevent the British–French–Israeli operation against Egypt, but that was in large part due to the allies' faulty appraisal that the United States would come to accept the operation once it really got under way. When that proved a serious misreading of Eisenhower's attitude, and Washington instead refused financial support through the International Monetary Fund, threatened to withhold deliveries of oil and cut off the supply of intelligence information in this very tense period, this American response became the crucial factor behind the British and then in turn the French decision to halt the operation and pull out. The lesson was clear. Britain "could never again resort to military action outside British territories, without at least American acquiescence."[99]

IX The United States and Its Allies: If so Strong, Why so Many Concessions and Why Such Problematic Allies?

America was the undisputed leader of the "free world." It exerted great power over the economic, political, and military structure within which all members of the American "empire" had to operate. The United States had tremendous influence in the occupied countries, and this influence continued in somewhat modified form even after West Germany and Japan became formally independent again. Frequently Washington had a significant impact on matters in the non-occupied countries, too. This was particularly true when Washington had considerable local support for its position, as was often the case.

Yet, the most far-reaching American objectives were clearly beyond the reach of any policymaker. The United States was far from being omnipotent. The wartime planners' dream of an effective world organization came to nothing. Instead of "one world" there would be two, East and West. In the East the United States had very little influence indeed. The ideal of free trade multilateralism was more realistic in that the communist countries were not really a basic part of such a system anyway. Washington was certainly able to advance this set of ideas, but still the results tended to fall short of what was desired. It was not simply for the United States to mold the world in its own image.[100]

Despite its tremendous strength, particularly in relations with its European allies, the United States frequently compromised and sometimes it even met with outright refusals to heed American advice. There were American half-successes, such as the increasing cooperation and integration of the Western European countries, the introduction of full currency convertibility in 1958, the imposition of restrictions on trade with Eastern Europe, and the increased defense expenditures in Western Europe. These were only half-successes in that Britain, and the smaller countries that still followed Britain in such matters, refused to join any tight European grouping, be this the European Coal and Steel Community, Euratom, or the European Common Market; the full currency convertibility came at least ten years later than the Americans had hoped; as soon as the Cold War subsided somewhat, particularly after Stalin's death and the end of the Korean War, the European trade restrictions and defense increases were modified much more than Washington would have liked. The different countries simply followed different policies, although some attention was still paid to what the Americans wanted.[101]

Then there were the refusals to heed American advice. The French National Assembly refused to ratify the plans for the European Defense Community (EDC) despite Dulles's threat of "an agonizing reappraisal" of America's attitude to Europe. The troop issue was quite problematic. Eisenhower insisted that the American troops were in Europe only as a temporary measure. The Europeans ought to handle the long-term problem by themselves. As early as the end of his first year, the President was forced to conclude that "Unhappily, however, the European nations have been slow in building up their military forces and have now come to expect our forces to remain in Europe indefinitely." As Ernest May has noted, in an imperial context American troops carried a surprisingly large share of the burden of protection against the enemy and local forces a rather small share. The British had been much more successful than the Americans were now in enlisting local forces. In the nuclear field, first the British and then the French built their own forces, generally to Washington's dislike. Finally, there was the challenge from President de Gaulle. The US could not stop him from taking France out of the military part of the NATO alliance; neither could it make him accept Britain as a member of the EEC, when the British finally decided to apply for membership. This ensured that Kennedy's Grand Design for two-pillar Atlantic interdependence would remain at the rhetorical stage.[102]

Early in his presidency Eisenhower blurted out that "I get weary of the European habit of taking our money, resenting any slight hint as to what *they* should do, and then assuming, in addition, full right to criticize us as bitterly as they may desire. In fact, it sometimes appears that their indulgence in this kind of criticism varies in direct ratio to the amount of help we give them." The whole thing made him wonder "whether the Europeans are as grown up and mature as they try to make it appear."[103]

Not only did the United States suffer disappointments in relations with its allies, but to some extent the American expansion also carried within it the seeds of its own destruction. Historically this was nothing new. Thus, on the economic side British investments in American canals, railroads, and heavy industry contributed to the rise of the US as the world's leading economic power. On the political side, both Napoleon's empire and the *Pax Britannica* led to the spread of liberalist-nationalist ideas which undermined the basis of imperial rule.[104]

It can be argued that the freer trade which was so strongly promoted by Washington, but was certainly accepted by many other countries as well, in the long run, and somewhat contrary to what many had expected, actually led to stronger economic growth in Western Europe and Japan than in the US itself. Despite Washington's emphasis on reciprocity, the US sometimes found itself making most of the concessions necessary to bring about the desired state of affairs. Thus, in the original 1947 GATT negotiations the American delegation had the authority to negotiate a 50 percent reduction in all US tariffs in return for the elimination of Britain's Imperial Preference System. In the end Washington gave up the entire 50 percent in return for only a slight reduction in the preferences. Similar outcomes followed from later GATT rounds as well.[105]

In some cases the United States actually promoted arrangements which even more directly undermined its position. Rarely did American policymakers pursue such policies with the explicit purpose of reducing the American role. Instead the reduction was implicit in their actions. If other parts of the world were strengthened, this simply had to weaken America, at least in relative terms. The American push for European reconstruction and integration and the arrangements undertaken to strengthen the Japanese economy can be seen as the most clear-cut examples of the United States thus organizing its own decline.

In the European context the Truman administration worked to promote reconstruction and economic growth even before the Marshall Plan, although the Plan in some ways represented a dramatic stepping-up of this effort. The European Recovery Program probably contributed 10–20 percent of capital formation in the member countries in the first two years, then the percentage tapered off to less than ten. What was even more remarkable was that Washington pushed so hard for European integration. In a historical perspective it has been rather unusual for a Great Power to promote unity and strength rather than discord and weakness in the most important areas it controlled.[106] Both the British and the Soviet experience provided many examples of "divide and rule."

The United States wanted a stronger Organization for European Economic Cooperation than the one actually established; it supported the European Coal and Steel Community, despite its fear of a European cartel that could hurt American economic interests; the Eisenhower administration pushed the European Defense Community and applied considerable pressure to get it through the French Parliament; Washington favored the Economic Community over the looser European Free Trade Association; after the trade split became a reality, it encouraged Britain to join the EEC on what would basically have to be the continentals' terms.

In the Japanese context both the Truman and the Eisenhower administration tried to stimulate the Japanese economy. In the early years after the war production declined dramatically, more than the occupation authorities desired. In 1949–50 the Toyota company almost folded up. Japan's difficult economic situation was one factor behind the so-called "reverse course." With the Korean boom the economy improved, but well into the 1950s Washington worried about the political and economic effects of the depressed Japanese economy. Both Eisenhower and Dulles frequently referred to the "Communist efforts to win over Japan by economic proposals, and the extremely dangerous current economic position of that country." Japan was dependent on foreign trade. The problem was that trade with China was to be curtailed for political reasons and, as Dulles put it, "Japan should not expect to find a big US market because the Japanese don't make the things we want."[107]

On this background Washington worked hard to support the Japanese and, particularly, to open up various markets to Japanese goods. The Southeast Asian market was seen as the most important, but the US itself also had to do more. In 1953 the United States granted MFN-status to Japan; in 1954 Japan was included in the Mutual Security Administration aid program; in 1955 Japan was finally given full membership status in GATT as a result of American efforts, despite European fears of Japanese competition; in the same year the US signed fourteen trilateral agreements with Asian and European nations, in which Washington granted tariff concessions to the third party in return for that country giving concessions to the Japanese. Some trade was even permitted with China and extra efforts were made to bring Japanese goods into the United States. Japanese industry benefited from the American arms buildup and the Eisenhower administration agreed to let the Japanese do less rearming than originally planned.[108]

These policies helped bring about the dramatic growth in the Japanese economy from the mid-1950s on. From 1955 to 1960 production more than doubled. Much of this growth was export-led and from 1955 Japan actually started to run balance of payments surpluses. Contrary to the forecasts, exports to the United States came to surpass those to Southeast Asia. Congress was less happy than the administration about exports that threatened American producers and in 1956 the Japanese in fact imposed the first "voluntary restraints," in textiles.[109]

Certain American producers were very successful in using US aid programs to promote their own economic interests (agriculture, shipping). In other fields, however, the United States gave assistance which directly strengthened foreign competition against American companies. The steel industry provided an example of this. Steel was considered the linchpin of many foreign economies and, thus, reconstruction of these economies meant support for their steel industries. From 1947 to 1960 the United States and international agencies very much influenced by Washington contributed more than USD 1.4 billion in direct aid to foreign steelmakers. In the early years most of this assistance went to Western Europe; later it went to Japan. In Japan's Second Modernization Program this aid accounted for 10 percent of total investments in steel. The Treasury Department warned that Congress was not too happy about such support and that US business would "strenuously object to our using their tax money to finance additional steel competition from abroad."[110] These warnings carried only limited weight, however. In addition, the United States offered technical know-how and stimulated advances in productivity. It also agreed to provide Japan with much needed scrap iron. The rise of foreign competition was certainly one of the many problems the American steel producers came to face. In 1950 the US output constituted 46.6 percent of world steel production (in 1945 it was 63.7 percent); in 1970 the percentage was 20.1.[111]

Several private American companies also entered into comprehensive agreements with Japanese firms. In 1953 General Electric bought into Toshiba and by 1970 owned the single largest bloc of shares in the Japanese electronics firm. Westinghouse negotiated its first licensing agreement with Mitsubishi as early as 1923 and by 1970 was a principal shareholder. Naturally, these agreements were meant to serve the American companies, but they may well have benefited their Japanese partners even more.[112]

There could be no doubt about the dominating role of the United States. Yet, there *was* a discrepancy between America's vast strength and the rather more limited influence it frequently came to exert over its allies and friends. Many reasons can be found for this discrepancy. One set of reasons had to do with the ways in which Washington more or less directly weakened its own leverage.

First, the overall American design was rather loose and flexible. The overriding objectives quickly became to secure international support against the Soviet Union and to limit the influence of communists and their "fellow-travelers." The American policy was in fact based on the assumption that the United States, Western Europe, and Japan had the most basic interests in common. As Truman put it in a 1952 meeting with Churchill, "The United States wants to keep the free world free and believes therefore that this rehabilitation of the free world is the most important task of the Twentieth Century."[113] Then the United States also pushed for freer trade. These objectives were all largely fulfilled, although most countries went shorter on the road to economic multilateralism than Washington desired. In this rather comprehensive perspective most of the rest could be seen as details which did not really warrant all-out stands.

Second, the United States consciously promoted arrangements

which reduced its role because it recognized its own excessive strength. As William Borden has argued, "the sheer economic supremacy of the United States . . . caused a tremendous imbalance in the world economy that threatened both the prosperity of the United States and its foreign policy objectives." Yet, there is nothing automatic here. Both the United States in the interwar period and Japan in the 1980s have shown that it is quite possible to pursue policies entirely different from those of Washington in its heyday.[114] At the same time, the emphasis on integration and union was also a natural consequence of America's strength, of America's own history and the desire to see the US serve as a model for others.

Third, Washington in general and Congress in particular were determined to reduce the costs of whatever responsibilities they were taking on. Certain "isolationist" remnants worked in the same direction. This kind of thinking was most clearly seen with the Republican right. For Taft, its most prominent spokesman, the Truman Doctrine was much too expansive, the Marshall Plan cost too much, and NATO stretched both the American constitution and US resources. They all diminished Washington's freedom of action.

In modified form all these elements could also be found within the American mainstream. At Yalta FDR stated that the American troops would have to return from Europe within two years. After the war the American forces were rapidly demobilized. Until the Korean War Truman insisted that the defense budget be kept below a somewhat magical and rather arbitrary limit of USD 15 billion.

Eisenhower represented the best example of the perceived need for restraint. He frequently worried about the United States overstretching itself. First as Supreme Commander of NATO, then as President he liked to point out that the American forces were in Europe on a "temporary or emergency basis." Occasionally he expressed the hope of having them out in three to four years. He even suggested that NATO itself might be needed for only ten to twenty years. Eisenhower's reasoning was in great part economic. If the Europeans did more, the United States could reduce its defense expenditures and taxes could be cut. The American troops remained in Europe, but Eisenhower still succeeded in cutting the defense budget, even in absolute terms. In relative terms—military spending as a percentage of GNP—defense spending was cut by about one-third from 1952 to 1960.[115]

Kennedy's starting point was different. The federal government could do more and it ought to do more. Defense spending increased substantially. America had to move with "vigor" on many fronts at the same time. Yet, America was beginning to experience balance of payments problems for the first time after the war. It was having difficulties paying for its "empire." Kennedy came to underline even more clearly than his predecessors that America had to move from domination to cooperation. A new bargain had to be struck with the Europeans (and with the Japanese). The United States was ready "to discuss with a United Europe the ways and means of forming a concrete Atlantic partnership, a mutually beneficial partnership between the new union emerging in Europe and the old Union founded here 173 years ago." Circumstances had changed. Europe was stronger economically and more demanding politically. In practice, however, Kennedy favored increased allied cooperation under strong American leadership.[116]

Fourth, American leverage was limited by the official ideology, by the right any country had to choose its own government and policies. (This applied especially in Western Europe vis-à-vis the democratic governments there.) Cold War revisionists are fond of quoting William Clayton, the negotiator of the 1945 loan to Britain, when he stated in response to criticism that he had not done enough to stop socialism that "We loaded the British loan negotiations with all the conditions that the traffic would bear." He went on to say, however, and this part is less frequently quoted: "I don't know of anything that we could or should do to prevent England or other countries from socializing certain of their industries if that is the policy they wish to follow. The attempt to force such countries to adopt policies with respect to their domestic economies contrary to their wishes would, in my opinion, be an unwarranted interference in their domestic affairs."[117] Similarly, in France, Washington certainly regretted the de Gaulle anti-NATO and anti-US policies, but there was very little it could do as long as the French people had expressed their preference as clearly as they had.[118]

Fifth, occasionally the American political system was an obstacle to strong and concerted action. America is strong internationally, but in many ways weakly organized to exert this strength. The many checks and balances frequently made decisionmaking a rather slow process. The divided nature of the American system, in addition to its openness, also gave foreigners a rather unique chance to influence the outcome. Within the executive branch there would almost always be some who defended the position others wanted to modify. Just to mention some examples: The Treasury Department on the whole favored a relatively pure multilateral world open to American business, while the State Department showed much greater sympathy for political considerations, including the views of foreigners. The latter tended to receive the support of both Presidents Truman and Eisenhower. Truman and Eisenhower wanted to bring American troops home from Europe as soon as the Europeans could take over, but the US army did what it could to keep the troops there (to protect its mission and budget). "Localitis" was widespread within the relevant geographical office of the State Department and the local US embassy. Then there was the occasional rivalry between the executive and the legislative branch. For instance, in 1948 Congress refused to ratify the International Trade Organization. Still, this rivalry was rather less pronounced in this period than in earlier and later ones, but attempts to put pressure on, for instance, Chiang Kai-shek or on Israel was bound to run into congressional criticism.[119]

Sixth, partly as a reflection of these other factors, on many occasions Washington actually circumscribed its own influence quite directly. Thus, the European Recovery Program, which undoubtedly represented the single strongest American lever, was to be worked out primarily by the Europeans themselves. Although the American role clearly exceeded the "friendly advice" foreseen, much was actually left to the Europeans. For instance, to a large extent they decided how the American aid was to be divided up among the participating countries.[120] In a rather paradoxical twist, Belgian leader Paul Henri Spaak in 1954 blamed the United States for the lack of unification in Western Europe. The alleged reason was Washington's "over-generous policy," the Americans "had missed a golden opportunity when at the outset of the Marshall Plan they did not make all Marshall aid contingent upon the creation of a unified political community in Europe."[121]

Then there was another related set of reasons which served to weaken the bargaining power of the US and to strengthen that of the allies. These reasons were not, as the first set, primarily products of Washington's own decisions. Instead they either flowed from more indirect circumstances or had to do with the nature of America's partners.

First, since the Europeans well realized that Washington had essential reasons of its own for pursuing the policies it did, any American threat to back out of Europe tended to lack credibility. This is another way of saying that before the United States was really committed to Europe, it had great leverage. Once the commitment had been made, the leverage became much smaller. Whatever leverage may have remained after the formation of NATO and the buildup of American strength in 1950–51 disappeared with Eisenhower's election in 1952 and the virtual disappearance of the unilateralist-isolationist alternative.

This point was well illustrated in the French EDC debate. Dulles's threat of an "agonizing reappraisal" of the American role in Europe was quite simply not credible. Even before the negative vote in the French assembly the key American ambassadors in Europe reported that "the agonizing reappraisal had not in general been taken seriously."[122] The alternative of bringing West Germany directly into NATO was well known in advance and was seen by quite a few on both sides of the Atlantic as possibly just as satisfactory as the EDC, although this was not brought out because so much prestige had been committed to the EDC and because it was feared that to suggest alternatives would only prolong the French process further.[123]

Second, with the US in, Washington was bound to dominate the alliance. Political economists have made us realize that public or collective goods theory applies to alliances as well as to national and local matters. One aspect of the domination was that since the "hegemon"—the United States—could provide the good in question—for instance security—virtually on its own, there was less of an incentive for the allies to come up with substantial contributions, particularly if these were controversial domestically, as they often were. The temptation was great for the allies to take America's role for granted and pursue policies which demanded less of themselves.[124]

Third, some countries were so strong and so insistent on certain points that if the United States were to have its way, this would at best be only after a bitter struggle. Britain was America's closest ally, but on some questions also its main problem. It was financially weak, but it still carried considerable political weight. In 1947 the British were forced to make sterling convertible, but when this led to the collapse of Britain's foreign exchange position, Washington agreed to suspend convertibility. It could not well drive Britain into bankruptcy. Britain also simply refused to join continental schemes which would dilute its sovereignty. Here too Washington eventually adjusted. Finally, the Attlee government had established a comprehensive system of social welfare and economic regulations. Many US policymakers thought this system went too far. They could do little to change it, however, and once it was "permitted" in Britain, it had to be permitted in the smaller Western European countries as well. The protection offered by the British in this respect was a prominent element in the thinking of the Scandinavians in particular.[125]

Fourth, there is the phenomenon of what is sometimes referred to as "the tyranny of the weak." Attempts to apply pressure on the Europeans might, as one official put it, be a "successful operation, but the patient would be dead." This was a primary reason why, for instance, the many ways of using Marshall Plan counterpart funds to pressure various centrist governments in France more or less collapsed. Again, the alternatives, the communists on the left and the Gaullists on the right, were simply unpalatable to Washington.[126] In the EDC debate both Eisenhower and Churchill referred to what they called "the tyrannical weakness of the French Chamber."[127]

Even Germany had considerable leverage in its dealings with the United States. Adenauer was dependent on the United States, but the United States also became dependent on Adenauer. If the "Allied" Chancellor did not do well, he might be succeeded by Kurt Schumacher and the SPD. Early on Washington had preferred a CDU–SPD coalition government, but with the SPD coming out so strongly against NATO, support for Adenauer's party was stepped up. In a longer perspective, to hold Germany down could lead to renewed nationalism, possibly even to a new Hitler, or, more likely, bring about increased cooperation with the Soviet Union, another Rapallo. Thus, one State Department memorandum concluded that Adenauer was "bargaining with us from what is essentially a position of strength."[128]

Even in Japan's case the United States had to be careful that it did not undermine its own best friends. The Japanese had to agree to rearm, but the extent of the effort became the product of endless discussion. The final outcome was certainly less than Washington had hoped for. Many of the reasons for this were spelled out by Ambassador Allison in Tokyo: "In formulating our position we compelled face Japanese realities, particularly constitutional problem [the ban on armed forces], unreadiness of large part of public opinion, and vulnerability of conservative forces to leftist attack if build-up too rapid, at this time. Moreover, we cannot ignore widespread fear here, shared by Yoshida himself, of return of military clique if build-up too rapid, and impact on budget of irresistible demands for relief from this year's great flood damage and crop failure which will require heavy expenditures next fiscal year."[129]

It sometimes seemed that the weaker the government, the greater the leverage. By "threatening" to collapse, Washington's pressure could be counteracted. In 1953 Dulles told the Senate Foreign Relations Committee that a Syngman Rhee or a Chiang Kai-shek "are not the people, under normal circumstances, that we would want to support." Yet, he went on to say, they were the "lesser of two evils." That left the US with very little choice. As Kennedy expressed the same dilemma in May 1961 in the context of the Dominican Republic, there were three choices in descending order of preference: "a decent democratic regime, a continuation of the Trujillo regime or a Castro regime. We ought to aim at the first, but we really can't renounce the second until we are sure that we can avoid the third." In crisis situations Washington frequently felt less than certain that it could avoid this third alternative. That meant that it would often be stuck with the Trujillos of the world.[130]

X Disinterest and Defeat in America's Heyday

Thus, after 1945 the United States expanded on a scale which in important ways surpassed even that of 19th century Britain; the expansion was facilitated by the fact that quite frequently, and especially in Europe—the key area—this was an expansion by invitation. Yet, even in its "imperial" heyday there were areas in which the United States took little interest. There were also areas where it suffered serious defeats.

It is not very surprising that there were limits on America's interests and power. No Great Power has ever been omnipotent. Great Britain suffered a serious setback when the United States broke away from its first Empire in the American War of Independence. Later the limits on Britain's power were to be illustrated not only by its relatively weak position on the European continent, but also by events in South Africa and Ireland. The Boer War (1899–1902) was won, but the victory exhausted much of the earlier imperial enthusiasm. Next-door Ireland was more or less a continuous problem. Even the most loyal members of the Empire, the white dominions, could be kept loyal only by wide concessions to their self-government.

The Soviet Empire too faced rather immediate setbacks. In 1948 Tito's Yugoslavia was expelled from the Cominform. The expulsion was probably accompanied by the expectation that Tito would fall and complete loyalty then restored within the communist world. That was not to be. Instead Tito signalled the problems the Soviet Union would have with communist rulers with an independent power base. In China, as Mao Tse-tung himself said in 1958, with only slight exaggeration, "The Chinese revolution won victory by acting contrary to Stalin's will."[131] Sino-Soviet cooperation lasted barely a decade. Even little Albania could break away from the Soviet fold with impunity. The Soviet Empire expanded again, particularly in the 1970s, but the 1980s underlined how vulnerable Moscow was in most of these new areas of expansion. In the 1970s and particularly in the 1980s many of the rulers of Eastern Europe who in earlier years had been so dependent on the Soviets, were to show dramatic signs of independence.

In principle the United States was a global power from the Second World War on, the Soviet Union only from the 1960–70s. Yet, it was evident that some areas were of little interest to Washington. This fact was most clearly seen in Africa. The United States had military bases in Morocco and later in Libya; it had broad and longstanding interests in Liberia and certain economic and strategic interests in South Africa. That was about it.

The independence process changed this situation only slowly. In 1957 the United States had more foreign service officers in West Germany alone than in all of Africa; only in 1958 was a separate Bureau of African Affairs created within the State Department; economic support for the new states was quite limited. Washington still left the lead in Africa to the colonial or ex-colonial powers. The few signs of interest that could be witnessed, such as Vice President Nixon's visit to Ghana's independence celebration in

1957 (and to Ethiopia, Liberia, Libya, Morocco, the Sudan, and Tunisia) and Eisenhower's speech on Africa at the UN in 1960, were determined largely by Cold War considerations.[132]

Kennedy was to step up the American involvement. The post of Assistant Secretary of State for African Affairs was created; aid was increased; Kennedy spoke out against colonialism much more forcefully than Eisenhower had done. Yet, Washington still showed considerable deference to the colonial powers, and now the powers in question were Belgium and Portugal, not Britain and France. Washington often followed Brussels in matters related to the crisis in the Congo; the American position on Angola was softened after Salazar had made it clear that American base rights in the Azores could be affected. President Johnson became increasingly consumed by Vietnam. As late as 1973 the Assistant Secretary for African Affairs still spoke about "the feeling that Africa is largely a European preserve." He did conclude, however, that "There are several reasons why we should not leave Africa *entirely* [my emphasis] to others."[133]

The two big defeats for the United States occurred in Eastern Europe and in China. In Eastern Europe the United States was prepared to let the region gravitate toward the Soviet Union, but at the same time wanted to protect American interests and ideals. Moscow made certain concessions in favor of the West, but came to insist on firm control particularly in the countries closest to the Soviet Union. The United States applied various economic levers to strengthen its position, but to little avail. The region was not sufficiently important for it to use the military levers which could possibly have balanced the presence of the Red Army, but then only at the risk of war. Despite America's strength and global interests, in Eastern Europe—Moscow's backyard and high priority area—the Soviets were dominant, but that was also the only area in which the Soviet Union "defeated" the United States.[134]

China was the most populous country in the world and not to be controlled by anyone. The United States had long taken an interest in China. After the Second World War an initial optimism could be found that events would go in the right direction. Thus, in August 1946 Truman remarked that "For the first time we now have a voice in China and for the first time we will be in a position to carry out the [Open Door] policy of 1898." The civil war soon dampened any such optimism, but in that war America gave far more assistance to its side than the Soviet Union did to its. Not even three billion dollars could keep Chiang Kai-shek afloat, however.

China was certainly important to the United States. Yet, Washington did not intervene militarily or extend the kind of assistance to China it did to Western Europe. There were many reasons for this. American resources were vast, but still limited; Western Europe was even more important than China; the Soviets stayed out of the civil war; Chiang's was not the kind of regime the US wanted to make a large-scale commitment to; and last, but certainly not least, China was of such size that it was impossible to tell what would be needed to turn the civil war around.[135]

So, in Moscow's backyard and in the world's most populous country the United States suffered defeat. But those were really the only places. In the Korean War the American forces were nearly thrown out to sea, but General MacArthur made a brilliant comeback and soon the United States was crossing the 38th parallel, for the first time actually "liberating" communist territory. The Chinese intervention stopped that, and after two years of stalemate a cease-fire was finally worked out. The Korean War was to cost more than 50,000 American lives and more than USD 50 billion. Yet, the United States (with support from South Korea and smaller contributions from many other countries) held the North Koreans and the Chinese to a draw in a country very far from America, but right on the Soviet and Chinese borders.[136]

At the Geneva Conference of 1954 the North Vietnamese were given control over Vietnam down to the 16th parallel. Based on the war situation that was less than Hanoi had expected, but it still represented a formal extension of communist territory. The Eisenhower administration therefore tried to play down its involvement in Geneva. The defeat was blamed on various French political and military shortcomings. After 1954 the United States became the leading outside power in South Vietnam, working in cooperation with "its" local ruler, Diem. In his first few years Diem, and the United States, appeared to be quite successful.[137] That was soon to change, however.

Developments in Cuba were in many ways the biggest setback for the United States. Castro's take-over was at first seen as an improvement over Battista's corrupt rule, but soon American–Cuban relations went from bad to worse. The traditional way of solving such problems in the Western Hemisphere, an American-backed invasion, failed in the Bay of Pigs in 1961. Various attempts were then planned on Castro's life; they too failed. The non-invasion pledge that helped end the Cuban missile crisis ensured Castro against future invasions.

The Cold War had started in Moscow's backyard. Now it had come to Washington's backyard. A little country a few miles from Florida had successfully challenged Washington's role in the Western Hemisphere. Did this signal a more general American decline?

Early 1960s – 1990:
The "Empire" in Decline

XI The Debate about America's Decline

The debate about America's decline has really been carried out in two rounds. The first round started in the mid-1970s and was largely a debate among American political economists. The most important of these contributors were probably Charles Kindleberger, Robert Gilpin, David Calleo, Stephen Krasner, and Robert Keohane. Although their views differed on many concrete issues, they practically all agreed that in recent years at least the relative position of the United States had been declining. Most of these scholars were particularly interested in the question of whether the existing international economic regime could be maintained when the country that had done so much to set up this regime, was losing some of its leadership basis. Although Robert Keohane was fairly optimistic on that point, the title of his book *After Hegemony. Cooperation and Discord in the World Political Economy* summed up some of the issues these writers were concerned with. In this first round there was surprisingly little opposition to the dominant view of US decline. A few scholars did disagree, however, and the most seminal of these contributions came from Bruce Russett and Briton Susan Strange.[138]

The second round was initiated in 1987 with the publication of British historian Paul Kennedy's bestseller *The Rise and Fall of the*

Great Powers. Economic Change and Military Conflict from 1500 to 2000. There was relatively little new in Kennedy's overall views on the rise and fall of the Great Powers. Although in quite rudimentary form, Robert Gilpin in *War and Change in World Politics* had at least touched upon most of the themes presented by Kennedy (the parallels between earlier empires and post-1945 USA, the historical importance of uneven growth rates, the question of the discrepancy between commitments and resources, and the mechanisms which led to cycles of rise and fall.) Kennedy's approach was much more historical than Gilpin's; this was history on a vast canvas. Yet, it was also policy-oriented and futuristic. It is a safe assumption that most of the tremendous interest in Kennedy's 677-page book spanning more than six centuries had to do with the final 100 pages on the present and future roles of the United States and its rivals for superpower status.[139]

Kennedy's position was clear. America was in decline: "The task facing American statesmen over the next decades, therefore, is to recognize that broad trends are underway, and that the need is to 'manage' affairs so that the *relative* erosion of the United States' position takes place slowly and smoothly, and is not accelerated by policies which bring merely short-term advantage but longer-term disadvantage."[140]

Kennedy's *Rise and Fall of the Great Powers* became a focal point of political and academic debate. "Everybody" had to declare his or her position on whether the United States was declining or not. Ronald Reagan explicitly rejected the view that America was in decline. So, apparently, did a host of prominent scholars, such as political scientists Joseph S. Nye and Samuel Huntingdon, and economist-historian Walt W. Rostow. Politicians out of power found it easier to admit decline than those in power. Thus, former Secretaries of State Kissinger and Vance wrote that "despite our vast military power, our ability to shape the world unilaterally is increasingly limited."[141]

From the tone and range of the debate, it was difficult indeed to see that there was actually general agreement on two very basic points. First, America had been declining compared to its heyday in the 1950s. Second, it was still clearly the strongest power on earth.

The debate was to a large extent one about what America's position in the 1970s-1980s should be compared to. Russett pointed out that if the basis of comparison was 1938 or earlier instead of 1945, it was far from evident that the United States had declined. Nye and Huntingdon agreed that there had been a decline compared to the 1950s and 1960s, but went on to argue that the American position then had been "artificially high."[142]

So, almost everything depended on your reference points. My purpose is to analyze the development of the American role after 1945, when a new era was generally seen as having begun. America's position in the 1930s had not been very important militarily and diplomatically, so a comparison of the 1930s with the 1980s is really of limited interest. Instead the 1950s and 1960s become crucial and cannot simply be written off by them being characterized as years when America's position was "artificially high."

Rostow, who appears to take strong exception to Kennedy's general perspective of decline, has at the same time actually argued that power started to drift away from both the United States and the Soviet Union as early as 1948, when the US undertook the Marshall Plan and Stalin expelled Tito from his Eastern European Empire. That makes you wonder when America's heyday really was.[143]

At the same time, however, there is agreement that the United States is still the world's strongest power. Only the United States has all the qualifications of a true superpower, with its military force, its economic strength, its political organization, its ideological foundation. Even Kennedy wrote explicitly that "the United States is at present still in a class of its own economically and perhaps even militarily."[144]

XII The Declining Relative Strength of the United States

Compared to its position in the first two decades after the Second World War, there can be no doubt that the relative position of the United States declined. On the military side, the Soviet Union achieved rough strategic parity in the late 1960s–early 1970s. The Soviet Navy also increased considerably in the 1960s and 1970s, as did other forces of so-called power projection. (So, absolute, not just relative power counted. Now, as opposed to earlier, the Soviet Union had the capacity to intervene in most parts of the world. This mattered more than the fact that the US was still far

ahead in both naval and general power projection strength.) Cou-
pled with the opportunities provided by the "local" situation, this
meant that the Soviet Union, too, could now act as a global superpower. In the 1960s the Soviet Union had sent forces to Cuba. In
the 1970s Moscow cooperated militarily with Cuba in substantial
operations in Angola and Ethiopia. Such operations would have
been both unheard of and virtually impossible in the 1950s. In this
geographic perspective, the largest of all the Soviet interventions,
the sending of more than 100,000 soldiers to Afghanistan, was actually a somewhat more traditional operation close to Soviet
borders.[145]

The Soviet military buildup was the result of a consistent 3–4 percent yearly increase in defense spending from the early 1960s and
well into the mid-1970s. American spending vacillated much more,
with increases under Kennedy and during the Vietnam War, but
with in fact absolute decreases both in 1965 and in the early 1970s.
After Vietnam the political climate was quite cool to defense spending. The fact that the United States could not keep up with the increases on the Soviet side was undoubtedly one factor which stimulated the interest of Nixon–Kissinger in arms control. Qualitatively,
however, the United States still led in most fields.[146]

While the Soviet Union was moving toward nuclear and military
parity with the United States, Western Europe and Japan were
strengthening their economic positions vis-à-vis the US. In 1960 the
French, West German, Italian, and Japanese economies had constituted respectively 17, 26, 10, and 15 percent of the American
economy. In 1975 the corresponding percentages stood at 22, 28, 13,
and 33. Thus, the Japanese growth was particularly impressive. The
only major industrialized country that lost ground to the United
States was Britain, whose respective percentages were 17 and 15.[147]

American economic assistance to Western Europe stopped in
the 1950s and military assistance in the 1960s. Western Europe's
and Japan's new prosperity was bound to reduce Washington's leverage and influence in these crucial areas. Soon the Europeans
and the Japanese were in fact providing more foreign assistance
than the US itself. In the 1950s the United States had provided
over half of the world's development assistance. In the 1980s the
percentage was around 30. In 1989 Japan became the single largest
donor and the European Community combined provided more
than either of the other two.[148]

The American percentage of world production continued to go down, although much more slowly now than in the first two decades after 1945. In 1960 it had been at around 30 percent; in 1970 it had declined by 3–4 percentage points. The decline from 1970 to 1980 represented another 1–3 percentage points. In the 1980s economic growth in the United States was relatively high and the drop in the American gross national product as a percentage of world GNP therefore stopped. The estimates of what that percentage actually is today vary from 23 to 26 percent depending on the method of calculation used, but the important thing here is more the trend than the overall level.[149]

While the overall decline was no longer as dramatic, in some important fields the decline of the United States was quite remarkable. In 1950 the US had held 50 percent of the world's international monetary reserves; in 1970 this percentage stood at 16. America began to run investment "deficits" with Japan and Western Europe, and in 1990 it in fact appeared that for the first time since the First World War foreigners in general would own more of the American economy than Americans would own of theirs. Japan was not only producing more cars, that traditional field of American domination; more importantly, it also had all ten of the world's ten largest banks and the Tokyo stock exchange was worth more than the New York Stock Exchange. West Germany rivalled the United States as the world's largest exporter. America was probably still holding an overall lead in inventions and patents, but even the so-called patent balance had become negative with Germany in the mid-1960s and with Japan in the mid-1970s. In the 1980s Japan's share of the world's semiconductor market nearly doubled to 49 percent, while that of the US declined from 55 to 39 percent. Increasingly, the United States had to turn to other countries not only for standard parts for major weapons systems, but also for many of the highest forms of technology. This was an entirely new situation for the United States.[150]

The United States became more interdependent with the outside world. The big jump took place from 1970 to 1980, when exports increased from 6.6 percent of GNP to 12.9 percent and imports from 5.9 to 12.1 percent of GNP. In the 1980s the export share actually declined to 9.5 percent in 1987, while the import share held steady at 12.1. The United States was still far less dependent on foreign trade than Western Europe, but more so than the Soviet Union. America's overall position most resembled that of Japan, a Japan that was less dependent on foreign trade than was often assumed. Japanese imports were particularly low, but that was the reverse of the situation in the US. In fact, in the few years from 1982 to 1986 America went from still being the world's largest creditor to being its largest debtor.[151]

The consequences of commercial and financial interdependence are less obvious than one might think. Thus, the big importer and even the big debtor may hold considerable power and debt and imports may be used to strengthen the long-term prospects of an economy, as was the case in the United States in the 19th century. Yet, normally the greatest leverage would clearly seem to lie with the net exporter and the net creditor.

While the United States had earlier been able to use its creditor position to influence the economic and political behavior of other states, it now became dependent on foreign creditors. These creditors invested in the US because the American economy was growing at a satisfactory pace, but the whole question of dependence and foreign leverage represented a dramatic reversal of roles. And the American borrowing was largely for personal consumption; very little went toward investment which could later help turn the trade and investment deficits around.[152]

In oil, a particularly sensitive product, the reversal in the American position was stunning. In 1953 the US still produced more than 50 percent of all the oil in the world and imports were quite limited; in 1976 the US produced only 14 percent of world production; imports increased dramatically and peaked in 1977 at 46 percent of total American consumption. The Middle East now dominated production and, even more, world exports. This was an important part of the background for the rapidly rising role of the Organization of Petroleum Exporting Countries (OPEC). The organization had been formed in 1960, but only in the 1970s did it come to exercise a basic role in the petroleum trade. The 1973 Middle East crisis helped bring about a tripling of oil prices and in 1978–80 the fall of the Shah and the Iran–Iraq war led to another tripling. After a decline in American imports in the early 1980s due to higher prices and conservation, imports then began to increase again and projections for the 1990s indicated that imports would come to surpass 50 percent of consumption.[153]

This change in America's interdependence with the rest of the world coincided with a huge increase in international capital mobility. During a serious exchange crisis in 1961 USD 0.3 billion were converted into Swiss francs during a four-day period; in the 1973 currency crisis USD 3 billion were converted into European currencies in one day; in 1986 the foreign exchange volume on the London, New York, and Tokyo markets alone reached nearly USD 200 billion a day. The internationalization of the money markets lessened the financial freedom of action of any individual country, certainly including the US.[154]

The relative military and economic decline of the United States coincided with a breaking-up of the domestic foreign policy consensus based on executive leadership and bipartisanship. The Vietnam War was the single most important factor behind this breakup, but Watergate and a general swing against the "imperial" presidency were also important. Congress tried to strengthen its position again at the expense of the President. The War Powers Act of 1973 was the most clear-cut expression of this; all kinds of oversight committees were also set up. One problem with the role of Congress, however, was that its leadership had been fragmented. Many more senators and representatives had to be consulted at an earlier stage than under the old system. Finally, the Vietnam War led to a division between conservatives who supported the war and interventions in general and liberals who not only opposed the Vietnam War, but also became skeptical of most (Third World) interventions.[155]

The decline in general and the Vietnam War in particular changed both America's self-image and the world's image of the US. (The latter will be discussed in part XIV.) America was far from omnipotent. In 1971 Richard Nixon described the situation in 1947, when he entered Congress, in these terms: "We were number one in the world militarily, with no one who even challenged us because we had a monopoly on atomic weapons. We also at that time, of course, were number one economically by all odds. In fact, the United States was producing more than 50 percent of all the world's goods." Now, however, and looking five to ten years ahead, he stated: "First, instead of just America being number one in the world from an economic standpoint, the preeminent world power, and instead of there being just two super powers, when we think in economic terms and economic potentialities, there are five great power centers in the world today."[156]

In the 1970s there were many references to America's reduced role, whether in the form of Nixon's five centers (the United States, the Soviet Union, Western Europe, China, and Japan) or Carter's "malaise" affecting the nation. In 1965, 79 percent of the American people had wanted the United States to take an active role rather than to stay out of world affairs. This figure reached bottom in 1982 at 53 percent.[157] Among historians a whole school developed which argued that the United States, not the Soviet Union, was primarily to blame not only for Vietnam, but also for the Cold War. The self-doubts about America's role and mission in some ways resembled the British doubts before and after the First World War. In Britain these doubts increased further during and after the Second World War. In America, however, they appeared to recede.[158]

Ronald Reagan changed the rhetoric dramatically. America was celebrated in terms even more extravagant than those used by Kennedy twenty years earlier. True, there had been setbacks in the 1970s. "How did all this happen?", Reagan asked rhetorically. He gave the answer himself: "America had simply ceased to be a leader in the world". Self-criticism had to stop. For eight full years the President kept up his nationalist rhetoric. And in surveying his own accomplishments in the 1988 State of the Union address, he was very proud of the results: ". . . there is only one description for what, together, we have achieved: a complete turnaround, a revolution. Seven years ago, America was weak and freedom everywhere was under siege; today, America is strong and democracy is everywhere on the move . . . We have replaced 'Blame America' with 'Look Up to America.'"[159]

Reagan was actually able to restore some of the self-confidence of America. In 1986 64 percent wanted the United States to take an active role in world affairs.[160] The partly renewed self-confidence was an important factor of strength in itself. The American defense budget increased by about a trillion dollars in Reagan's first four years. Still, in 1984 the United States was spending "only" 28 percent of world military expenditures as compared with an estimated 51 percent in 1960. In Reagan's second term there was actually a slight *reduction* in military spending in real terms. On the economic side, after the recession of 1981–82 the United States experienced one of its longest economic expansions, but the total historical budget deficit almost tripled and, as we have seen, the balance of payments deficit was so huge that America turned from being the world's largest creditor to its largest debtor. The air was rife with references to America's alleged fall from its Number One position. In a longer historical perspective Reagan's celebration of America showed that developments in the US perhaps resembled those in Britain in the late 19th century in that celebration of the leadership role increased with declining relative material strength.[161]

XIII Contraction and Partial Expansion

The declining American strength was reflected in many policy areas. At the global economic level, in the years 1971–73 the United States suspended the dollar's convertibility into gold and introduced a system of widespread currency floating. This decision was similar to the one Britain had taken in 1931 when it went off gold. Both decisions reflected a weakening of the economic "hegemon's" position; this weakening made it necessary to pursue more nationalistic policies. The United States was running big payments deficits, and needed to suspend rules which limited its freedom of action. Thus, the system which the United States had been the primary creator of had actually come to undermine its position.[162]

Although free trade remained the dominant American ideology, protectionism was rising. The free trade coalition which had dominated post-war economic policies was beginning to fray. Industries that were facing increased foreign competition were dropping out. To reconcile the new protectionism with the free trade ideology, the system of "voluntary restraints" came to include not only textiles, but also steel and automobiles. The implication was clear. If Japan, Western Europe, or the Newly Industrialized Countries (NICs) concerned did not agree to such restraints, Congress would come to pass even tougher ones. In the late 1980s the United States was increasingly insisting on enforcing the rules of international trade on its own, not through the multilateral organizations it had done so much to establish and promote.[163]

The international property regime was changing. From the late 1960s an increasing number of nationalizations were taking place. The American response could still be seen as including open interventions (Dominican Republic in 1965), more "covert" ones

(Chile in 1973, Nicaragua in the 1980s) and economic sanctions (Jamaica and Guyana in 1974). This is not to say that economic reasons were the only ones or even the primary ones for these responses, only that they had an economic dimension too. Yet, by and large Washington had to accept the dramatic increase in nationalizations, the modified rules of compensation, and the many changes short of full nationalization. The American accommodation was most dramatic in the oil sector where demand was great, the united front of the oil companies breaking up, and the local governments often conservative and loyal to the United States in their foreign policy.[164]

Vietnam was the most significant American defeat. Despite the presence of more than 500,000 soldiers, direct expenditures of more than USD 110 billion (the indirect expenditures—including veterans' benefits—would total another USD 240 billion) and more bombs dropped than during the Second World War, the United States and its South Vietnamese ally were not able to defeat North Vietnam and the Viet Cong. When Nixon took over as president in 1969, the American ground troops were gradually pulled out; the air and naval war was intensified and military support to the South Vietamese also increased. The 1973 ceasefire quickly collapsed. A well-equipped South Vietnamese force consisting of one million men proved insufficient to resist the 1974–75 North Vietnamese offensive.[165]

The defeat in Vietnam was to have major consequences for American foreign policy, consequences quite different from those brought about by the Korean War. Korea led to widespread rearmament and several new alliances; Vietnam led to disillusionment and aversion to new commitments. Korea was seen as a direct East–West conflict, with the Soviet Union standing behind North Korea and Washington therefore receiving broad domestic and international support; Vietnam was perceived more as a conflict between a superpower and a small country, with international support, and soon also support inside the United States, flagging.

Vietnam showed the limits of America's power. Détente was, among other things, an effort to come to terms with the relatively declining power of the United States. SEATO and CENTO collapsed. According to the Nixon Doctrine, the United States would still balance the Soviet Union, but regional and local powers would have to handle "local" challenges. The primary regional powers were Western Europe and Japan, Brazil, Indonesia, Iran, and even Zaire.[166]

The fall of Saigon led to the fall of Laos and Cambodia, but outside Indochina there was really no domino effect. When India became independent in 1946–47, this had important effects not only in Asia, as was recognized at the time, but, contrary to expectations, also in Africa. Once India had set the pattern, many felt there was little point in using any considerable force to hold back developments which had to come sooner or later anyway. The situation after Vietnam was different. Indochina was unique. With only a few exceptions, there was little enthusiasm for the Vietnamese model of national liberation and, despite its skepticism to new commitments, the United States did not really see itself as another Britain, or even as an imperial power at all, whose withdrawal from one area would necessarily be followed by retreats from others as well.

The more careful attitude to new and even to some of the old commitments continued under Carter. The Carter administration too stressed the importance of the "regional influentials." The new list overlapped with Nixon's, but Carter also included India, Saudi Arabia, and Nigeria. The new president promised to withdraw the American troops from Korea and to reduce American arms exports. Little was done to stop Soviet–Cuban expansion in Angola and Ethiopia, a dramatic reversal of traditional US Cold War policies. As Henry Kissinger argued with reference to Angola, this was "the first time since the aftermath of World War II that the Soviets have moved militarily at long distances to impose a regime of their choice. It is the first time that the US has failed to respond to Soviet military moves outside their immediate orbit." In Iran, one of the most important of the "regional influentials," the Shah's regime collapsed in 1978–79, with the United States being able to do very little, not even free the American hostages who were held captive for more than a year or, for that matter, give the Shah asylum in the United States.

Carter also concluded the drawn-out and controversial negotiations—which had started under Johnson—about the ultimate transfer of the Panama Canal to Panama. Conservatives reacted very negatively to any such prospect. In his 1976 campaign for the Republican nomination Ronald Reagan stated that "We bought it, we paid for it, it's ours and we are going to keep it." In the end

Carter was just barely able to get a treaty through the Senate which gave Panama control over the Canal after 31 December 1999.[167]

In the Middle East the Carter administration initially wanted to involve the Soviet Union in an attempt to provide a comprehensive peace solution for the region. President Sadat put an end to that approach by his dramatic trip to Israel, a move which in turn made possible the Camp David agreement mediated by Carter. In Africa Nixon had started out by showing even less interest than his predecessors. Washington moved closer to the white rulers of South Africa and even Rhodesia as well as to the Portuguese masters of Angola and Mozambique. With the collapse of Portugal's colonial empire and the earlier strategy in shambles, Kissinger came to take a greater interest in Africa. Under Carter pressure on South Africa and Rhodesia was considerably stepped up. At least parts of the administration showed a commitment to Africa not seen before and this was a commitment not primarily tied to the East–West conflict. But despite the emphasis on "racial equality and social justice in southern Africa," even the Carter administration recognized that in most instances the interests and influence of the traditional European powers "greatly exceed our own."[168]

Around the turn of the century, when Britain was declining and the threat from Germany was increasing, London had withdrawn from some areas where the threat was perceived as small (the strategic withdrawal from the Western Hemisphere, 1904–06). It had also given up its policy of "splendid isolation," first in Asia through the alliance with Japan (1902) and then in Europe through the *entente cordiale* with France (1904) and with Russia (1907).

The United States was forced to withdraw from much of mainland Asia. It tried to work with the "regional influentials." The opening to China was the one American move that corresponded most closely with Britain's policy of diplomatic adaptation to declining status. This rather obvious (in the light of the Sino-Soviet split), but still dramatic (considering past Chinese–American relations) move was based on the realization that "in a triangular relationship it is undeniably advantageous for us to have better relations with each of the other two actors than they have with one another." Moscow had to worry about being outflanked. The opening to China provided a dramatic illustration of how diplomacy could change military requirements. Washington's war plans had earlier been based on the possibility of having to fight two and a half wars at the same time (with the Soviet Union, China, and a local war); the requirement was now scaled down to one and a half wars. China could be taken out of the equation.[169]

In the end the rhetoric of withdrawal was stronger than the action. Carter decided against bringing the troops home from Korea; arms exports increased instead of decreased, as did the defense budget. Moscow's interventions in Angola, Ethiopia, and, especially, in Afghanistan in December 1979 were to bring about a more united perception of the Soviet threat again. After the invasion Carter proclaimed that "This action of the Soviets has made a more dramatic change in my own opinion of what the Soviets' ultimate goals are than anything they've done in the previous time I've been in office."

The intervention in Afghanistan was seen as a potential threat to basic American interests in the Persian Gulf area. The time had come to take on new commitments again. The Carter Doctrine proclaimed that "An attempt by any outside force to gain control of the Persian gulf region will be regarded as an assault on the vital interests of the United States of America, and such an assault will be repelled by any means necessary, including military force." Thus, the Carter Doctrine resembled the Truman and Eisenhower doctrines and represented at least in part a repudiation of the Nixon Doctrine. A Rapid Deployment Force was set up to provide concrete evidence of America's new will to defend its interests.[170]

The election of Ronald Reagan was in part a reflection of this new more activist mood, in part it came to strengthen it further. In fact, the new President not only stood by America's old commitments, but in the form of the Reagan Doctrine he also showed a willingness to roll back Soviet influence. Unlike Eisenhower's rollback strategy, Reagan's was backed up by considerable military and economic support to insurgents fighting communist/radical regimes, in Afghanistan, Nicaragua, Cambodia, and Angola. Nevertheless, this was to be war by proxy. Fears of a new Vietnam were still lingering. The American military were most reluctant to commit troops to major operations without a definite expression of public support and such support did not exist.

The results of the Reagan Doctrine were mixed. In Afghanistan the Soviets actually pulled out in February 1989; in Angola–Namibia the Cubans and the South Africans agreed to a mutual withdrawal; in Cambodia there was Vietnamese disengagement. Yet, the existing regimes remained in power. In Nicaragua Washington's support for the Contras proved both halfhearted and ineffective. Congress and the American people had little desire to intervene militarily even in Central America. In related actions the Reagan administration invaded Grenada and bombed Libya, operations which were criticized even by most of America's allies but were great successes in a domestic American context. The administration did take on significant new commitments in the Persian Gulf in protecting Kuwaiti and even non-belligerent shipping against Iranian attacks. It was much easier for the Reagan administration to use the Air Force and the Navy for limited action than to bring in combat troops.[171]

Thus, the United States met with some successes under Reagan. The new American ambition was probably part of the explanation; so was certainly the desperate state of the Soviet economy and Gorbachev's strong determination to improve the East–West climate and cut both arms and expensive commitments. The superpowers still exercised considerable power. Yet, the importance of the local dimension was clearly underlined too. The Soviet withdrawal from Afghanistan was the result of the indomitable will of the mujahedin (strengthened by advanced American technology). In Libya the American action was relatively limited while in tiny Grenada it was impossible not to succeed. Against a well-organized regime with considerable support, as in Nicaragua, Washington long accomplished little. In Lebanon a President who often stressed the importance of the American presence there, decided in favor of a quick withdrawal after 241 US soldiers were killed in a suicide mission. Lebanon showed that even small groups, if sufficiently determined, could make the American superpower give up what was considered an important commitment. So, paradoxically, the superpowers demonstrated their influence more by pulling out of situations than by imposing their control locally.

Prominent members of the new Bush administration openly admitted that both superpowers were faced with "a frankly diminished capacity to influence events." As a result, US diplomacy came to rely more on local actors than before. In the Arab–Israeli conflict the initiative was left largely with the regional politicians, in Lebanon the Arab League took the lead, in Central America regional leaders and the Organization of American States played important roles. In Europe the EC coordinated Western assistance to the countries in Eastern Europe, all of which now defined their own policies. Japan's role was rapidly being strengthened in Asia.[172]

XIV   Invitations, Interference, and Superpowers versus Local Forces

The United States had to redefine its relationship with the world, including its allies. The Soviet threat was receding, there was not the same need for unity any more. America's relative power had been reduced while that of Western Europe and Japan had increased. America's ideological appeal declined from its high point under Kennedy, although it probably recovered somewhat in the 1980s compared with the 1970s. The invitations issued by the allies to Washington to continue its leadership role became more ambiguous.

Repeatedly Washington referred to the need to redefine the relationship with Western Europe and Japan. Kennedy had proposed his Grand Design and Atlantic interdependence, Nixon proclaimed a "Year of Europe," and Carter a "trilateral" relationship between the United States, Western Europe, and Japan. Little came out of these efforts. The basic structure remained the same. The United States still provided the nuclear deterrence and the troops that could trigger the nuclear response. In somewhat modified form the United States maintained its leadership.

Washington certainly wanted to continue to lead, but it also wanted to cut the expenditures involved. It wanted "hegemony on the cheap." The Europeans, and the Japanese to a lesser extent, insisted on being consulted much more frequently, but were less willing to increase their defense spending. While no Western country became as free in its ways as de Gaulle's France, practically all countries now took more independent positions vis-à-vis Washington than before. Even West Germany, which had been both most dependent on and most loyal to the US chartered its own course. In fact, within a 15 to 20-year period from the early

1960s it went from the hardest of the Cold War hardliners to being the leader in the rapprochement with the East.

In 1962–63 Washington was able to stop the export of German oil and gas pipelines to the Soviet Union. Twenty years later the Reagan administration had to abandon a similar effort. The Europeans did increase their share of NATO's defense expenditures, but still paid less than the Americans argued for. When the United States pressed for economic sanctions after the invasion of Afghanistan in 1979 and again after the introduction of martial law in Poland in 1981, the Europeans followed only part of the way.[173]

The changes in allied relations were greatest on the economic side. The creation of the European Economic Community in 1957 and its later enlargements in most respects established a European economic pillar. In the 1980s the GNP of the combined EC rivalled that of the United States. The growth of Japan remained spectacular and in the late 1980s Japan was in the process of surpassing the Soviet Union for the second largest GNP in the world.

In the mid-1970s regular seven-power economic summits were initiated. In part this mirrored the devolution of economic power within the Western Alliance. Matters which Washington had frequently dealt with on its own or in bilateral consultations were now discussed in a more formal setting with the leading Western European powers, Japan (and Canada). In 1979 these economic summits began to discuss foreign policy issues as well. Discussion and consultation led to better understanding of each other's viewpoints, rarely to full agreement and harmonization of policies.[174]

What happened to the invitations that had formed such an important part particularly of the early American–European relationship? As soon as the Americans had committed themselves economically, politically, and militarily, there was a growing tendency to complain about the strings attached to America's assistance. Once the benefits of the American presence were taken for granted, cries about American interference would be louder and more frequent and they would no longer come just from the minority on the left, which all along had protested against the American role. As British historian Michael Howard argued, a significant element behind American–European difficulties was "the degree to which we Europeans have abandoned the primary responsibility for our defense to the United States; have come to take the deterrence provided for granted, and now assume that the dangers against which we once demanded reassurance only now exist in the fevered imagination of our protectors." Vietnam became a focal point for the younger generation in the same way the Second World War, the Marshall Plan, and NATO had been for the older, but with totally different results as far as the attitude to the US went.[175]

Nevertheless, the changes in the relationship between the United States and its allies can easily be overdone. First, as we have seen, even in its heyday Washington had not really dominated this relationship to the extent that its vast resources would have led one to believe. Second, in some areas it was evident that the Americans were still invited to play important roles.

In the strategic area, the European governments wanted to be protected by the American nuclear umbrella. European worries, more than American insistence, led to the 1979 decision to deploy Intermediate Range Nuclear Forces (INF) in Western Europe, and the 1987 INF-treaty was more popular in America and with the European peace movements than with some of the leading European governments. True, in the 1980s public opinion in several European countries was skeptical of the American nuclear presence. Special problems existed in West Germany—in part as a result of new attitudes to the East–West conflict, in part as a result of a vast military presence in a country about the size of Oregon—and in Spain and Greece, where the US had been associated with the pre-democratic regimes. Yet, support for NATO as such and for the American troops remained strong in practically all the Alliance countries.[176]

On the political side the relationship between Reagan's America and Thatcher's Britain was particularly close, but after a shaky start even American–French relations improved considerably under Reagan and Mitterrand. On the economic side American investments in Western Europe increased rapidly. As late as 1957 they stood at only USD 1.7 billion. This rose to USD 24 billion in 1970 and USD 149 billion in 1987. In the 1960s fears were expressed about "the American challenge," and certain weak restrictions emerged, but the slower economic growth of the 1970s and 1980s largely dispelled these fears and in fact often stimulated competition for new US investment. It is another matter that in these two decades European and Japanese investments in America increased even more rapidly than the other way around.[177]

Similarly, the invitational part was still clearly present in the

American role in Japan as well. Tokyo relied even more than the European capitals on Washington for its strategic deterrence; the security connection with America was fairly broadly accepted, although it was bilateral, not multilateral as in Europe. While Japan in 1986 abandoned its self-imposed limit of defense expenditures not exceeding one percent of the country's GNP, in relative terms it still spent much less on defense than the Europeans. Despite Japan's economic rise and its increasingly active economic diplomacy, it remained dependent on the US not only in military matters, but to a large extent also in its general foreign policy orientation.

In sum, the picture varied a great deal, but there was still an interest in both most of Western Europe and Japan in maintaining and even in strengthening at least certain aspects of the American presence. On the other hand, little or nothing remained of the urge to involve the Americans that had characterized the early period of the Atlantic relationship.

Generally the US still supported both European integration and access to the American market for Japanese goods. But no longer was Washington willing to make the sacrifices of the past. In connection with its integration goals for 1992, the EC was told that "The creation of a single market that reserves Europe for the Europeans would be bad for Europe, the United States, and for the multilateral economic system." Japan was warned much more bluntly that it had to open its own economy to American goods and services if it wanted continued access to the American market. Trade disputes became increasingly numerous both with Europe and Japan. Economic considerations could no longer be made so clearly subordinate to foreign policy reasons. There was to be no more decline by design.[178]

The early American expansion had, especially in the crucial areas, been largely by invitation, although, as we have seen, there were certainly examples of intervention and interference as well. Many of the early covert operations had been successful. "Successes" could still be found. The CIA did play a role in the overthrow of Allende in 1973, but his fall was primarily due to his minority support in Chile and to his country's worsening economic situation and political polarization. The more open American support for the mujahedin in Afghanistan could also be seen as at least partly successful.

Yet, the failures were more noticeable now, thus in a way illustrating America's decline even in the field of covert operations. This was only in part due to the fact that after Vietnam and Watergate Congress took a much greater interest in overseeing the CIA and severely circumscribed the administration's freedom of action (including a ban on further assassination attempts).[179] The "success" from Guatemala in 1954 could not be repeated either in Cuba in the early 1960s or in Nicaragua in the 1980s. In 1953 the CIA had played a central role in bringing the Shah back to power; in 1978–79 the United States could do little to prevent his fall.[180]

Iran illustrated the fact that even "successes" were temporary. In the long run American-sponsored coups created a backlash of anti-Americanism. However, the basic explanation for the changing fortunes of covert operations probably lay in a relative strengthening of local forces vis-à-vis that of the superpowers. In the early years after the Second World War the United States had suffered setbacks in Moscow's own backyard—in Eastern Europe—and in the world's most populous country—China. Starting in the 1960s even small countries were able to make the US suffer defeats: the existence of Castro's Cuba in Washington's backyard, the trauma of Vietnam, the humiliation in Iran, the withdrawal from Lebanon, the collapse of ANZUS due to New Zealand's anti-nuclear policies, the failure of the Contras in Nicaragua, the survival of Panama's Noriega in 1987–89 despite several rounds of very strong American pressure (until he was finally brought down in December 1989 through direct American military intervention).

The situation was rapidly becoming even worse for the other superpower, the Soviet Union, which had to pull out of China in 1959–60, Egypt after the 1973 war, and Afghanistan in 1988–89. The situation in Eastern Europe was becoming increasingly difficult with each country in the region more or less staking out its own course. Once Moscow signalled that there would be no further interventions, the old system was bound to crumble. The climax came in 1989, when in the course of half a year, from the free elections in Poland in June to the fall of Ceausescu in Rumania in December, new and more democratic governments came to power in all the Eastern European countries.

The Soviet Union was certainly much more vulnerable in its key region than the United States was in Western Europe and Japan, despite great changes being under way in the other two areas as well. America's "empire" by invitation, although in decline, proved to have a longer life than the Soviet Union's by imposition. The Soviet economy was still only half the size of the American one, and it seemed to be facing vastly greater problems. In the short run at least, *perestroika* did not lead to growth, but rather to confusion. And one of the most dramatic expressions of *glasnost* was the full revival of the long-suppressed nationalities question. Not only the Soviet Empire in Eastern Europe, but also the Soviet state itself was in serious danger of breaking up. The Baltic states, Moldavia, several republics in the Caucasus region, even Russia itself, all threatened to leave the Union of Soviet Socialist Republics.

It was simply becoming increasingly difficult for the superpowers to control events. At the same time, Washington and, particularly, Moscow clearly wondered whether their partners and clients were not becoming too expensive in relation to the rather uncertain benefits they often seemed to provide.

The decline of the Cold War lessened the importance of the security dimension and thereby weakened the roles of the two superpowers since the security area was where their primary strength lay. Both superpowers faced economic problems while some of their key economic challengers did not. Economic conflicts cut across the military blocs. In fact, the major conflicts here were among the trilateral partners of the United States, Western Europe, and Japan. The strengthening of popular sovereignty, especially in Eastern Europe but, on a much smaller scale, also in Latin America helped push the old order aside.

In the Third World the number of independent countries had increased dramatically; they now held a majority in most international forums. Flagrant interference in their affairs was becoming more difficult. Nationalism strengthened resistance to most forms of foreign rule and often made it difficult even for superpowers to acquire and certainly to manipulate clients. Local regimes were generally better organized and could mobilize larger parts of the population than before, some on the basis of political, others religious doctrines.

Technology was being diffused, particularly modern weapons. Whereas in 1950 only five Third World countries (Argentina, Brazil, Colombia, India, and China) could build anything more than small arms, by 1980 that number had increased to twenty-six and the range of products had grown to include much heavier weapons. Not only countries, but even small groups could now, through modern weapons technology, cause losses unacceptable to a superpower. And the locals were generally much more committed to their cause than was the outside power. As Ho Chi Minh told a French diplomat in 1945, "You will kill ten of our men, but we will kill one of yours and it is you who will finish by wearing yourself out." Admittedly Vietnam was an extreme case, but Ho's basic point applied to other areas as well.[181]

XV The Future of America and the Costs of Empire

In the first round of the debate on America's decline the question of what the future held for America was not particularly important. Most of the political economists involved in the debate were more interested in the future of international regimes than in the future of America. Still, they clearly expected the decline to continue. In the academic-political debate of the late 1980s the future really held center stage. On the political side, Reagan reacted very negatively to any suggestion that America's days might be over even at some distant point in the years to come. Kissinger and Vance were also fairly optimistic: "Far into the future, the United States will have the world's largest and most innovative economy, and will remain a nuclear superpower, a cultural and intellectual leader, a model democracy and a society that provides exceptionally well for the needs of its citizens." President Bush too wanted to sound optimistic, but there was still a change from the Reagan years. Deputy Secretary of State Lawrence Eagleburger received particular attention for a speech he gave on 13 September 1989, where he described "a world in which power and influence is diffused among a multiplicity of states" and concluded that "If it is true that we have emerged victorious from the Cold War, then we, like the Soviets behind us, have crossed the finish line very much out of breath."[182]

On the academic side, Samuel Huntingdon was the most bullish on America: "The image of renewal is far closer to the American truth than the image of decadence purveyed by the declinists." Walt Rostow made it clear "that my most fundamental disagreement with Kennedy is his tendency to regard history as linear. He

regards calls for regeneration as the providence of right-wing pa-
triotic politicians trying fruitlessly to swim against the tides of history." Even the more moderate Joseph Nye argued that "it is important not to mistake the short-term problem arising from the
Reagan period's borrowed prosperity for a symptom of long-term
American decline. The latter need not be the case unless Americans react inappropriately to global changes and inflict the
wounds upon themselves."[183]

Kennedy did tend to regard history as linear and America's decline as inevitable: "the only answer to the question increasingly
debated by the public of whether the United States can preserve
its existing position is "no"—for it simply has not been given to
any one society to remain *permanently* ahead of all the others, because that would imply a freezing of the differentiated pattern of
growth rates, technological advance, and military developments
which has existed since time immemorial." True, the United
States would not "shrink to the relative obscurity of former leading Powers such as Spain or the Netherlands." It also had certain
advantages compared to 19th century Britain, but, Kennedy argued, it had some weaknesses too: the budget deficit, a weaker
political and constitutional system, and a much more challenging
and competitive world environment.[184]

Some of the predictions about the future were based on general
theories about how empires rise and fall. Among political economists the most stimulating contribution came from Robert Gilpin,
among historians from Paul Kennedy.

Gilpin argued that at first empires will yield a surplus for the ruling country, but ultimately the costs of empire will exceed the surplus. A whole host of internal and external mechanisms make it
more or less inevitable that decline will ultimately set in. Security
is expensive and it costs more as the periphery keeps being extended; spending on protection and consumption will crowd out
investment; affluence and preeminence have corrupting effects,
the entrepreneur becomes rentier; challenger countries will rise
and develop new and improved technologies. The international
system is also in a constant state of flux. The challengers tend to
gang up on the leader and wars will speed up changes tremendously. The United States was faced with a particular problem in
that it had to compete with the Soviet Union militarily and with
Western Europe and Japan economically.[185]

Kennedy focused more specifically on the two factors that in his opinion bring empires into decline. First, a gap tends to develop between a "nation's perceived defense requirements and the means it possesses to maintain those commitments." The United States, like former Great Powers, runs the risk of "imperial overstretch." Second, the patterns of global production are constantly shifting and the leading country's technological and economic bases of power are all the time being challenged.[186]

I do not have much to say explicitly about the future. In addition to summing up some of the main points of this study, I shall merely offer a few comments on decline in general and on the "costs of empire" or "imperial overstretch" as a mechanism of decline in particular.

Decline is rarely absolute, in the sense that a country becomes poorer economically and weaker militarily than it was before; more frequently decline is relative in the sense that the leading country is overtaken by challengers economically and militarily.

In this perspective Britain's decline is not really that difficult to understand. Britain was actually becoming richer economically and stronger militarily, but its population, size, economic base, and natural resources were simply too limited in comparison with those of other powers, first Germany, then the United States and the Soviet Union. Indeed, the most remarkable thing about the British Empire may well have been that it lasted as long as it did. What brought about its final collapse was the combined effects of the Second World War on the British economy and on British political attitudes, on the colonies, and on the positions of the United States and the Soviet Union.

The question, then, becomes much more limited: Did the costs of empire contribute to Britain's relative economic decline? While the Empire undoubtedly buttressed Britain's political status, recent research has tended to stress the costs involved in running it. Individuals may have profited, some even considerably, but economically Britain as a whole probably did not benefit much, if at all, and the trend was clearly in favor of expenses outrunning income more and more. Defense was the big item. It has been estimated that in the late 19th and early 20th centuries the costs of British defense were almost twice as high as those borne by the French and the Germans. The white dominions secured particularly good deals from the British. Even India, the only country that the British tried to make self-financing in defense, paid on a per capita basis only a third of what Siam paid for defense. The celebrated Royal Navy was costly and it is not obvious that British shipping, insurance, banking, and other invisible exports were really dependent on the superiority of the Navy to prosper. Then the colonies received cheap loans and administrative subsidies. Taxes were relatively low. Thus, taxes in British India were generally lower than in the Princely States.[187]

On the other hand, the expenses involved were probably not so high that the costs of empire should be ranked among the most important factors for Britain's economic decline. Adequate statistics are not really available, but some estimates put the expenses of the entire public sector at 10–11 percent of the national income in the 1880s and 1890s and at 14–15 percent in the decade 1900–10. The mix between military and civilian expenditures varied considerably from year to year, but military expenditures only rarely made up 50 percent or more of this total and debt payments another 10–20 percent.[188]

It is in fact likely that changes in the tax system could have spared Westminster from making some of the cuts it felt compelled to undertake both on the naval and the army side. Only belatedly did the politicians make such changes. Generally they chose to muddle through, on combinations of tax increases, reductions in commitments, elements of diplomacy, and simply wishful thinking.[189]

The most stunning reversal has taken place in evaluations of the Soviet role. In the 1970s, talk was widespread not only in Moscow, but also in many Western capitals of "the correlation of forces" running in the Kremlin's favor. The Soviet Union was becoming the military equal of the United States; it was making advances in Asia, in Africa, even in Latin America. In the 1980s the popularity in the West of the new leader, Mikhail Gorbachev, far surpassed that of all previous Soviet leaders—and of many Western leaders in their own countries for that matter—but virtually no one was arguing that the correlation of forces was running in favor of the Soviets any more. In fact, military and political commitments were being rapidly scaled back as the state of the Soviet economy went from bad to worse. The Soviet Union's basic problem was that it was trying to be militarily and politically equal with the United States with an economy only half that of the US and with economic problems greatly surpassing even those of the other superpower.

In the early years after 1945 the Soviet Union probably benefited from its (Eastern European) Empire. Reparations were paid by some and resources transferred from all of the countries in the region through war booty, one-sided trade agreements, and joint ventures. One study has argued that the Soviet Union took just about as much out of Eastern Europe as the United States put into Western Europe under the Marshall Plan.

With the death of Stalin, Soviet controls were relaxed and many of the Soviet privileges abolished. On the expense side, the costs rose steadily as did the size of the empire. Military expenses were always high; in the early 1980s they were estimated at 15–17 percent of Soviet GNP. Soviet military expenses were two to three times higher than in the Eastern European countries. Additional expenses went to civil defense and other civil-military functions. The more direct costs of the empire—trade subsidies, trade credits, economic aid, military aid, Afghanistan, covert operations— were even more difficult to calculate and varied considerably over time. One estimate has these expenditures reaching a peak in 1980–81 around 7 percent, then declining to 4 percent of Soviet GNP. Eastern Europe now received considerable subsidies from the Soviet Union, particularly in the form of oil, which was being exported at prices below world market levels, and manufactured goods, which were being imported at higher than world market levels. Overall Soviet security and empire expenses thus totalled about 20–25 percent of GNP.[190]

Whether defense spending has a negative effect on economic performance is a hotly debated topic. A good theoretical case can be made that it has, particularly in highly developed economies operating at or near full capacity. The high growth rates and low defense spending of Japan and, to a lesser extent, West Germany can be used to support this case. On the other hand, some countries, such as for instance Taiwan and South Korea, have been able to combine high growth and high defense spending. Defense spending is only one among a host of relevant variables and is therefore practically impossible to isolate. Much of its effect will depend on the exact nature of the defense expenditures involved, their spillover effects to the civilian sector, the alternatives to defense spending, and so on.[191]

In the rather extreme Soviet case, however, where defense spending has remained so high over such a long period, it would appear that defense has cut heavily into not only consumption, but also investments. With lower growth rates the defense burden became more difficult to carry. In the 1980s few, if any, in the Kremlin appeared to argue that defense spending should be increased to stimulate the Soviet economy. The shoe was definitely on the other foot. Under Gorbachev there were strong signs that the Kremlin was trying to shift expenditure from the military to more productive sectors.[192]

The American case is clearly different from the Soviet one. US military and "empire" expenses have fluctuated considerably, but in normal periods defense expenditures have been around 8–9 percent of GNP and other empire costs around 1–2 percent. While in the 1980s total Soviet expenses have been estimated at 20–25 percent of GNP, the comparable US figure would be around 8 percent.[193]

Such a low percentage would not seem to present any great problems for the American economy. Yet, the answer is not that simple. Thus, the American economy is a research intensive one. To have around one-third of all engineers and scientists working for the military, as is the case in the United States, could have rather negative consequences for the civilian economy, particularly with diminishing spillover from the military to the civilian sector. And, America's economic competitors spent even less on defense. The Europeans spent 3–5 percent of GNP and the Japanese only 1 percent. If defense expenditures were less productive than most other investments, then the competitors could use the "savings" to build a stronger economy.[194]

The American figures for defense and empire spending would seem to be roughly comparable to the British figures. Rostow has argued that American and British costs were so low because the two countries pursued "balance of power" instead of "hegemonic policies." The choice of terms may be somewhat problematic in that both the British and the Americans exercised an influence in their heyday which surpassed that of virtually any other Great Power in history, including the Soviet Union. It can well be argued that Britain and the United States pursued balance of power and hegemonic policies at the same time, depending on the specific area and context we are discussing.[195]

The relatively low spending figures would, however, appear to be another way of stating that the British and American Empires, as opposed to the Soviet, depended on rather limited use of force. The number of British troops was small outside of India and even in India most of the troops, and the financing, were local. Britain's Empire rested on the notion of British superiority being accepted both by the rulers and the ruled. When this was no longer the case, the empire quickly crumbled. The American "empire" went one step further in that many of the participating countries, particularly in Western Europe, invited the United States to play an active role in their affairs. For instance, the American troops stationed abroad certainly represented an expression of Washington's own interests; but they were also encouraged to be there by the Europeans and generally also by the Japanese. Increasingly the host country would also cover much of the American expenses involved. The West German offsetting payments were the clearest example of this. Still, intervention and interference were also integral parts of both empires. Force was there, readily available, and occasionally used, in the US case particularly in Latin America.

The British Empire had been characterized by expansion on the periphery and balance of power policies in Europe. The American expansion after 1945 was really most noticeable in the key areas, in Western Europe and Japan. So close was the relationship between the United States, Western Europe, and Japan that Washington supported the economic reconstruction and growth of the other two power centers, encouraged Western Europe's political integration, and promoted more active political and military roles both for Western Europe and Japan. This friendly attitude was based on Europe's and Japan's role within a wider America-dominated order and on the assumption that all three shared basic interests—preferably as defined by Washington. By strengthening Western Europe and Japan, the US hoped to reinforce the anticommunist front and to limit American expenditures. Under the order set up by the United States, many countries actually prospered more than the US itself, a fact which in turn tended to undermine this order, most clearly on the economic side. Thus, while it was not Washington's objective to reduce America's influence as such, in many ways this policy could nevertheless be described as decline by design.

Outside Western Europe and Japan, most locals perceived the Soviet threat as not very acute, overall political attitudes were generally less friendly to Western powers and ideals, and the ties of economic (inter)dependence with the United States were weak. (Heavy economic dependence could also create problems, as in Cuba and Central America.) Here the United States more frequently came into conflict with local forces, particularly those that desired radical change. Sometimes these conflicts ended in defeat for the US. In Eastern Europe, China, Cuba, Vietnam, and Nicaragua (until the 1990 elections) communists/radical socialists triumphed with varying degrees of nationalist support. But Washington was also humiliated by fundamentalist nationalists, as in Iran, and by fundamentalist terrorists, as in Lebanon. Sometimes the US had difficulties in maintaining good relations even with moderate nationalists, as illustrated by Nehru's India and Nasser's Egypt. The nationalist challenge was in part economic, but Washington was able to adapt to quite dramatic economic changes—as witnessed in relations with the conservative oil countries--when the overall political climate was right. It was generally more difficult for America to accept foreign policy challenges, although frequently economic and foreign policy considerations went hand in hand.[196]

The First and particularly the Second World War had a very negative impact on Britain's world role. By this standard, the effects of America's armed conflicts were much smaller, as were the wars. The wars in Vietnam and Korea were costly, but even during these wars Washington's relative military and imperial expenses remained far below Moscow's ordinary peacetime expenditures. The political-psychological effects of Vietnam were in many respects similar to those the Boer War had on the British and, one might guess, Afghanistan had on the Soviets. These wars were also somewhat similar in that they illustrated the imperial capital taking on ever new commitments and thereby becoming dangerously overextended and vulnerable.[197]

On the whole the American superpower position has rested and still rests on a much firmer basis than that of Britain ever did. In the foreseeable future no country is likely to combine superpower status in so many areas as does the United States. The Soviet Union is equal to the US only militarily, and even in this area the equality is now maintained with increasing difficulty. (This is illustrated by, for instance, the technological challenge of the Strategic Defense Initiative and, even more striking, the dramatic withdrawals of the Red Army from Eastern Europe. For the first time since 1945 these withdrawals will probably leave the United States with greater forces in Western Europe than the Soviet Union will have in Eastern Europe.)

The European Community surpasses the United States in population and, more importantly, rivals the US in the size of its GNP, but still lacks a great deal of the political organization and also some of the military strength necessary to become a superpower. The EC's economic power will probably only continue to grow with the enlargement of the Community and the coming of the integrated market of 1992. Yet, despite the development of closer political consultations, its political strength will still lag considerably behind its economic strength. A united Germany will certainly represent a dramatic new factor, but its combined GNP will still be smaller than that of, for instance, Britain and France together.

Japan has experienced dramatic economic growth, rivals the US in high-tech, and has become the world's primary creditor, but these are only a few of the dimensions of a superpower. Japan is falling short along several other dimensions and even its GNP is still only about half that of the US. As Huntingdon has argued, Japan "has neither the size, natural resources, military strength, diplomatic affiliates nor, most important, the ideological appeal to be a twentieth-century superpower."[198]

Although Kennedy overdoes the parallels between 19th century Britain and 20th century America and does not sufficiently appreciate the strong basis for the US to stay in the Number One position, Washington's problem too has been to "preserve a reasonable balance between the nation's perceived defense requirements and the means it possesses to maintain those commitments." This is the gap Walter Lippmann described as early as 1943 in his now often quoted phrase, "Foreign policy consists in bringing into balance, with a comfortable surplus of power in reserve, the nation's commitments and the nation's power."[199]

While the United States has declined relatively and has suffered defeats, it did not really scale back its commitments significantly (with the exception of Southeast Asia). Even more clearly than in the British case, the problem in maintaining these commitments was not so much an economic as a political one. From the 1960s on, but accelerating dramatically in the 1980s, the American people and their political representatives just refused to pay for their total military and civilian commitments. This fact was most explicitly expressed in the budget and payment deficits.[200]

The "eat, drink and be merry" mentality of America in the 1980s has been compared with Spain in the late 16th century, France in the 1780s, and Britain in the 1920s. To Kennedy the deficits became a symptom of America's failure to adjust sensibly to the inevitability of a new world order, in the way Britain adjusted to the rise of new successor states. Huntingdon has taken the most optimistic approach to the deficits: "The deficits stem from the weaknesses, not of the American economy, but of Reagan economics. Produced quickly by one set of policies, they can be reversed almost as quickly by another set of policies." The problem is actually being taken care of. "America is not in decline, it is in a process of renewal."[201] As is so often the case, the "truth" would seem to lie somewhere between these two extremes. The United States has certainly been in decline, but for the foreseeable future it is still likely to remain Number One and it is indeed much easier to cut taxes than to raise them.

The passing of the Cold War means that in all likelihood the military dimension will become less important and the economic one more so. This will have the most dramatic consequences for the Soviet Union, but will probably also affect the United States negatively. The new East–West climate may well come to have more important consequences for the US role in Western Europe and Japan than America's economic problems have had so far.

Thus, the payment deficit produced considerable pressure in Congress both in the 1970s and 1980s to reduce the number of US troops in Western Europe in particular. These Congressional efforts (Mansfield, Nunn Amendments) were consistently blocked by all administrations from Nixon's to Reagan's. With the dramatic change in the East–West climate and the Soviet willingness to make vastly asymmetrical cuts, the Bush administration proposed to scale back the number of US troops dramatically. Western Europe did not see the same need to have as many American troops as before and there was little chance of the Europeans compensating for the reduced American presence. The new political climate meant reduced defense expenditures on both sides of the Atlantic. In the Japanese case there was still talk of Tokyo picking up the slack resulting from the reduced American role. These withdrawals may improve the American balance of payments, but, as I have tried to stress, America's leading role has in part hinged on its position exactly in Western Europe and Japan. Although the basic commitment to Western Europe and Japan will remain, the troop reductions are quite likely to reduce America's influence especially in these two crucial areas of course, but possibly also more generally. The withdrawals, then, may become more than simply a reflection of the passing of the Cold War; they could also push America's decline further along.

Still, the United States remains *the* superpower. Even at Britain's imperial zenith, predictions about the United States and Russia, and also Germany, coming to succeed Britain were quite frequent. Today there is still no evident successor state to the United States.

This study has not really tried to deal with the future. It has been concerned with the past, with the relationship between the United States and the world in the period when, everybody agrees, the United States was clearly Number One among countries. If there is one lesson to be learned here, it would have to be that America, or any other Great Power for that matter, exerted great influence when it worked *with* local forces. When it worked *against* these forces, it tended to meet with defeat, at least in the long run. Thus, the British Empire collapsed and the fate of the Soviet Empire now provides another dramatic illustration of this fact. Since the American "empire" has generally been more flexible and more in accordance with the will of the local populations—less of an ordinary empire if you will—it has, despite America's obvious decline, nevertheless held up much better than its Soviet counterpart. Still, empires come and go.

But before we historians become too involved in trying to answer a question we cannot really answer, that of America's future, we should try to deal with America's past, its unrivalled strength, the nature of its expansion, its relationship with the countries and peoples of its "empire," the seeds of its decline.

3

Uniqueness and Pendulum Swings in US Foreign Policy*

I Is American Foreign Policy Unique?

Americans have tended to answer this question in the affirmative. This is true of both proponents and opponents of official policy, of whom the former have been by far the most numerous. They have generally seen America as special in its defense of general values and principles: democracy, the rights of neutral countries and the right to self-determination. We are all familiar with some of the images used to describe the special mission of the United States in the world: "a city upon a hill," "a chosen people," "the Israel of our time," "God's own country." While other states had interests, the United States had responsibilities. Its prime mission was nothing less than to save the world.

On the political side an abundance of quotations can be used to illustrate this sense of uniqueness. Woodrow Wilson proclaimed that "Whenever we use our power, we must use it with this conception always in mind—that we are using it for the benefit of the persons who are chiefly interested, and not for our own benefit." John F. Kennedy referred to " . . . our right to the moral leadership of this planet."[1] Ronald Reagan again and again reaffirmed the basic creed, the "undeniable truth that America remains the greatest force for peace anywhere in the world today . . . the American dream lives—not only in the hearts and minds of our countrymen but in the hearts and minds of millions of the world's people in both free and oppressed societies who look to us for leadership. As long as that dream lives, as long as we continue to

---

* This study was originally published in *International Affairs,* Vol. 3, 1986. It is published here in a revised and updated version.

defend it, America has a future, and all mankind has reason to hope."[2] Tension may easily develop between being unique on the one hand and defending universal values on the other. This tension is rarely explored.

For a long time the picture of America presented in American history textbooks did not differ very much from that of the politicians. The authoritative textbooks saw the United States as the young Siegfried, "magically strong, and innocent of the burdens of history, yet at the same time an orphan, surrounded by potential enemies in an unrecognizable world."[3] Although leading academic historians have usually been wary of such generalizations, numerous "traditionalist" historians put the responsibility for the origins of the Cold War squarely on the Soviet Union. It was, in the words of Arthur M. Schlesinger, Jr., long seen as " . . . the brave and essential response of free men to communist aggression."[4]

Hardly anyone among the minority of the critics of American foreign policy has argued that the United States is the most evil country in the world. Instead critics have tended to agree that America had a service, even a mission, to perform. The problem was that America's true values had been corrupted by certain evil interests—flawed presidents, the capitalistic system, "merchants of death" or the military-industrial complex. In the 1972 presidential campaign George McGovern compared Richard Nixon to Hitler, but a more basic theme was his "Come home, America." The father of Cold War revisionism, William Appelman Williams, called his seminal book *The Tragedy of American Diplomacy*.[5] The main tragedy, he wrote, was the way in which sincere idealism had been subverted by ulterior forces, in his opinion by the overvaluation of power and the greed of capitalism.

Most European observers have been rather skeptical about the American claim to uniqueness, particularly as it usually implied American superiority. To many Europeans, what was unique about America was its uncanny ability to make the most inspiring idealism coincide almost perfectly with rather ordinary national objectives. American leaders lectured the world on the dangers and immorality of spheres of influence, except of course the United States' sphere of influence in Latin America. Or they pressed for the internationalization of waterways, except for the Panama Canal. They argued for the principles of free trade, except in those few fields where the United States stood to lose from international competition. And, at the top of its hierarchy of values, the United States always stood for democracy, except when a popularly elected left-wing government could be seen as working closely with the Soviet Union or when authoritarian law-and-order regimes were supported, for various reasons.

My introductory question about the uniqueness of America cannot be answered by logical exercise. We have to look at history. The surprising thing is how little has actually been done in the way of direct comparison between US policies and those of other great powers. Americans undoubtedly have perceived themselves as special. Most courses at American universities in US foreign relations are implicitly and often explicitly based on that premise. Has the United States really behaved very differently from other great powers?

II Great Powers and Constant Objectives

In British foreign policy, it is generally alleged, balance-of-power considerations have been the guiding star. We are all familiar with Lord Palmerston's famous dictum, that Britain has "no permanent friends . . . only permanent interests," and Churchill's description of Britain's alliance policy:

> For four hundred years the foreign policy of England has been to oppose the strongest, most aggressive, most dominating power on the Continent . . . it would have been easy and . . . tempting to join with the stronger and share the fruits of his conquest. However, we always took the harder course, joined with the less strong Powers, . . . and thus defeated and frustrated the continental military tyrant whoever he was . . .[6]

Britain thus tried to prevent Europe from falling under the domination of one country or one ruler, whether the Spain of Philip II, the France of Louis XIV and Napoleon, the Germany of William II and Hitler, or the Soviet Union of Stalin and Khrushchev.

The French have always been preoccupied with the grandeur of their nation. Of more immediate concern, at least since 1870, has been the protection of their natural frontiers and, particularly in that context, the role of Germany. Only after the Second World War were French fears partially relieved. As the French writer

Francois Mauriac put it: "I love Germany so. Every day I thank God that there are two of them."[7]

Russian, as well as Soviet, foreign policy appears to have been guided by that old axiom, "That which stops growing begins to rot." Force often provided the instrument and Pan-slavism and orthodoxy the rationalizations for Russia's expansion. The Soviet state combined force with what its leaders called "the laws of the class struggle", or what a Western observer has described as Soviet convictions "both of the infallibility of the communist word and of the inevitability of a communist world."[8]

What are the corresponding constant factors in American foreign policy, besides the sense of uniqueness? Isolationism was long seen as such a factor. Not any more. Instead, in the 1960s and 1970s we heard much of American expansionism.

Certain constant objectives can be found in American foreign policy. Three in particular are often picked out: the physical survival of the United States, the perpetuation of the American way of life, and the promotion of the economic well-being of the American society.[9] At least since the Russian revolution of 1917, the containment of communism could be listed as a fourth objective.

These factors, however, are so general that with the possible exception of the term "the American way of life" and its many ramifications, their various national counterparts could apply equally well to a great number of other states. Let me therefore introduce my favorite: the pendulum swings. Here is the argument: While there are of course elements of change in the foreign policies of all countries, the swings of the pendulum have been wider, not to say wilder, in the United States than in other Great Powers. Many states move from one position to a different one. In America the pendulum swings back and forth repeatedly.

Many observers have noted the swings of the American foreign policy pendulum. As early as 1951 the historian Dexter Perkins published his account of a "cyclical theory of American foreign policy" where he distinguished between periods of peace, periods of rising nationalism that precede war, and periods of nationalism that follow war.[10] In 1952 Frank L. Klingberg divided the history of American foreign relations into periods of "extroversion" and "introversion," both of approximately 25 years duration.[11]

Policymakers have noticed the same swings. In their first meeting after Richard Nixon had been elected President in 1968, Henry

Kissinger told the President-elect that "the overriding problem was to free our foreign policy from its violent fluctuations between euphoria and panic, from the illusions that decisions depended largely on the idiosyncrasies of decision-makers." Kissinger recommended a "British" approach: "Policy had to be related to some basic principles of national interest that transcended any particular Administration and would therefore be maintaned as Presidents changed."[12] Later Secretary of State George Shultz stressed the same theme, although he felt that this was as much a problem for all democracies as specifically for the American one.[13]

So there is little really new in a theory of American foreign policy swings. What this chapter attempts to do is, first, to give specific examples of such swings; secondly, to provide some of the badly needed comparisons with policies of other great powers; and, thirdly, to review some of the explanations for the swings on the American side being so much wider.

III Some Basic Policy Swings

The basic swing on the American side in the last fifty years is the one from the isolationism of the 1930s—and the Neutrality Acts of 1935–37 represented the most extreme point of this isolationism—to America's very expansive role after the Second World War, a role which culminated in the dispatch of more than 500,000 men to that less than strategically vital area, Vietnam.

It has been argued, with considerable justice, that America's basic assumptions about the outside world changed far less than the dramtic shift in its outward appearance might indicate. The sense of being special, even morally superior, remained untouched. Under isolationism America had to be protected from the corrupting influences of the traditional Great Powers. After the Second World War most of these powers lay shattered. Now America was in a position of such strength that there was little chance of corruption by its evil surroundings. In fact, in many parts of the world the United States was invited by various local governments to play a larger role to forestall the spread of communism, to strengthen their national economies, to reduce colonial influence and to accomplish an assortment of other objectives.[14]

Although the "involvement" pendulum has fluctuated considerably, internationalism and globalism have clearly maintained their position in American foreign policy since 1945. On this specific point, therefore, the swing on the American side is similar to some of the predominantly one-directional swings we have witnessed in the policies of the other powers. The Soviet role in the world has also been growing. In the 1920s and 1930s Moscow partly isolated itself and partly was kept in isolation by others. In the 1940s this changed dramatically, but the Soviet Union still counted for little outside its border areas. Only in the 1950s and 1960s did it develop both the interest and the capabilities necessary to play a global role similar to the one which the United States had already been performing for some time.

The importance of the old powers has declined. British foreign policy traditionally moved within three circles: the Atlantic, the Commonwealth, and Europe. The European dimension gradually became more and more important at the expense on the other two, particularly the Commonwealth. Britain and France have both experienced sweeping changes in their colonial roles. Their empires have gone, and so have most other empires.

In West Germany the pendulum swung from Konrad Adenauer's staunch anti-communism to Willy Brandt's détente-oriented *Ostpolitik*. But, here again, the basic change was in one direction only. The Christian Democrats came to adhere to the basic course set by Brandt. In Britain, both the Conservatives and Labor moved closer to Europe. No party could reverse the colonial decline of the European powers.

In China, policy swung from the pro-Soviet line of the 1950s to the anti-Soviet attitude of the 1960s and 1970s, and from anti-Americanism to the opening to America in 1971–72. In the late 1980s, however, Sino-Soviet relations swung back to a clearly more relaxed state of affairs and the repeated Chinese shifts between isolationism and involvement seem to approach the American swings which are the subject of this chapter.

Even movements from one position to another would normally be more dramatic on the American side. During the Second World War few countries pressed harder than the United States for the unconditional surrender of Germany and even for its deindustrialization in the form of the Morgenthau Plan. After the war, it took only a few years before the United States argued more strongly than anyone for the removal of most of the restrictions on

West Germany's freedom of action, including the right to bear arms. Developments in Japan followed a rather similar pattern. Nowhere was the fascination with China and the support for Chiang Kai-shek greater than in the United States. After "the loss of China," no European capital could measure up to Washington in its insistence on isolating the new rulers. Finally, in 1945 no people had higher hopes than the Americans for the United Nations. Again, disillusionment soon set in more severely here than in almost any other country.

IV The American Attitude to the Soviet Union and to Defense Spending

But the focus of this chapter is on recurrent change, swings back and forth, not simply from one position to another. It is here that the special nature of America's foreign policy is most pronounced. My examples and comparisons will come from two crucial fields, East-West relations and defense spending.

In Soviet-American relations since the Second World War at least five periods, or swings of the pendulum, can be detected: the period during the war, the years from 1945/6 to 1963, from 1963 to the middle to late 1970s, the period from the late 1970s until about 1984, the years from 1984 to 1990.[15]

America's conduct in the Second World War was characterized by faith in the possibility of cooperation with the Soviet Union. To give only a few, rather over-simplified, expressions of this: In March 1942 Franklin Roosevelt told Churchill, "I know you will not mind my being brutally frank when I tell you that I think I can personally handle Stalin better than either your Foreign Office or my State Department. Stalin hates the guts of all your top people. He thinks he likes me better, and I hope he will continue to do so."[16] In March 1943, *Life* published a special issue on the Soviet Union in which, among other things, Lenin was proclaimed "perhaps the greatest man of modern times," the Russians "one hell of a people . . . (who) to a remarkable degree . . . look like Americans, dress like Americans, and think like Americans," and the NKVD "a national police similar to the FBI."[17] As late as August 1945, 54 percent of a sample of the public thought that the Soviet Union could be "trusted to cooperate with us after the war is over." That figure was only one percent less than the wartime high immediately after the Yalta Conference. Thirty percent did not have such trust, while 16 percent were undecided.[18]

Then in late 1945 the pendulum began to swing towards the other extreme. Soon "Uncle Joe" Stalin was seen as another Hitler. As Truman later wrote about his own thinking after the North Korean attack on South Korea on 24 June 1950:

> In my generation this was not the first occasion when the strong had attacked the weak. I recalled some earlier instances: Manchuria, Ethiopia, Austria. I remember how each time that the democracies failed to act it had encouraged the aggressors to keep going ahead. Communism was acting in Korea just as Hitler, Mussolini and the Japanese had acted ten, fifteen and twenty years earlier.[19]

A student of Hollywood films has noted of this period: "Gone are the brave Russian women fighters, the happy villagers, and the democratic allures of the rulers. In their place somber, bureaucrats, counterparts of the Nazis, spread an atmosphere of oppression."[20] The number of people who believed that the United States could cooperate with the Soviet Union fell rapidly. In 1957, only 3 percent had a highly or even mildly favorable opinion of the Soviet Union, while 74 percent expressed a highly unfavorable opinion.[21]

Then, after the Cuban missile crisis of 1962, the pendulum slowly began to swing the other way. Détente was arriving. Its climax was probably reached in 1972–73. At the signing of the SALT I agreement Richard Nixon waxed lyrical: "The historians of some future age will write of the year 1972 . . . that this was the year when America helped to lead the world up out of the lowlands of constant war and onto the high plateau of lasting peace."[22]

Below the official level, détente and the Vietnam War caused Americans much soul-searching. To mention one example, revisionism flourished in historical writings on the origins of the Cold War, and a rapidly growing group of American historians told a somewhat startled world that the United States, not the Soviet Union, as most of Western Europe had always believed, was to blame for the Cold War. In 1972, 40 percent of a sample expressed a favorable opinion of the Soviet Union, while 32 percent had a very unfavorable and 22 percent an unfavorable one. As late as 1967, only 19 percent had been favorable.[23]

In the late 1970s the pendulum started to swing the other way again, and it swung all the way to the other extreme. The swings did not get smaller, as many observers had argued they would. The new climate was clearly noticeable in the last years of the Carter administration, but the climax was reached with President Reagan. In June 1982 Reagan described to the British parliament " . . . the march of freedom and democracy which will leave Marxism-Leninism on the ash heap of history as it has left other tyrannies which stifle the freedom and muzzle the self-expression of the people."[24] In short, the Soviet Union represented the "focus of evil in the modern world . . . and evil empire."

Again public confidence in the Soviet Union plummeted. After the Soviet invasion of Afghanistan, only 13 percent of a sample had a favorable opinion of the Soviet Union; in September 1983, after the shooting down of the KAL airliner, only 9 percent. This was the lowest level since the 1950s.[25]

Then, in 1984 the pendulum began to swing the other way again. The Reagan administration softened its rhetoric and in November 1985 Reagan and the new Soviet leader, Mikhail Gorbachev, met for the first time. They were to meet four more times and the swing of the pendulum was almost as dramatic and rapid now as it had been in 1945–46 when Stalin changed from "Uncle Joe" to the new Hitler. The evil empire disappeared and instead Ronald and Mikhail were walking hand in hand on Red Square. "Gorbamania" swept the United States. Harper & Row sold Gorbachev's book *Perestroika* as "the book of the year by the statesman of the year." Gorbachev was running behind Reagan but ahead of most other US politicians in American popularity polls. Still, public opinion changed less than did President Reagan and Gorbachev was clearly far more popular than was the Soviet Union as such.[26]

At first the Bush administration appeared to modify this course somewhat. After an initial period of evaluation Gorbachev was clearly seen in a favorable light, but the overall attitude was still more cautious than in Reagan's final year and it was evident that several members of the administration were far from willing to declare the Cold War over. Now Congress and the public came to feel that Bush was just too slow in responding to the vast changes in the Soviet Union and in Eastern Europe. But soon Bush picked up where Reagan had left off in trying to establish close bonds with Gorbachev. The administration made it quite clear that it wanted *perestroika* to succeed.

There have been as many as seven or eight different periods in the pattern of American defense spending since 1945, an observation which seems to indicate that levels of American defense spending do not depend exclusively or even primarily on perceptions of the Soviet Union. After the Second World War Truman thought USD 15 billion the absolute maximum figure that the United States could spend on defense, despite the fact that the 1945 defense budget had surpassed USD 80 billion. With the Korean War, defense spending more than tripled in the course of three years, and in 1953 it came to USD 50 billion. That constituted 13.8 percent of the American GNP, the highest ever since the Second World War. (In 1945, 38.5 percent of GNP had been allocated to defense.)[27]

Then Eisenhower brought "fiscal responsibility" back again, and the "New Look" strategy was drawn up to reflect "sound budgetary policies." The result was that as late as 1960 the defense budget stood at only USD 46 billion (in current prices). John F. Kennedy proclaimed that "We shall pay any price, bear any burden, meet any hardship, support any friend, oppose any foe, in order to assure the survival and success of liberty. This much we pledge—and more."[28] Even if, as with so much American rhetoric, this remark was not to be interpreted literally, in the early 1960s defense expenditure again increased fairly rapidly. The war in Southeast Asia soon made it rise even more steeply.

In the 1970s the defense budget declined. Although this was partly the result of reduced expenditure on the war in Vietnam, after inflation is taken into account it becomes clear that the budget had suffered a marked decline. When the 1978 defense budget passed the USD 100 billion mark the figure represented only 5 percent of GNP, the lowest level since 1948.[29]

Under the late Carter administration and even more under President Reagan, defense expenditure just could not be increased fast enough. Reagan's total of USD 1,007,900 million over his first four years represented the biggest buildup in peacetime in modern American history.[30] Reagan told the American Legion: "Possibly some of you remember drilling with wooden guns and doing maneuvers with cardboard tanks. We must never repeat that experience."[31] In constant dollars the defense budget was to peak in 1985, however.

After 1985 Congress and the American people refused to agree to any real growth. In January 1981, 61 percent of a sample of the American public had favored increased defense spending. In February 1985 this figure was down to 16 per cent.[32] In Reagan's last four years the defense budget actually declined slightly in real terms. Bush's first year was a zero growth year and the 1–2 percent increases foreseen by the new administration for the coming years seemed uncertain at best. In fact, the domestic budget crisis and the political upheavals in the Soviet Union and Eastern Europe soon made it obvious that the defense budget would see significant cuts.[33]

V Western Europe, the Soviet Union, and Defense Spending

If we compare American attitudes to the Soviet Union and to defense spending with attitudes in Western Europe, and Britain in particular, pendulum swings appear here, too, but they seem to be on a smaller scale than in America. In "soft" periods in the United Kingdom, British attitudes to the Soviet Union were generally "harder" than in the United States, while in "tough" periods they tended to be more conciliatory. This tendency was most noticeable at the top policymaking level, and is probably less pronounced in a comparison of public opinion in the two countries.

To simplify matters vastly: during the Second World War there was less faith in Britain than in America in the lasting nature of the common objectives of the Grand Alliance. As Churchill said in 1941 about his purpose in cooperating with the Soviet Union: "I have only one purpose, the destruction of Hitler, and my life is much simplified thereby. If Hitler invaded Hell I would make at least a favourable reference to the Devil in the House of Commons."[34] Balance-of-power considerations had brought Britain and the Soviet Union together. In the United States the balance of power was an evil concept. In Britain there was a less pronounced tendency to assume that the allies were becoming more and more alike as a result of sharing the same overriding objective in war. Most Cabinet members, both Conservative and Labor, the

Foreign Office, the top military leaders, and most of the establish-ment in general maintained an evident skepticism about Soviet in-tentions, although they—and Churchill himself—were certainly in-fluenced by the climate of wartime cooperation. At the level of public opinion, however, strong signs of a pro-Russian mood could be found.[35]

In 1945-early 1946, British-Soviet antagonism was more pro-nounced than the American-Soviet version. While during the early years after the war the British, like most West Europeans, were worried that the Americans might not show sufficient interest in containing the Soviet Union, they soon came to fear that they would do too much. In part this reflected European ambivalence toward the United States, an ambivalence most strongly expressed in non-European matters. But Europe's fears also illustrated the sweeping anti-communist mood in the United States. In Decem-ber 1950 Attlee flew to Washington to warn against American use of atomic weapons in Korea and to encourage the exploration of a settlement with the Soviet Union.[36] After Stalin's death in 1953 the British, again under Churchill's leadership, showed greater inter-est than the Americans in East-West summits and agreements. This shift toward dialogue continued under the Premiership of An-thony Eden and Harold Macmillan. It was undoubtedly stimulated in part by a lingering desire for Britain to play a world role and for a chance for the Prime Ministers to exercise their considerable diplomatic skills.[37] Again, at the level of public opinion the British change in attitude was probably similar to that in the United States, although direct comparisons are difficult. Any pro-Soviet mood gradually disappeared, and in the 1950s only 3 or 6 percent approved and 70 to 80 percent disapproved "of the role the Soviet Union is now playing in world affairs."[38]

This pattern was repeated in the period of detente in the United States, and London differed not only from Washington, but also from Paris and Bonn. Joseph Frankel has concluded that "Whereas British governments used to lead during the previous at-tempts at an East-West detente, ever since 1968, they had begun to lag behind their partners.[39] There were many reasons for this lag, which was apparent under both the Wilson and Heath govern-ments: a strong reaction against the Soviet invasion of Czechoslo-vakia in 1968, a certain fear of what the detente policies pursued by de Gaulle in France and Brandt in West Germany could lead to, a preoccupation with the "east of Suez" debate, the expulsion of 105 Soviet representatives in 1971. Public opinion probably changed less in a pro-Soviet direction than it did in the United States. While in 1973–74 disapproval ratings of the Soviet Union had fallen to 39 percent, approval had increased only to 17–18 percent, with over 40 percent answering "don't know."[40]

In the late 1960s and early 1970s the British, like most Europeans, may have expected less from detente than many Americans. Nor, for many different reasons, was there the same need in Britain to oversell detente in order to undermine opposition to agreement with the Soviet Union, as was the case in the United States.

The Europeans possibly expected less and they certainly gained more: normalization of relations in Germany and Berlin, increased trade and human contacts across the East-West divide. For this and other reasons, events outside Europe—Soviet policies in Angola, Ethiophia, and Afghanistan—brought about less of a conservative detente backlash in Western Europe than in the United States. Even Prime Minister Margaret Thatcher, so close to President Reagan on many questions, wanted to maintain more open lines to the Soviet Union, as was illustrated in the gas pipeline dispute.[41]

When in 1984–85 the Reagan administration changed its course so dramatically, this then brought the US and Western Europe closer together in their policies toward the Soviet Union. Naturally the Gorbachev phenomenon had a major impact in Western Europe too, particularly in West Germany, but also in Britain. Yet, since Europe had not really moved so much away from detente, the swing of the pendulum was not so violent here, although the detente policies of conservative Chancellor Kohl were particularly far-reaching. Mrs Thatcher combined an early appreciation of Gorbachev's qualities with insistence that the West should not drop its guard. Like most other Western European leaders she was shocked by Reagan's declared objective at the Reykjavik summit of eliminating all ballistic missiles from the face of the earth and even, ultimately, creating a world without nuclear weapons. (And this was done without any consultation with the European allies.) Again the attitude of the British public probably changed more than that of the government. In March 1981, 70 percent thought that the Soviet Union wanted to extend its power over other countries. Eight years later only 35 percent thought so as compared with 33 percent who said the same about the United States. The French moved the least of all in that de Gaulle's France had been a "soft" deviator in the late 1950s–60s, while in the 1980s the French were relatively skeptical of Gorbachev's Soviet Union.[42]

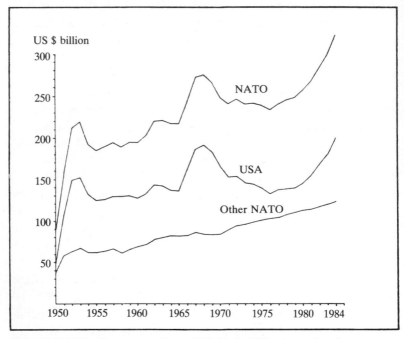

Figure 1 NATO military expenditure, 1950–84. At 1980 prices and exchange rates. *Source:* This figure is gratefully reproduced by permission from *SIPRI Yearbook 1985* (London, 1985), p. 229.

The smaller swings of the pendulum on the European side (plus Canada) with regard to defense expenditure are represented in Figure 1. The ups and downs on the American side are clearly visible. On the European side, the stability is quite remarkable: here there has been a fairly consistent though small, increase in most years since 1950. (With a few exceptions the same basic pattern is found if we look at individual countries in Western Europe.) To mention one example: while in the late 1970s the Americans came to feel rather strongly that they had to reverse an earlier decline, the Europeans pointed out that they had in fact been increasing their defense budgets all through the 1970s. But Figure 1 also illustrates the "American" point that the United States continued to outspend the Europeans, despite the roughly equal size of America's economy and that of its European NATO partners. (There are many reasons for this, one being the fact that the United States is a superpower with global commitments, the European countries are not.)

The same trend would also seem to hold true for the latter half of the 1980s with the stagnation in defense spending being more marked in the United States than in most Western European countries, although in this case the cuts in Britain have been at least as big as in the US, despite the defense rhetoric of the Thatcher government.[43]

VI Soviet Attitudes to the West and to Defense Spending

Winston Churchill described the Soviet Union as "a riddle wrapped in a mystery inside an enigma." In the analysis of political processes and the motivations behind actions, we in the West have traditionally been dealing in varying degrees of ignorance, although the situation has certainly improved under Gorbachev.

Yet it can also be argued that Soviet actions are or at least have in the past been more predictable than American ones. To quote James Schlesinger: "The passage of almost half a century has provided sufficient experience to make Soviet policy almost predictable. There is persistency, perhaps even consistency—and remarkably few sharp turns. Can the same be said of US attitudes and US policy? Hardly so."[44]

The Soviet foreign policy pendulum has certainly swung, but more narrowly than the American one. Soviet attitudes to the United States appear to have followed the overall pattern and to have fluctuated less than American attitudes to the Soviet Union. The pattern probably also applies to Soviet defense spending.

During the Second World War and again in the period of detente in the late 1960s and early 1970s, euphoria about East-West cooperation was rather more controlled in Moscow than in Washington. Even in the struggle against Hitler's Germany the Western allies were kept at arm's length. The basic antagonism between capitalism and communism had not ceased to exist. The most significant lowering of the Soviet ideological guard was probably immediately after the invasion of Normandy in June 1944. For the first time, *Pravda* published figures on the massive aid the Soviet Union had been receiving from the West, primarily from the United States. Stalin even suggested that the Soviet Union, Britain, and the United States should establish a joint staff to coordinate their operations. This new climate lasted only a few months. Soon Moscow reverted to the established line. The Red Army was the only decisive force in the war. Stalin was no longer interested in a joint military staff.[45]

A similar pattern was repeated in the 1970s, although Leonid Brezhnev certainly saw greater advantages in peaceful coexistence than Stalin. On 30 August 1973, in an editorial entitled "Peaceful coexistence and the class war," *Pravda* praised East-West cooperation, but went on to state: "The struggle between the proletariat and the bourgeoisie, between international socialism and imperialism, will continue until the complete and final victory of Communism throughout the world."[46] At the 25th Party Congress in 1976, Brezhnev warned, "Detente does not in the slightest way abolish and cannot abolish or change the laws of the class struggle. We do not conceal the fact that we see detente as a way to create more favorable conditions for peaceful socialist and communist construction."[47]

Yet, in the 1980s, for the first time, the swing in Soviet attitudes may well have rivalled if not surpassed American ones. In his early years Reagan was attacked in the Soviet press in the crudest of terms and in September 1983 party leader Andropov stated that "if anyone had any illusions about a possible evolution for the better in the policy of the present American Administration, such illusions have been completely dispelled by the latest developments."[48] Gorbachev changed all this. Soon the international class struggle was more or less declared over and instead the need for cooperation was stressed. In one journalist's phrase, the Soviet caricature of America changed from Rambo to Mister Rogers, and Gorbachev was as effusive in praising his superpower counterpart as was Reagan. There are indications that the Soviet public had difficulties in adjusting to the dramatic change in climate.[49]

Knowledge in the West about levels of Soviet defense spending is limited, and estimates concerning this are subject to a minefield of methodological problems. Still, to quote from a study by the Stockholm International Peace Research Institute (SIPRI), "More trust can be placed in the trend than in the absolute level."[50] Figures 2 and 3 illustrate the trend of the Soviet defense budget compared with that of the United States.

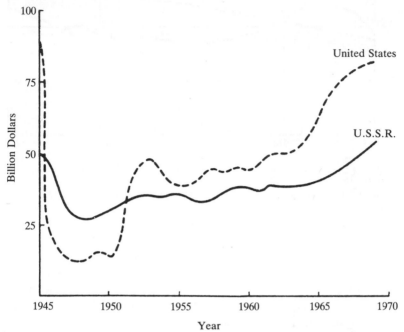

Figure 2 Military spending, United States and the Soviet Union, 1945–68
Note: Soviet spending is nominal defense category, plus defense-related research and development. Figure is given in dollars, converted from rubles at ratios of domestic purchasing power, rather than legal exchange rates.
Source: I am grateful to George H. Quester for allowing me to reproduce this figure from his *Nuclear Diplomacy: The First Twenty-five Years* (New York, 1970), p. 293.

One fact seems to stand out from Figures 1, 2, and 3, as well as from most other studies: the swings on the Soviet side are less violent. The decline in Soviet defense spending after the Second World War was much smaller than on the American side. The wartime level had been lower, and Soviet spending remained higher in the immediate postwar period. In the late 1940s and early 1950s the Soviet defense budget did increase, but considerably less than in the United States. There was modest growth in the 1950s and somewhat quicker growth in the 1960s and into the 1970s, although this development was neither sudden nor dramatic. A 3–4 percent increase sustained over a long period will yield

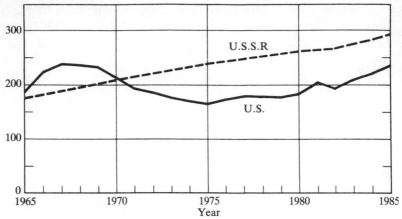

Figure 3 US and Soviet military outlays compared, 1965–85 (in billions of constant FY 1985 dollars)
Source: This figure is gratefully reproduced by permission from John M. Collins and Patrick M. Cronin, *U.S.–Soviet Military Balance 1980–1985* (Washington, D.C., 1985), p. 24.

significant results. On the American side, defense spending fell in real terms in the 1970s after the buildup of the 1960s. Partly in order to compensate for this, in his first administration President Reagan increased real spending by an average of nearly 9 percent, while the Central Intelligence Agency has estimated that Soviet defense expenditure, adjusted for inflation, grew at about 2 percent a year from 1976 to 1983.[51]

Although Gorbachev announced various unilateral reductions in Soviet forces, for some time it was unclear whether the Soviet defense budget was actually cut—as was claimed by many sources—or still increased at the 2–3 percent rate—as was long argued by the Pentagon in particular.[52] In the course of 1989 consensus was finally reached even in Washington that the established pattern of growth in Soviet defense spending had indeed been broken. Still, despite the changes brought about by Gorbachev, the point remains that on the whole the fluctuations on the Soviet side have been much smaller than on the American side.

VII The American Swings Explained

How then do we explain these violent swings on the American side? Many different explanations have to be taken into account, each of which could justify a separate article, even a book.[53] I shall offer only some brief comments on what I consider the most important of all these factors.

Countries have to change policies because the international environment changes. It would be a strange policy indeed which had remained unchanged in spite of the changes in the political and strategic map of the world since 1945. But why should this factor result in wider pendulum swings in America than in other countries?

Part of the answer could well be that the United States has enjoyed greater freedom of action than most other countries. Its location in the Western hemisphere—plus the British Navy—made it possible for the United States to choose isolationism. After the Second World War its new position as by far the world's strongest power formed the material background for the informal American "empire".[54] The Europeans, on the other hand, simply had to involve themselves in each other's affairs. Isolationism was not a real option. After 1945, neither was empire.

The Soviet Union was the only country which resembled the United States in these respects. Its size, strength, and geographical location made it possible for Moscow to choose at least "semi-isolation." After the war the Red Army controlled most of Eastern Europe, and the Soviet Union was the second strongest power in the world. Its "semi-isolation" came to an abrupt end. Again, the Soviet Union was dominated by an ideology with globalist aspirations, a source both of strength and of a sense of vulnerability. In the Soviet Union, as in the United States, there were fierce policy debates about the proper attitude to the outside world. To stretch the likeness a little further, the isolationists in the United States can in some ways be compared to the Slavophiles in Russia, and the internationalists to the Westernizers.[55]

America acted while Europe reacted. The counterpart of the American policy swings could perhaps be found in what might be called European dependency swings. Whatever Washington did was bound to result in some European criticism, at least in part as a result of Europe's dependence on the US. Thus, in periods of East-West tension the Europeans tended to see America as overly rigid and ideological. Then, when Washington and Moscow cooperated, fears quickly arose that the superpower duo would operate at the expense of European interests. This had been de Gaulle's criticism going all the way back to the alleged division of Europe at Yalta in February 1945, but in milder forms this kind of response could be found also outside France. (Similar dependency swings could be said to exist in other policy areas as well. American leadership was fine, but there also had to be consultation. Too much consultation, however, showed a lack of leadership. When the dollar went down, that could be bad for Europe. It could also be bad when it went up.)

On the defense side, some of the fluctuations in American spending were due to commitments (e.g. Korea, Vietnam) which the United States arguably undertook at least in part as leader of the "free world." Since the Americans did this, the Europeans could do less than they might otherwise have had to. This, then, can help explain some of the "highs" on the American side and also some of the "lows" in the form of the defense cuts after the commitments had ended.

Then, a whole host of other factors have been seen as contributing to the wider swings on the American side. Party politics have been mentioned as one such factor. The definition of what constituted American national interests was undoubtedly influenced by the existence of and rivalry between the two parties with their different geographical, class, and ethnic bases. But, on the other hand, ideological differences between the major parties are rather smaller in the United States than in most other democracies.

Three slightly different institutional explanations would seem to be more important. First is the so-called presidential "predecessor" argument. As John Gaddis has written, " . . . incoming administrations tend to define their geopolitical codes, not by an objective and dispassionate assessment of what is going on in the outside world, but by a determination not to repeat what they see as their immediate predecessor's errors."[56] Every president has his own foreign policy. Regardless of what course Washington comes to pursue, the newest "new" policy is always here to stay because, it will be argued, it is most directly in tune with the deepest desires of the American people. Often the road to the very political top is also different in the United States from what it is in Western Europe. Most European leaders have served in several national offices before they become president or prime minister. In the US Carter and Reagan are examples of recent presidents without any such previous national experience. Experience probably tends to reduce swings. On the other hand, too much should not be made of this factor in that many of these "predecessor" changes have been primarily cosmetic, and have had more to do with presentation than substance.

The second explanation concerns the sharing of power. Arthur Schlesinger, Jr., has focused on one part of this: the ebbs and flows in the struggle for power between the president and Congress. Strong presidents will, sooner or later, provoke a reaction from Congress, and congressional supremacy will, in turn, lead to a resurgence of presidential authority. The interventionism of Theodore Roosevelt and Woodrow Wilson stimulated the congressional isolationism of the 1920s and 1930s. Then, " . . . the memory of the deplorable congressional performance in foreign affairs . . . gave Americans in the postwar years an exalted conception of presidential power." This led to Vietnam and, in turn, to the War Powers Act of 1973.[57]

Another aspect of power-sharing and of other constitutional arrangements is the fact that it is relatively easy to block legislation and appropriations. Strong action has to be taken or at least strong words used to overcome all the domestic obstacles. The result is that, in Joseph Nye's words, "In order to shorten the lags in formulating consensus in our democracy, the political leadership must exaggerate the degree of external threat,"[58] or, for that matter, exaggerate the possibility of cooperation in periods of detente.

There is much to Schlesinger's point, but this chapter deals primarily with the many swings *within* presidential congressional swings. Even in the period of executive leadership and relative bipartisanship, from the 1940s to the mid- to late 1960s, the swings of the policy pendulum were pronounced.

Nye's explanation, although important, as a general element probably lets the top political leadership off too lightly. Various administrations have undoubtedly, for tactical reasons, painted the international picture with a broader brush than was done in internal analyses. The public presentation of the Truman Doctrine in 1947, of the ideas behind National Security Document 68 in 1950, and of the prospects for detente in the early 1970s provide three examples among many.

On the other hand, the first two presentations in particular were not really that different from what policymakers actually believed

at the time. And there are examples of an administration swinging
further out than Congress and public opinion (most recently, the
policies of the Reagan and possibly even the Bush administration).
Congress and the public wanted both "strength" and "peace."
Only gradually did Reagan come to favor the latter.[59]

The third institutional factor concerns the politicized nature of
large sections of the American executive branch, sections which
would be staffed by permanent civil servants in most West European countries. The stabilizing influence of the permanent career
officials has been particularly strong in Britain (it was exaggerated
only slightly in the popular 1980s TV series, *Yes, Minister*). Although the spoils system has been pushed back, many Europeans
still find Harold Nicolson's comment that "the American diplomatic service . . . (is) staffed by a constant succession of temporary amateurs . . ." not only witty but, frequently, all too true.[60]
The civil servants act as stabilizers vis-à-vis both the politicians and
the public while in America the latter two often feed on each
other. As we have seen, the changes in attitudes to the Soviet
Union have probably been more dramatic among the British public than on the level of the government.

An abundance of examples of incompetence on the part of political leaders and their appointees has led many American foreign
policy experts (and State Department career officials) to argue
that the "experts" should be given more power, that the influence
of Congress should be reduced or even, as George Kennan has argued, that a parliamentary system should be introduced in
America.[61] Most such proposals are politically unrealistic, to put it
mildly. And it is necessary to remember that this is only one of a
complex set of factors.

VIII The Importance of American Cultural Factors

Frank Klingberg has related his extrovert-introvert cycles to
swings in many other fields of human behavior: the alternating
strength of major political parties, war cycles, business fluctuations, even the rise and fall of civilizations. In Hegelian fashion
he argued that "the principle of rhythm" is perhaps a basic law in
human society.[62]

Klingberg's pattern of extroversion-introversion generational
swings, each about 25 years long, breaks down for the years after

the Second World War. More specifically, the swings in American attitudes to the Soviet Union and to defense spending have been much shorter than 25 years.

Although a general theory about rhythms can provide useful insights, I would play down the universality of the swings, seeing them instead as rather more typical of the United States. Then I would relate the rhythm theory to certain American cultural factors and argue that it is here we find perhaps some of the deepest explanations for the swings of American foreign policy.

American society, it can be contended, in many ways adheres to one overall ideology, and Americans are quite satisfied with the fundamental structure of their political system. But it is also possible to argue that the country is built on conflicting cultural sub-values. The exact mix between these values will vary from person to person, but, to a larger extent than in most other countries, the basic conflict can probably be found even within most US citizens. In some periods certain values will be emphasized, in other periods the opposite values will tend to dominate.

One such pair of cultural values is moralism vs. pragmatism.[63] On the moralist side (again to simplify matters vastly), just as in 1862 the United States could not remain half free, half slave, so in 1917 and in 1941 Washington concluded that the world could not remain half free, half slave. After the Second World War the crusade against communism was based on a similar dichotomy.

On the pragmatic side, Americans used to feel (they are probably not so sure any more) that they were the world's leading "how-to-do-it" people. If one approach does not work, you try something different. Since most Americans are not terribly patient—US athletes have traditionally been better sprinters than marathon runners—they will not wait long for the desired results. This impatience in itself provides an additional explanation for the swings. Aspiring politicians cater to this mood: "If you elect me, the problem will go away." This attitude has probably been even more pronounced in American-West European than American-Soviet relations, since the differences with Moscow are recognized as much deeper than any with the West Europeans.

A second pair of cultural values is optimism vs. pessimism. As citizens of God's own country, most Americans take it for granted not only that the United States is the "best" country in the world, but also that it is bound to prevail in the long run. That old Army

Corps of Engineers slogan, "The difficult we do immediately; the impossible takes a little longer," has become part of the national creed. There is a solution to every problem. Europeans are less certain. America's foreign policy optimism has not been tempered by foreign occupation, nor even by invasions or defeats.

The conflict with the Soviet Union will be long and tough but, to quote George Kennan, a strong critic of the moralistic-legalistic tradition in American foreign policy:

> Surely, there was never a fairer test of national quality than this . . . the thoughtful observer of Russian-American relations will find no cause for complaint in the Kremlin's challenge to American society. He will rather experience a certain gratitude to a Providence which, by providing the American people with this implacable challenge, has made their entire security as a nation dependent on their pulling themselves together and accepting the responsibilities of moral and political leadership that history plainly intended them to bear.[64]

Caspar Weinberger even wrote about "prevailing" in a nuclear war, and Reagan assigned Marxism-Leninism to the ash heap of history.

At the same time, pessimism or, perhaps, rather a strong sense of vulnerability is often expressed. America is a fragile experiment and can be threatened so easily, either by infiltration from within (McCarthy's communists in the State Department) or by attack from without—Pearl Harbor in 1941 or, according to the extreme version of Reagan's early "window of vulnerability" rhetoric, a Soviet first strike out of the blue. So, while the United States will win, threats are to be found everywhere.

Many other similar pairs of values could be mentioned: power (in the sense of how many troops you have) vs. ideas (often expressed in the form of a world community of interests); change (America as the world's most revolutionary country) vs. stability (the United States as the prime defender of the status quo); good vs. evil, war vs. peace.[65]

The last two of these pairs would seem particularly important. There is a deep-rooted feeling in America (though not only there) that peace is the normal condition. Certainly wars and conflicts interrupt the normal, ideal state of affairs, but somehow the expectation remains that once the enemy is defeated—and its surrender should be unconditional—"normalcy" will be brought back. As Henry Kissinger has argued "Our deeper problem was conceptual. Because peace was believed to be 'normal', many of our great international exertions were expected to bring about a final result, restoring normality by overcoming an intervening obstacle."[66] The United States itself—and most democracies, for that matter—is considered almost constitutionally incapable of aggressive action. Thus in the postwar world only the Soviet Union stood between America and this world of "sweet reason and peace." Or, as Ronald Reagan phrased it in 1980 in a simplistic restatement of this belief: "Let us not delude ourselves. The Soviet Union underlies all the unrest that is going on. If they weren't engaged in this game of dominoes, there would not be any hot spots in the world."[67]

Either there is peace or there is war (or at least serious conflict). If the Soviet Union is an "evil" power, then the United States has to respond accordingly. If the Soviet Union is a "good" country, as was believed by so many during the Second World War and during the heyday of detente, then conflicts will disappear. The world is black or white, seldom grey. Americans apparently feel uncomfortable with the idea of cooperation in some fields and conflict in others. This underlying dichotomy of black or white would appear to be an important explanation for the violent shifts of mood in the United States.

IX   Conclusion

It is implicitly assumed in some European quarters that its excessive foreign policy swings are the result of America's short history of close involvement in world affairs. The expectation is that with tradition will come wisdom. Perhaps the swings of the pendulum will lessen (though there have been few signs of this so far). Yet there are absolutely no grounds for arrogance on the part of Europe. As early as 1826, British Foreign Secretary George Canning declared with a flourish, "I call in the New World to redress the balance of the old." He was really a bit premature. But the crucial role of the United States, or of the Soviet Union for that matter, in European politics since 1945 can only be understood in the light of the Europeans' self-inflicted destruction of their own European-dominated world system.

4

The United States, Great Britain and the Origins of the Cold War in Eastern Europe*

The fate of Eastern Europe was not decided at Yalta. It was determined primarily by the military situation, by the fact that the Red Army was in control of most of Eastern Europe when the war ended. While the United States was the strongest of the two new superpowers, especially in economic, but even in military terms, there was at least one area where the global supremacy of the United States could not balance the regional domination of the Soviet Union, namely in Eastern Europe. The decisive factor was the strength on the spot.

In addition, I shall attempt to show that the outcome was influenced by the fact that while the Soviet Union had Eastern Europe as its top priority area, the United States and Britain had their basic priorities elsewhere. Eastern Europe was important for the United States and Britain as well. They could not simply cede the region to the Soviet Union. But the point that their primary interests lay elsewhere showed in the nature of their acceptance, al-

---

* This article was originally prepared for the conference "Yalta: A Myth that Resists", held in Cagliari, Italy, 23–26 April 1987. The conference papers were published in 1989 in a volume edited by Paola Brundu Olla, *Yalta, Un Mito Che Resiste*. It is published here in a slightly altered form and represents an attempt to update and revise my earlier study *The American Non-Policy Towards Eastern Europe, 1943–1947. Universalism in an Area Not of Essential Interest to the United States*, Oslo/New York, 1975, in the light of the numerous relevant studies which have been published after 1975. Considerably more emphasis is placed here on the British role than was the case in the original study. As is evident, I feel that most of the conclusions of my study have held up pretty well. Points that have been documented in detail in *The American Non-Policy Towards Eastern Europe 1943–1947* will not be documented again in full here. On these points I shall only briefly refer to the relevant pages in my book.

though reluctant, of Soviet domination in the region. Not only that, to protect their more important interests, the United States and Britain entered into several understandings and agreements which actually served to strengthen the Soviet role in Eastern Europe. This pattern was evident before Yalta, at Yalta and after Yalta.

I Idealism — The Starting Point

There was no doubt about the starting point, particularly on the American side. Washington wanted to promote a world organization, political democracy, and multilateralism. Spheres of influences represented an evil and dangerous concept. The basic creed, whether we call it universalism, perfectionism, globalism or the Open Door, was repeated again and again, in the Atlantic Charter, in the United Nations Declaration, in Article 7 of the Master Lend-Lease Agreement with Britain and in the other Lend-Lease agreements as well, in the Four Power Declaration from the meeting of the foreign Ministers in October 1943, and in the Yalta Declaration on Liberated Europe. This was the side the Roosevelt administration wanted to present to the outside world, especially to the American public. Progress was allegedly being made. As the President told Congress after his meeting at Yalta with Stalin and Churchill, "it spells the end of the system of unilateral action, exclusive alliances, and spheres of influence, and the balance of power and all the other expedients which have been tried for centuries and have failed."[1]

The British were rather skeptical about this combination of claims to American uniqueness and an uncanny ability to make the most inspiring idealism coincide with rather ordinary national objectives. Yet, to a very large extent the British shared the American ideals. Britain consented to all the general statements mentioned above. Churchill wanted to protect the Empire from certain of these ideals, but Eastern Europe was different. There even the British could let idealism prevail, at least as a point of departure for its policies. Poland was of particular importance for the British. As the Prime Minister told the House of Commons in *his* report upon the Yalta Conference,

. . . even more important than the frontiers of Poland, within the limits now disclosed, is the freedom of Poland. The home of the Poles is settled. Are they to be masters in their own house? Are they to be free, as we in Britain and the United States or France are free? Are their sovereignty and their independence to be untrammelled, or are they to become a mere projection of the Soviet state, forced against their will by an armed minority to adopt a Communist or totalitarian system? I am putting the case in all its bluntness. It is a touchstone far more sensitive and vital than the drawing of frontier lines. Where does Poland stand? Where do we all stand on this?[2]

II Idealism Modified

Even in American thinking rejection in principle of spheres of influence was tempered in practice by many different currents. Washington combined the rejection of spheres with what seemed very much like spheres both in the Western Hemisphere and in the Pacific. But even with regard to other powers the United States was prepared to enter into arrangements, which although theoretically in accordance with American ideals, tended to undermine these very ideals. Such deviations came even more naturally to the British. For instance, Churchill fiercely tried to protect the British Empire against any interference from outside powers, including the United States.

Firstly, Washington and London accepted the idea of areas of military responsibility. As Secretary of State Cordell Hull phrased it, "our military authorites are extremely reluctant to have their hands tied by the necessity of waiting for decisions from other than the Governments under which the Combined Chiefs are operating."[3] Therefore, the United States and Britain insisted on keeping the Soviet role in the occupation of Italy limited. This they did even though they appreciated that the Soviet Union would probably promote arrangements in the Eastern European Axis satellites similar to those the Western Powers were establishing in Italy.

Therefore, the United States and Britain were prepared to grant a dominant position to the Soviet Union in the occupational regimes established for the Eastern European satellites. But in these cases the US and Britain tried increasingly hard to make a clear distinction between military and political matters. In the September 1944 armistice for Rumania, the relevant clause simply stated that the Control Commission would operate "under the general direction and orders of the Allied (Soviet) High Command, acting on behalf of the Allied Powers." In the 28 October Bulgarian armistice, the United States was able to secure a distinction between the "military" period until the end of the war and the "political" period from the fall of Germany to the conclusion of peace. But this distinction was rather hazy, due to the strong local position of the Soviet Union, the Italian precedent and the weakening of British support linked to the October percentage agreement between Churchill and Stalin. The Hungarian armistice of 20 January was somewhat more satisfactory, but even there the leadership role of the Soviet Union was repeated, although it would, presumably, be reduced at the "conclusion of hostilities against Germany."[4]

The same principle applied in the civil affairs agreements with the Allied countries. In 1944 both the United States and Britain refused to sign civil affairs agreements with Czechoslovakia. This negative attitude was in part related to the fact that the two Western Powers wanted to keep the Soviet Union out of such agreements for the countries in Western Europe. The United States and Britain also refused to give aid of any significance to the rebellion in Slovakia in the fall of 1944. As Slovakia lay within the Soviet sphere of operations, the United States and Britain felt that it was Moscow's responsibility to support the insurgents. Similar considerations also influenced the American and British stand as to assistance to the Warsaw uprising.[5]

Secondly, the principle of areas of political gravitation was accepted both in Washington and in London. The three Great Powers simply could not have the same amount of influence everywhere. The United States and Britain had areas they wanted to protect. A certain reciprocity for the Soviet Union was only natural. In the Yalta briefing papers the State Department, with reference to the Balkan states, thus stated that "politically, while this Government probably would not oppose predominant Soviet influence in this area, neither would it wish American influence to be completely nullified."[6] The British, as we shall shortly see, consented even more readily to such ideas.[7]

Thirdly, and related to the previous point, the need to put first things first represented another set of circumstances strengthening

Moscow's role in Eastern Europe. On the British side, Churchill's percentage agreements with Stalin sprang from a combination of local Soviet domination and a wish to protect British interests in Greece and Italy in particular, countries of greater importance than those in the Balkans. On 4 May 1944 the Prime Minister asked Foreign Secretary Eden for a short paper on

"the brute issues between us and the Soviet government which are developing in Italy, in Roumania, in Bulgaria, in Yugoslavia, and above all, in Greece . . . Broadly speaking the issue is: are we going to acquiesce in the Communisation of the Balkans and perhaps of Italy? . . . I am of the opinion on the whole that we ought to come to a definite conclusion about it, and that if our conclusion is that we resist the Communist infusion and invasion we should put it to them pretty plainly at the best moment that military events permit.[8]

In May the deal was to be limited to Greece versus Rumania where, as Churchill told Roosevelt, the Russians "will probably do what they like anyhow." In October the Soviet negotiating position had improved considerably and the 90 percent in Greece and the 50 percent in Yugoslavia had to be exchanged with 90 percent in Rumania and 80 percent in Bulgaria and Hungary for the Soviet Union.[9] Roosevelt had been ready to try the May arrangement for a three-month period. In October he again, at least indirectly, indicated his consent, but he never, except in the vaguest of terms, even hinted publicly at what he thought would be the future realities in Eastern Europe. He tried to evade the State Department. And the Department's day-to-day policies were not based on any American consent to the October percentages. Thus, Roosevelt's realist impulses were effectively circumscribed by his advisers and the general impact of public opinion.[10]

Fourthly, and most important, Western ideals were up against the forceful reality of the Red Army's presence in ever larger parts of Eastern Europe. On 31 August 1944, Bucharest fell to the advancing Soviets. In early September, Bulgaria switched sides and the Red Army occupied the country. On 19 September the Finnish armistice was signed. In January 1945 the Hungarian armistice followed and Warsaw was finally taken after the uprising of the previous August-October had collapsed.

The Soviets were on the spot. In the final analysis they had the power to determine events. On the American side no one could speak more strongly in favor of universalist-perfectionist ideas than the President himself. But, at the same time, few rivalled FDR in understanding local realities in Eastern Europe. As he told Hull in September 1944

> in regard to the Soviet government, it is true that we have no idea as yet what they have in mind, but we have to remember that in their occupied territory they will do more or less what they wish. We cannot afford to get into a position of merely recording protests on our part unless there is some chance of some of the protests being heeded.

Or as he told Democratic and Republican Senate leaders during a private meeting just prior to his departure for Yalta, " . . . the Russians have the power in Eastern Europe, . . . it was obviously impossible to have a break with them and . . ., therefore, the only practicable course was to use what influence we had to ameliorate the situation."[11]

Churchill was even more clearly aware of the effects of the Red Army's presence. As he commented privately when Roosevelt wanted to postpone a meeting between themselves and Stalin until after the American presidential election, " . . . the Red Army would not await the result of the election."[12]

III The Yalta Conference

This was the background to the Yalta Conference. There could be no break with the Soviet Union. The local situation was rapidly evolving in Moscow's favor. Since the Red Army ultimately had the power to control events in the region, almost any agreement would be better than a projection of this kind of a *status quo*.

The military situation and the lack of alternatives thus strengthened the Soviet position in Eastern Europe. In addition came the fact that, with the partial exception of Poland, the United States and Britain really had their priority objectives outside Eastern Europe. Only the Soviets put Eastern Europe at the very top of their agenda.

If we study Yalta as a "tripartite negotiating experience," the conclusion would seem to be, as Diane Shaver Clemens has argued, that "each nation had an issue of overriding importance to it, and each gained support from its other two Allies".[13] The British secured a role for France in the occupation of Germany and thereby also in European politics; the Soviets did not get exactly what they wanted in Poland, but the agreement on the Polish government was undoubtedly biased in favor of the Soviets. The Americans got support for their voting formula in the United Nations and agreement on Soviet participation in the war against Japan.

Most likely there was a connection here, particularly between the settlements regarding the United Nations and Poland. It may also be true, as Fraser Harbutt has recently argued, that this connection goes back to the Teheran Conference. "Its basis was the exchange of some as yet only partially defined American support for Stalin's aspirations in Eastern Europe in return for the Russian promise for participation in a postwar United Nations."[14] At Yalta, Stalin started out by placing primary emphasis on the German situation, especially on the question of German reparations. It was actually FDR who brought up Poland. This he did, as he often argued, from a position of "great distance" and with reference to the state of "opinion in the United States." But at least indirectly Stalin linked an American high-priority item, the voting procedure in the Security Council, with what most likely must have been his high-priority item, the composition of the Polish government. Stalin also tried to associate Poland with the high-priority British item, the role of France, when he argued that "We have considered it possible to deal with de Gaulle and make treaties with him. Why not deal with an enlarged Polish provisional government? We cannot demand more of Poland than of France".[15]

In the negotiations on the Polish government the United States and Britain wanted to establish an entirely new government, while the Soviet Union wanted the Lublin government to continue in power. The key sentence of the Yalta Protocol read that "The Provisional Government which is now functioning in Poland . . . should be reorganized on a broader democratic basis with the inclusion of democratic leaders from Poland itself and from Poles abroad." It is difficult to escape the conclusion that this was putting most of the emphasis on Lublin. Both the Soviet Union and the London Poles considered the Yalta agreement a victory for

Lublin. Roosevelt too, although not before late March, told Churchill that "as clearly shown in the agreement, somewhat more emphasis [is placed] on the Lublin Poles than on the other two groups from which the new government is to be drawn."[16]

But, again, what could be done? As Richard Law and Sir Orme Sargent of the Foreign Office explained the day after the Yalta Conference ended to the London Poles still recognized by Britain and the United States: the alternative to the agreement just concluded on the Polish government "could only be that the London Government would remain in permanent exile from Poland and that the Lublin Government would establish its position more and more strongly inside Poland." Thus, "there was really no alternative to the suggested procedure."[17]

Regarding Rumania, Bulgaria, and Hungary the State Department clearly felt that problems were arising, but these were minor compared to the issues discussed at Yalta. In the Briefing Book papers the Department noted that the Allied Control Commissions operated "on the same general pattern as . . . in Italy, with Russia playing the leading role which Great Britain and the United States have in Italy." The big change would have to come when the military phase was over, "following Germany's surrender the United States would like to see the Control Commissions become genuinely tripartite in character." The Foreign Office feared that if Britain complained about Rumania and Bulgaria, the Soviets would respond by criticizing British behavior in Greece. There is every reason to believe that the percentages agreement lay behind this argument.[18]

Therefore, very little was said at Yalta about these countries. The British actually took the lead. Bulgaria received passing notice due to the British airing of grievances against Soviet domination of the ACC, against Yugoslav-Bulgarian treaty cooperation, and against non-agreement on Bulgarian reparations to Greece. The United States did not present any definite viewpoints on these topics, but it is clear that the State Department sympathized with the British positions.[19]

At Yalta Roosevelt also proposed that London and Moscow accept some of the general principles which the United States had been promoting during the war, such as Allied responsibility for the problems of liberated Europe, the formation of representative governments, and the holding of free elections. Both Stalin and

Churchill quickly agreed to the proposed Declaration on Liberated Europe, although Churchill again wanted it understood that "the reference to the Atlantic Charter did not apply to the British Empire."[20]

The State Department had originally promoted the idea that the Declaration be backed up by an Emergency High Commission for Europe. Roosevelt rejected the Commission for reasons which are still unclear. In part he probably disliked delegating responsibility away from himself. In part he may have reacted negatively against the pattern established by the European Advisory Commission. Finally, the High Commission could easily come to involve the United States more closely in European affairs than Congress and public opinion were willing to accept.[21] Molotov weakened any enforcement machinery further when he moved, and promptly had accepted, that the words "they will immediately establish appropriate machinery for the carrying out of the joint responsibilities set forth in this declaration" be replaced by "they will immediately take measures for the carrying out of mutual consultation." Later the British were able to change this slightly so that the final wording read that "they will immediately consult together on the measures necessary to discharge the joint responsibilities set forth in this declaration."[22]

The Declaration on Liberated Europe was to apply to all the liberated parts of Europe, although Poland was frequently mentioned as a particular case. State Department officials hoped that it could prevent "Soviet domination and control in an extreme sense."[23] So, the Declaration on Liberated Europe presented some American-inspired ideals, the interpretation of which would most likely prove controversial, without any agreed upon machinery to interpret, let alone enforce, these ideals. The same was in part true for that part in the agreement on Poland which stated that "the Polish Provisional Government of National Unity shall be pledged to the holding of free and unfettered elections as soon as possible on the basis of universal suffrage and secret ballot." The United States had tried to have the ambassadors of the three Great Powers act as supervisors of the elections, but this had met with Soviet opposition and the American delegation, reluctantly supported by the British, had to settle for a rather weak clause as far as supervision was concerned.[24]

IV The Polish Government

The two overriding facts determining the situation in Eastern Europe, namely that the Red Army was already in control of most of the region and that the Western Powers had their most important interests elsewhere, continued to make their influence felt also after the conclusion of the Yalta Conference. The first set of circumstances was particularly noticeable in Poland, the second in the Balkans, although both pressures could be felt in both areas.

On the British side Churchill had felt that the Americans had gone somewhat too far in arranging a compromise on the Polish government. Nevertheless, the Prime Minister and his advisers came back from Yalta satisfied even with the sections on Poland.[25] But pessimism soon followed. The situation was probably most clearly expressed by Churchill in his letter of 24 February to Prime Minister Fraser of New Zealand. Fraser had expressed doubts whether the pledges on Poland would be kept. Churchill responded that the "force" of Fraser's criticism was "indeed inescapable" and "have throughout been very much in our minds." But Britain was not in a position to get "exactly the solution we wish" since

> Great Britain and the British Commonwealth are very much weaker militarily than Soviet Russia, and have no means, short of another general war, of enforcing their point of view. Nor can we ignore the position of the United States. We cannot go further in helping Poland than the United States is willing or can be persuaded to go. We have therefore to do the best we can.[26]

Churchill was to complain repeatedly that he did not receive the kind of firm support from the United States that he hoped for. His most immediate alternative, however, was simply to go public about the disagreements with the Soviets over Poland. That could easily become simply another way of advertising the impotence of the Western Powers in Poland.

The American side was also painfully aware of the fact that the Soviets were in control in Poland. On 7 March Ambassador Averell Harriman in Moscow cabled Washington that the Soviets and "their" Poles "consider time is playing in their favor. Every day the Lublin Government is becoming more and more the Warsaw Government and the rulers of Poland."[27] On 15 March Roosevelt told Churchill that we "are fully aware that time is working against us" and that "a stalemate . . . would only redound to the benefit of the Lublin Poles."[28]

It was just very obvious that a prolongation of the *status quo* was working in Moscow's favor. Anything would be better than simply letting the Warsaw Government continue its domination. On the Polish side, one study of the tactics of the Polish communists has argued that the period from October 1944 to May 1945 was dominated by their "aggressive posture toward the underground and . . . a policy of terror towards the AK" [The Home Army associated with the London Poles][29]

For more than a month after Yalta the United States and Britain were at odds on a number of questions related to Poland. On the key issue, however, the composition of the Polish government, they basically agreed. For the first month and a half the Commission agreed upon at Yalta of Foreign Minister Molotov and Ambassadors Harriman and Clark Kerr did not even get close to discussing this question. Moscow/the Lublin Poles insisted that they should have the right to veto the names of Poles invited to take part in the consultations in Moscow. The best indicator of the desires of the Great Powers as far as the composition of the Polish government is concerned is therefore found in the composition of the groups proposed to be called in the for the consultations about the future government.[30]

These rather detailed discussions have not received the attention they deserve. Even in detailed studies on Eastern Europe, such as Lynn Davis's *The Cold War Begins. Soviet-American Conflict over Eastern Europe* little space is given to these discussions.[31] Even in Harbutt's recent study *The Iron Curtain. Churchill, America, and the Origins of the Cold War* the generally accepted version is repeated: the United States and Britain held firm on strong representation for non-Lublin Poles until Harry Hopkins on 31 May accepted 20–25 percent representation, "far below anything envisaged by the Americans or British up to this point."[32]

As I have tried to show in my *The American Non-Policy Towards Eastern Europe 1943–1947,* Washington in fact gradually scaled down its criteria for what constituted an acceptable Polish government.[33] At first Washington seemed to work on the assumption that the Lublin Poles, the Poles abroad, and the democratic leaders in Poland were to be equally represented. The last two groups were considered as being basically opposed to the established Warsaw government. This would in fact have meant only about one-third representation for the pro-Moscow forces. As this state of affairs was naturally criticized strongly by the Soviets, Harriman and the State Department seemed willing to increase somewhat the representation of the existing Warsaw government. This could be done by including members favorable to that government in the groups from London and from inside Poland.

As early as 7 March Harriman suggested that a five to four constellation in favor of the Warsaw government be accepted "leaving open for future agreement the manner in which we would expand the list after consultation with these Poles [the 4] and the Warsaw representatives."[34] This proposal was accepted by the State Department, but did not get anywhere since Molotov was still insisting on the Warsaw Poles having a right to veto other Poles.

In many ways the American attitude on the Polish question hardened in the final weeks of Franklin Roosevelt's life. At the end of March Roosevelt finally gave in to British pressure to send Stalin a message about Poland. The wording had been worked out in cooperation with Churchill and had his support. In this message the responsibility for the impasse was placed squarely on the Soviets. For the first time after Yalta FDR personally made it clear to Stalin that "a thinly disguised continuance of the present Warsaw regime would be unacceptable and would cause the people of the United States to regard the Yalta agreements as having failed."[35] There are other indications as well that the President's attitude was changing.[36]

Many historians have argued that American policies hardened further under Truman. In some ways they did. Harbutt refers, largely correctly, to two characteristics in the new President, each a contrast with FDR, which exacerbated the situation: "a pronounced respect for and a rather literal approach to the law" and "a taste for forceful, sometimes rash action."[37] Truman was willing to employ a language quite different from that used by FDR. Since he was inexperienced in foreign affairs, he also had to rely on his advisers, most of whom were rapidly becoming more skeptical toward the Soviet Union.

Yet, in their concrete policies toward Poland neither Roosevelt nor Truman could get away from the realitites of the local situation. In a message to Churchill the day after he had taken over, the new President referred to "the danger of protracted negotiations and obstructionist tactics being utilized to consolidate the rule of the Lublin group in Poland." Then he went on to propose that Lublin and non-Lublin elements have four representatives each in the Moscow consultations.[38] With the exception of Harriman's 7 March proposal, which was meant only as a first step, this was not as favorable a situation as that which the United States had earlier appeared to regard as a minimum. However, due to pressure from the British, Truman's proposal was changed to a five to three composition in favor of the non-Lublin side.[39]

Moscow kept stepping up its commitments to the unreformed Warsaw government.[40] Washington's response was twofold. On the one hand, the Truman administration was willing to speak ever more bluntly to the Soviets about the situation in Poland. Truman's meeting with Molotov on 23 April was an illustration of this. On the other hand, further concessions had to be made. The Warsaw government was continuing in power unreformed, and, as Churchill told Truman at this time about another matter, the Trieste dispute, "Possession is nine points of the law. I beg you for an early decision."[41]

Stalin kept insisting on the Yugoslav pattern as the right one also for Poland. This was generally interpreted to mean 20 percent representation for the non-Lublin Poles. At the end of April Stalin finally agreed to let Stanislaw Mikolajczyk, the Peasant leader seen by both the US and Britain as the key figure on their side, participate in the Moscow consultations.

In the first days of May, Secretary of State Stettinius and Harriman formulated what they considered the absolute minimum the US could accept. This limit was defined as one-third or preferably two-fifths representation in the government itself for the non-Lublin Poles, and a definite inclusion of Mikolajczyk in that minority. Harriman now argued that Mikolajczyk's presence in the future government, as a rallying point for the opposition, was more important than "the details of the percentage of non-Lublin representation . . ."[42]

Eden, who was in San Francisco with the Americans at the UNO Conference, seemed prepared to agree to this plan. Churchill, however, was against such a weakening of the western position. As we shall later see, he was searching for levers which could strengthen their position. He wanted to postpone further negotiations until Potsdam. Yet, he expressed his deep worries to Eden, "I fear terrible things have happened during the Russian advance through Germany to the Elbe . . . After it was over and the territory occupied by the Russians, Poland would be engulfed and buried deep in Russian-occupied lands."[43] Harriman wanted to pursue the matter despite the Prime Minister's objections since "if we did nothing now, the matter might die and it was important to maintain our position and not give the impression by silence that we were accepting the Soviet thesis . . ."[44]

The presentation of this minimum plan was stopped, but only temporarily, by Molotov's statement on 3 May that sixteen prominent Poles who had been missing for some weeks had actually been imprisoned by the Russians. The Americans agreed to the British wish to suspend further talks on Poland, but they did this halfheartedly and with their minimum plan ready for later use. Eden even feared that the State Department might agree to Stalin's Yugoslav precedent.

At the end of May Truman broke the suspension by sending Harry Hopkins to Moscow. Hopkins and Stalin in fact managed to agree on the list of names to be invited for the consultations on the new Polish government. Of twelve names, they selected five who favored Lublin, four who could be placed in Mikolajczyk's camp, while the last three were apparently undecided. In the subsequent consultations, as seems to have been expected, two of the three supported Lublin. The result of the Stalin-Hopkins talks was vague as regards the elections promised in the Yalta agreement. The Soviet leader's support for elections and political freedom in Poland was hedged with several qualifications.

Thus, Hopkins actually did better than the one-third which was deemed the minimum acceptable to the United States. Both the President and the State Department were therefore relatively well satisfied with the outcome of the Hopkins mission. Churchill, with some resignation, also admitted that Hopkins "has obtained the best solution we could hope for under the circumstances."[45]

In addition, and this was considered no small accomplishment, Washington obtained a solution to the UN veto question. As we have seen, ever since Teheran Stalin probably made use of this question to strengthen his hand in Poland. Both questions had been "solved" at Yalta; then the agreement on Poland proved illusive and the veto problem was reopened. For tactical purposes

Stalin most likely exaggerated the importance which he actually attached to the details of the veto question. Now Hopkins got a satisfactory clause on voting in the UN while Moscow obtained an acceptable agreement on Poland. There was no direct deal, but there was a clear measure of mutual satisfaction.[46]

After agreement had been reached on the persons to be called in for the consultations, American and British leverage in the process which followed was limited. Furthermore, the Poles opposed to Lublin were anxious to break out of their isolation and get to work in Poland itself. The various factions therefore soon agreed that Lublin would control two-thirds of the new government. Actually non-Lublin representation was to fall just short of one-third. But Mikolajczyk had been accepted as Vice-Premier. And, again, what was the alternative? Significant gains had been made compared to the *status quo*. Harriman reported from Moscow that "Mikolajczyk and his associates have been wise in accepting the best deal they could make on their own and not coming to Clark Kerr and myself for direct assistance on improving the present agreement since it is the future decisions that are all important."[47]

On 5 July, Washington wanting to avoid Independence Day, the US, somewhat reluctantly supported by Britain, extended recognition to the new Polish government. The Poles had then in turn recognized the decisions made at Yalta. To Washington and London that primarily meant the holding of free elections. The elections were held only in January 1947 and then they were far from free.

V The Balkans

In the Balkans, as in Poland, the Western position was greatly undermined by the fact that the Red Army was already in control in Rumania, Bulgaria, and even Hungary. Furthermore, in these countries, much more than in Poland, Western diplomacy was also greatly weakened by the fact that important concessions had already been made in favor of Soviet supremacy.

Britain undoubtedly felt committed to the October 1944 percentage arrangement also after Yalta. In late February-early March Churchill repeatedly indicated that "as regards Poland we would have our say" while in Rumania he was "much concerned" lest Stalin should reproach Britain for breaking our understanding with him . . . We must keep our own word however painful if we are to use that argument [Greece and Poland] to him with effect. We really have no justification for intervening in this extraordinarily vigorous manner [as local British representatives suggested] for our late Roumanian enemies, thus compromising our position in Poland and jarring upon Russian acquiescence in our long fight in Athens. If we go on like this, we shall be told, not without reason, that we have broken our faith about Roumania after taking advantage of our position in Greece, and this will compromise the stand we have taken at Yalta over Poland.[48]

The same argument basically applied to Bulgaria, although Soviet intervention there had been less direct.

Such explicit references to the effects of the October deal would seem to have disappeared after late April, and British diplomacy toward Rumania, Bulgaria, and Hungary gradually became more active. But Stalin undoubtedly kept the arrangement in mind. And British policymakers came to realize that whenever they complained about conditions in Rumania and Bulgaria, the Soviet side would respond by bringing up the state of affairs in Greece. This pattern was very noticeable at Potsdam.[49]

The fact that first things had to come first and that matters in the Balkans ranked pretty low also on the American list of priorities showed in many different ways. After Yalta the United States certainly did not feel bound by the percentage agreement. In theory the Declaration on Liberated Europe was to be a prime guideline for American diplomacy toward this part of Europe. In practice, however, the United States too was to limit its role there.

At this time the limitations stemmed especially from two factors. The first concerned the war-time supremacy of military considerations, particularly in former enemy countries. Roosevelt expressed this point rather clearly in a cable to Churchill on 11 March:

> The Russians have been in undisputed control from the beginning and with Rumania lying athwart the Russian lines of communications it is moreover difficult to contest the plea of military necessity and security which they are using to justify their action.[50]

The War Department was even more influenced by such reasoning than the State Department, in large part because the military wanted Moscow kept to a most limited role in their areas of responsibility.[51]

Equally significant was the concentration on Poland. American interests were more important there and presented a much better test case than in a former Axis satellite where basic concessions had already been made in favor of Moscow. Thus on 14 March Harriman told the Secretary of State that

> I recognize that the Rumanian situation is in many ways secondary in importance to Poland and if we come to a point in our relations with the Soviet government where we feel we must make a major issue I believe that we would be on firmer grounds to do so in connection with Poland. Also, a serious and public issue over Rumania might prejudice our chances of a reasonable settlement regarding Poland.[52]

The situation in Poland therefore consistently took precedence over that in Rumania also as far as American complaints were concerned.

Yet, this did not mean that Britain and the United States would do nothing in the Balkans. The situation in Rumania was the most worrisome. In early March the Soviets had forced King Michael to appoint a new government headed by Petru Groza. Although communist representation was small, even most of the non-communists in the government looked to the Soviet authorities for guidance.[53]

On 6 March Churchill had told the Cabinet that

> It would be for consideration whether the Yalta Declaration on liberated territories could be construed as superseding previous arrangements such as that in respect of Rumania and Greece which had been made at a time when we could not rely on United States assistance.

The British *did* agree to use the Declaration "as a means of putting the Russians in the wrong and giving us a grievance which may be of use in the course of future bargaining."[54] The percentage agreement was to be played down.

After repeated hints, the United States on 14 March invoked the Declaration on Liberated Europe in an attempt to change the situation in Rumania. This was the first test of the Declaration. But the problem was that it did not commit the Russians to any definite course of action. This was admitted by Stettinius when he told Harriman that "the only reasonable interpretation of this language is that all three governments must agree as a prerequisite to setting the operative sections of the declaration in motion."[55] Harriman complained that the Soviets would never agree to do this and "thus one of the most widely approved actions of the Crimea Conference could be nullified."[56] The Ambassador was right. The Soviet Union would not agree to enforce an American interpretation of the Declaration. And, the United States and Britain could not enforce it on their own.

At the very same time, however, not only the British, but also several Western European governments feared that the Soviets could use the Declaration to insist on communist representation in Western Europe. This apparently made the Foreign Office somewhat less interested in pressing the potential of the Declaration.[57] And when Roosevelt on 21 March asked Churchill what he thought of sending a tripartite mission to look into the economic situation in Greece, the Prime Minister instead proposed a bilateral US-British commission. FDR opposed such a solution and stated that "This would look as though we, for our part, were disregarding the Yalta decision for tripartite action in liberated areas and might easily be interpreted as indicating that we consider the Yalta decisions as no longer valid."[58] Yet, no mission was sent to Greece. So, developments related to parts of Europe more crucial to the Western Powers than Eastern Europe also undermined the Declaration.

The United States and Britain had more or less given up on changing the war-time rules regulating the ACCs in the former Axis satellites. Moscow even refused to give the American and British representatives in Bulgaria and Rumania the same rights the Soviets enjoyed in Italy. The issue was more or less postponed until the war was over.

President Truman's immediate reaction to the unsatisfactory American-British status on the ACCs was the impulsive one of wishing to withdraw the American representatives in Bulgaria and Rumania, but the State Department persuaded him that this would only make matters deteriorate even further.[59] When the war was over, the decision was made to concentrate on the state of affairs in Hungary. The wording in the armistice about the nature of the Soviet lead in the so-called second period was somewhat more favorable here than in Bulgaria and, particularly, in Rumania. The Soviet Union acknowledged that changes in the operating rules were in order once the war against Germany was over. Significant changes were actually agreed upon for Hungary and at Potsdam the Soviets approved the introduction of this Hungarian model in Bulgaria and Rumania as well. But despite these changes, the Control Commissions remained instruments in the hands of the Soviet occupation authorities.[60]

Thus, both the United States and Britain maintained rather low profiles in Hungary, Rumania, and Bulgaria. The local representatives of both Powers were clearly more activist than the State Department and the Foreign Office. And the top military leaders, certainly in Washington, were even more reluctant to dramatize the situation. Despite the effects of the percentage agreement, the British were somewhat more interested than the Americans in the situation in Rumania. London had the best contacts with the King and the Western-oriented politicians. At Yalta the British were in the lead as far as ACC reform was concerned. After Groza's takeover Washington became more active and on 11 April Churchill told FDR that "in Roumanian affairs we have been following your lead . . . and we shall continue to do so." He referred to the percentage agreement as a main reason for this.[61] In March-April Washington also took the initiative in having the unsatisfactory elections planned in Bulgaria postponed.[62]

The differences between the two Western Powers were primarily tactical. This was also the case when the question of diplomatic recognition of the Axis satellites came up. On 27 May Stalin proposed that the governments of Rumania, Bulgaria, Finland, and, after a certain time, that of Hungary be given full diplomatic recognition. Churchill, as opposed to the Foreign Office, was in fact inclined to accept the Soviet proposal. In July London finally decided that little would be gained by opposition alone. Instead, Britain proposed to try to speed up the conclusion of the peace treaties, a process which in turn would result in the recognition of the existing regimes, however unsatisfactory. The important thing now was to get the Red Army out as quickly as possible.[63]

On the American side Harriman basically supported a policy of recognition. Other hard-liners, such as Acting Secretary of State Grew, and Soviet expert Charles Bohlen, also showed sympathy for this approach. This clearly showed that the differences were primarily tactical rather than political. The State Department, however, came out against any such policy. Truman was definitely not in favor of recognizing regimes which were not to his liking. Both recognition and speeding up the peace treaties were thus rejected in Washington. The British reluctantly agreed to support the American point of view.[64]

In the preparations for Potsdam, Washington concluded that the governments in Bucharest and Sofia were definitely unsatisfactory. The Miklos government in Budapest was clearly preferable to the other two, but fears were increasing that developments would take a turn for the worse even in Hungary. The American pre-Potsdam position was summed up as follows:

That the Allied Governments agree in principle to the reorganization of the present governments in Rumania and Bulgaria, and should it become necessary, in Hungary, and to the postponement of diplomatic recognition and the conclusion of peace treaties with those countries until such reorganization has taken place.[65]

At Potsdam the American negotiating position on Eastern Europe was considerably weakened by the strong American desire to normalize relations with Italy as quickly as possible. The Potsdam communiqué recognized "the preparation of a Peace Treaty for Italy as the first among the immediate important tasks to be undertaken by the new Council of Foreign Ministers," but, in return for this, Truman and Churchill/Attlee agreed

to examine each separately in the near future, in the light of the conditions then prevailing, the establishment of diplomatic relations with Finland, Rumania, Bulgaria, and Hungary to the extent possible prior to the conclusion of peace treaties with those countries.

Churchill feared that such an agreement might mislead the public, since the United States and Britain had already made it clear that they would not recognize the governments in Rumania and Bulgaria. Recognition of the government in Hungary would depend primarily on how the upcoming elections were conducted. After some hesitation, however, the British had given their support to the somewhat confusing Potsdam decision on recognition of these regimes.[66]

The Italian-Eastern Europe connection remained in force until the peace treaties for Italy, Finland, Hungary, Bulgaria, and Rumania were finally concluded in February 1947. Benefits could not be secured in Italy without granting the Soviets similar benefits in the Eastern European Axis countries. In November-December 1945 Washington's interest in maintaining a protected position, even in crucial Japan, further increased Soviet leverage in Rumania-Bulgaria.[67]

During the first meeting of the Potsdam Conference, Truman had presented a proposal for the implementation of the Yalta Declaration on Liberated Europe. Yet, Secretary of State James Byrnes, who was responsible for the "package deal" which made final overall agreement possible, withdrew all references to the Yalta Declaration. The Declaration on Liberated Europe was not even mentioned in the Potsdam communiqué. An American proposal for the supervision, mostly by members of the world press, of elections not only in Hungary, Rumania and Bulgaria, but also, to soften the Soviets, in Italy and Greece met with limited success. The only thing left of the American proposal was a vague reference to the freedom of the Allied press to report from the Eastern European Axis countries.[68]

The part of the package deal which concerned German reparations had the most striking sphere of influence overtones. The United States and Britain, desiring the exclusion of the Soviet Union from reparation payments from the Western zones, managed to secure an agreement which in fact represented a significant step towards separate spheres in Germany itself. More important with regard to Eastern Europe was the agreement on German external assets. The United States and Britain, again because they wished to prevent the Soviets from obtaining benefits and influence in the West, had in turn to renounce all claims in the East, thereby giving the Soviet Union unilateral claim to assets in the Eastern European countries. Even if the discussions on this point had the most striking political overtones, Washington and London did not, of course, intend to cede the area as such to Moscow, but the Potsdam decision nevertheless strengthened a spheres of influence approach to Eastern Europe.[69]

VI The Search for Leverage

In various ways both the United States and Britain tried to find means which could modify the regional supremacy of the Soviet Union in Eastern Europe. This is not the place to present in full the debates on the roles of the atomic bomb, ground troops, and the various economic levers in American-British diplomacy. I shall only superficially sum up my own position on these questions as they involve Western diplomacy in the period from Yalta to Potsdam.

On the atomic bomb, there now seems to be near universal agreement among the leading diplomatic historians that the most important motive in dropping the bombs on Hiroshima and Nagasaki was to end the war in Asia as quickly as possible. Yet, at the same time there has been growing agreement that many prominent policymakers were clearly aware of the advantages the bomb could represent also vis-à-vis the Soviets. Roosevelt had wanted to protect the bomb secret, and Truman, Byrnes, and Secretary of War, Stimson, among others, all welcomed the additional military-political strength which the new weapon would bestow on the United States. One major problem, however, was the simple fact that it was politically impossible for the United States to threaten the Soviet Union explicitly with the bomb, even after it had been used against Japan. If the Soviets simply refused to be impressed, as they did on the surface at least, there was not much Washington could do.[70]

The question, then, really becomes whether the United States escalated its objectives in Eastern Europe as a reflection of the development of the bomb. That seems unlikely. The basic objectives of the United States had been made clear before the bomb became a near certainty and the American negotiating positions both at Yalta and at Potsdam were drawn up by policymakers largely or wholly unaware of the bomb.

On the other hand, it seems possible, even likely, that key persons, such as Truman and Byrnes, gained increased confidence from the bomb, a confidence which was also reflected in their policies toward Eastern Europe. Even Herbert Feis suggests that the bomb may have "sharpened his [Truman's] tongue" as early as in his 23 April meeting with Molotov.[71] One reason for the American postponement of the Postdam Conference seems to have been a wish to complete the bomb before the meeting took place. The reports from Alamogordo about the successful trial explosion probably also strengthened the President's determination at the Conference. But it is impossible to single out specific instances where the influence of the atomic bomb was apparent. And the outcome of the Postdam negotiations was not in any way particularly advantageous to the United States. It may be that the bomb was one factor which invigorated the American policy towards Rumania, as evidenced in the August-September 1945 crisis, but if it did, it could not prevent Byrnes from backing down rather quickly.[72] Nothing could balance the influence of the Red Army.

There is a rapidly growing literature also on the role of ground forces in American and British diplomacy at the end of the Second World War. In this context the cruical point is the debate about the American "frontal" versus the British "peripheral" approach. This had been reflected in the debate over *Overlord,* the Normandy invasion, versus various Mediterranean thrusts. In March-April 1945 the related issue was whether to attack in Germany on a broad front, or, as Churchill argued, whether "from a political standpoint we should march as far east as possible, and hit".[73]

Eisenhower, the Supreme Commander, again stuck to the frontal strategy. His military and political superiors did nothing to change this. There were many reasons for the American attitude. A concentration on Berlin could cost extra lives. Western troops could easily get mixed up with the advancing Russians. Military considerations thus favored the broad approach and, politically, the zonal arrangement for Germany was already agreed upon and would presumably not be affected by a Berlin thrust.[74]

The capture of Prague presented a similar issue. Here Eisenhower proved willing to try to reach the city after it became evident that General Patton's Third Army could really get there before the Russians. But when General Antonov protested, Eisenhower agreed to stick to the original plan.

Such aloofness did not mean that the Americans were always against letting political considerations interfere with military campaigns. When Eisenhower felt that there was a less acute conflict between what was militarily sound and what was politically preferable than in the cases of *Overlord,* Berlin, and Prague, he was indeed willing to let political prizes influence his strategic thinking. Thus, Eisenhower too was interested in cutting the Red Army off at Lubeck so that Denmark would instead fall to General Montgomery's forces.

Even if Churchill was not successful in inducing the Americans to make a spearhead movement for Berlin, as a result of military developments American-British troops were nevertheless capable of moving beyond the zones of occupation which the three Great Powers had agreed upon. Again Churchill reflected on what leverage these troop positions could give in dealings with Moscow. As he cabled Eden on 4 May:

> the Allies ought not to retreat from the present position to the occupational line until we are satisfied about Poland, and also about the temporary character of the Russian occupation of Germany, and the conditions to be established in the Russianised or Russian-controlled countries in the Danube valley, particularly Austria and Czechoslovakia, and the Balkans.

To the Americans he did not initially present his plans for holding back the withdrawal of the Western troops in such a rather comprehensive light.[75]

At first Truman was hesitant to exploit even this question. The Great Powers had agreed on the zones of occupation, a rapid return of American soldiers from Europe was expected, and, in addition, Moscow held a number of strong cards with respect to Berlin and Austria which could be used to counteract demands by Britain and America. On 14 June Truman proposed to Stalin that Western withdrawal be tied to those points having to do with Berlin and Austria and the Soviet leader in the end agreed to this. In Czechoslovakia too the War Department was anxious to get the American troops out of the western part of the country as quickly as possible, while the State Department wanted this move timed with the Soviet withdrawal. Despite a rather weak negotiating position, in November Washington and Moscow actually reached agreement on coordinated withdrawals from Czechoslovakia.[76]

Various economic instruments constituted the third set of levers which could be applied to strengthen the Western position in Eastern Europe. A lot of thinking went into considering potential use of these instruments. On 30 March, after what was to prove his last Cabinet meeting, Roosevelt apparently favored the idea that post-war economic aid to the Soviet Union be withheld until the US had some knowledge of what the Soviet "peace objectives" would be. Harriman was the foremost proponent of an intimate relationship between economic aid and what the Moscow Ambassador liked to call "our overall relations with the Soviets".[77]

It is now well established that such ideas figured in many of the decisions taken in Washington on economic assistance to the Soviet Union. The Lend-Lease curtailment order of 11 May in part reflected Washington's dissatisfaction with Soviet foreign policy behavior. The answer to the Soviet application of January 1945 for a USD 6 billion loan was held up for similar reasons.

When Washington finally replied in June, the American note pointed out that "long term post-war credits constituted an important element in post-war relations between our two countries." On several occasions Harriman wanted to bring the aid connection directly into dealings with the Soviet Union over Eastern European questions. In late June Harriman held some hope for the future even in Poland. As he cabled Washington:

> It is impossible to predict the trend of events in Poland but I believe the stage is set as well as can be done at the present time and that if we continue to take a sympathetic interest in Polish affairs and are reasonably generous in our economic relations, there is a fair chance that things will work out satisfactorily from our standpoint.[78]

Yet, this anti-Soviet perspective can easily be carried too far. The May reduction in Lend-Lease was applied without formal discrimination among the many recipient countries, although some advisers had Moscow particularly in mind. The order was also carried out in a more extreme way by the bureaucrats than the policymakers had intended.[79] The Soviet loan question kept being postponed, but there was no sign that this moderated Soviet behavior, a fact which in turn led to further postponement. When the formal terms were finally stated in February 1946, they included, among other things, the following point:

> Determination of concerted policies to be followed by the US and the USSR together with the UK, under the terms of agreement reached at the Crimea Conference, in assisting the peoples liberated from the domination of Nazi Germany and the peoples of the former Axis satellite states of Europe to solve by democratic means their pressing economic problems.

The American-Soviet exchange of opinion led nowhere. The contacts with the Eastern European countries proved similarly unfruitful. Loans were sometimes given, other times not. Credits were suspended when they did not evoke the reaction hoped for. In many different ways financial assistance was dangled before the various governments as a reward for satisfactory behavior. The results, however, were to prove unsatisfactory almost without exception.[80]

On 25 April Harriman had recommended that "while we cannot go to war with Russia, we must do everything we can to maintain our position as strongly as possible in Eastern Europe."[81] "Doing everything" in fact meant doing rather little. The strong levers, the atomic bomb and the ground troops, could at best be hinted at, no more. The weak levers, such as economic assistance and withholding diplomatic recognition, were used to an ever increasing extent, but without any noticeable effect.

VII The Search for the Middle Road

The two Western Powers and the Soviet Union did not clash over all the Eastern European countries. In the period up to the Potsdam Conference there were at least two countries where Washington, London, and Moscow saw eye to eye, namely Finland and Czechoslovakia.

Thus, when at the end of May Stalin proposed that the Great Powers recognize the Eastern European Axis satellites, Truman could agree with regard to Finland. Elections had been held there in March and although they represented a swing to the left, the State Department took no offence. On 7 June Truman informed Stalin that "I am prepared to proceed with the exchange of diplomatic representatives with Finland at once because the Finnish people, through their elections and other political adjustments, have demonstrated their genuine devotion to democratic procedures and principles." Since Stalin, however, refused to single out one country only, American recognition of Finland was also postponed. At Postdam Finland was the only former Axis country where all the Great Powers agreed that conditions were satisfactory. When, following Postdam, the Soviet government announced its decision to restore diplomatic relations with Rumania, Bulgaria, and Finland, the United States and Britain were ready to follow suit with regard to Finland.[82]

In March-April 1945 the Czechoslovak government-in-exile was reorganized in Moscow. The communists were now brought in and the party and its sympathizers fell just short of controlling one half of the posts in the new Fierlinger government. From Moscow President Benes and the Czechoslovak government moved to Kosice in the home country where a new reform program was announced. The State Department and the Foreign Office were annoyed by the fact that Soviet authorities did not allow Western embassy personnel to travel with the government into Czechoslovakia, but this was blamed on the Soviets and not on the Czechoslovaks. The American policy paper for Postdam repeated what had been said before Yalta, that "relations between the United States and Czechoslovakia remain excellent as they have in the past."[83]

In theory there was no necessary conflict between "security" as defined by the Soviet Union, and "self-determination" as defined by the United States and Britain. Even in practice, as seen most clearly in the Finnish and Czechoslovak examples, the basic requirements of the two sides could be reconciled.

Based on the concessions the United States was ready to make in Eastern Europe, Eduard Mark has argued that Washington favored an "open" as opposed to an "exclusive" Soviet sphere in Eastern Europe.[84] In short, foreign policy leanings toward the Soviet Union were acceptable as long as basic democratic rights were observed. The "open" versus "exclusive" division is thus a division between foreign and domestic policy. This is a useful distinction, although somewhat oversimplified in that for instance areas of military responsibility were thought to have certain consequences also on the domestic side.

The trouble, however, was that the Finnish and Czechoslovak models could not be transferred. Attitudes in Allied Czechoslovakia were far different from those in Poland, and those in Finland differed from those in Rumania and Bulgaria. No one in Poland,

Rumania, and Bulgaria could play roles similar to those of Benes and Paasikivi. Anti-Russian sentiments were particularly strong in Poland and Rumania. Furthermore, the Soviet Union was probably more set on determining events in crucial Poland and Rumania than in Finland and Czechoslovakia. The Soviet means to do so were also stronger, in that Finland was not occupied at all while the Red Army withdrew from Czechoslovakia in November-December 1945. Finally, Western interests too were more important in Poland than in any other Eastern European country. But it appears likely that, from a Western point of view, a Finnish solution would have been quite acceptable also in Poland, Rumania, and Bulgaria. Yet, as I have argued elsewhere, the Czechoslovak model ceased to be acceptable to Washington from the fall of 1946.[85]

Therefore, in most Eastern European countries no compromise was possible if the Soviet Union was to define "security" and the United States and Britain "self-determination." Policymakers in Washington, and even in London, had done little to prepare public opinion for the concessions which would have been necessary to reconcile Western and Soviet policies. Roosevelt provided a clear-cut example of this. On many occasions, particularly in talks with Soviet representatives, he hinted at compromises with Moscow in Eastern Europe. This realism went against the grain of some of his advisers, and certainly against the way in which public opinion was perceived. To avoid having his hands tied by such strong domestic forces, if that had been possible at all, Roosevelt would have had to make his realist views quite explicit, also to the American public. This he never did. The same was actually true for Churchill. The British public would have been unprepared for anything like the percentage agreements.

The tension particularly in Washington's policy between perfectionism and realism, between universalism and its modifiers, was never resolved; therefore a "non-policy." To simplify matters vastly, the American public and the Soviet Union came to expect entirely different things from the Roosevelt administration, and, to a lesser degree, from the Truman administration. The public was shown the perfectionist side, the Soviets much more of the realist side. The Kremlin may well have seen the White House and Whitehall as having "ceded" at least some countries in Eastern Europe. Later attempts by the Western Powers to retrieve what they had "given up" were naturally resisted. As former Foreign Minister Maxim Litvinov asked American journalist Edgar Snow in June 1945: "Why did you Americans wait till right now to begin opposing us in the Balkans and Eastern Europe? You should have done this three years ago. Now it's too late and your complaints only arouse suspicion here."[86]

Both East and West were prepared to make concessions to the other side in Eastern Europe. Stalin was probably willing to accept the Eastern Neisse as the border between Poland and Germany. At Potsdam the Poles insisted on Western Neisse. The United States and Britain accepted the western line without Stalin really being tested on this point.[87] The Soviet Union was also willing to accept Western-oriented politicians in the governments of all Eastern European countries, although preferably in a minority position. When Washington and London protested against the biased elections that were planned in Bulgaria, first in March-April and then in August, Moscow agreed to postpone them. Later monarchy persisted in Bulgaria until the autumn of 1946 and in Rumania yet another year. In Hungary the Smallholders for a time had considerable influence after their electoral victories in October-November 1945. The Finnish and Czechoslovak experiences have already been mentioned.

Stalin was certainly ready to make "concessions" in Western Europe in return for Western concessions in Eastern Europe. Repeatedly he more than hinted at such a division of Europe. Stalin's message to Churchill of 24 April 1945, provides one case in point:

Poland is to the security of the Soviet Union what Belgium and Greece are to the security of Great Britain . . . I do not know whether a genuinely representative Government has been estalished in Greece, or whether the Belgian Government is a genuinely democratic one. The Soviet Union was not consulted when those Governments were being formed, nor did it claim the right to interfere in those matters, because it realises how important Belgium and Greece are to the security of Great Britain. I cannot understand why in discussing Poland no attempt is made to consider the interests of the Soviet Union in terms of security as well.[88]

Churchill recognized this for what it was, an attempt to get back to a spheres of influence approach. He still recognized the force of the percentage agreement of October. This became evident when he replied that "the way things have worked out in Yugoslavia certainly does not give me the feeling of a fifty-fifty interest as between our countries" and that "We have given repeated instructions that your interest in Roumania and Bulgaria is to be recognised as predominant." Yet, the emphasis was different now. Referring to Rumania and Bulgaria, Churchill continued that "We cannot however be excluded altogether . . ."[89] And there was Poland, where Western interests were the strongest and the fewest concessions had been made to the Soviets.

In the final analysis an explicit or exclusive sphere was out of the question. Deputy Under-Secretary of State Orme Sargent made the point most forcefully:

> It would no doubt be easy to strike a bargain with the Soviet Government if we were prepared to recognise their exclusive interest in certain countries. On such terms we might be able possibly to save Czechoslovakia, Yugoslavia, Austria, and Turkey at the cost of sacrificing Poland, Roumania and Bulgaria. But it is inconceivable that we should adopt this course.

Sargent saw three main reasons for this, reasons which other policymakers as well referred to again and again. One could never be sure how long the Soviet Union would observe such a bargain. It would also mean an abdication of the right for a Great Power to concern itself with the affairs of this part of Europe. And, "it would appear in the eyes of the world as the cynical abandonment of the small nations whose interest we are pledged to defend."[90]

Even on the American side, as we have seen, most prominent policymakers were in fact ready to make considerable concessions in favor of the Soviet Union in Eastern Europe. A few even suggested a spheres of influence deal with Moscow, although they did so quite reluctantly. For instance, Soviet expert George F. Kennan argued that Europe be divided, i.e. that the United States should write off Eastern Europe unless it possessed the will "to go whole hog" and oppose Soviet domination of the area.

As Charles Bohlen wrote after Yalta in reply to Kennan:

> The "constructive" suggestions that you make are frankly naive

to a degree. They may well be the optimum from an abstract point of view. But as practical suggestions they are utterly impossible. Foreign policy of that kind cannot be made in a democracy. Only totalitarian states can make and carry out such policies.[91]

From a certain *Realpolitik* point of view it may well be that the overall policy the United States and Britain pursued toward Eastern Europe was the worst possible. They made basic concessions, but did not accept a sphere. They were opposed to an exclusive sphere, but were not in any way prepared to force the issue with Moscow. But, more to the point, it may also have been the only course they could pursue. Simply to have ceded Eastern Europe was out of the question. On the other hand, it was virtually impossible to go directly from a joint war against Hitler to a full-scale conflict with Moscow over Eastern Europe.[92]

Eastern Europe was sufficiently important for the United States and Britain to make them take an interest in the affairs of the region. The Western response to Soviet policies led to the Cold War. Yet, Eastern Europe was not sufficiently important for the Western Powers to exploit their strongest levers. The Red Army was the final arbiter of events. American and British opposition to Soviet domination was on the rise. But the most basic Western interests lay elsewhere. The need to put first things first even stimulated Washington and London to enter into agreements which facilitated Soviet rule in Eastern Europe. This happened before Yalta, at Yalta, and after Yalta. The Moscow Conference of December 1945, the Axis satellite peace treaties, and even certain aspects of the Marshall Plan were to provide further illustrations of this point.[93] This, too, helped determine the outcome of the struggle over Eastern Europe.

Notes

Notes to Chapter 1

1 For fairly recent treatments of the theme of American uniqueness see Arthur M. Schlesinger, Jr., *The Cycles of American History* (Boston, 1986), esp. pp 3–110; Loren Baritz, *Backfire: A History of How Culture Led Us into Vietnam and Made Us Fight the Way We Did* (New York, 1985); James Oliver Robertson, *American Myth, American Reality* (New York, 1980); and "Uniqueness and Pendulum Swings in US Foreign Policy," chapter 3 of this book.

2 Sally Marks, "The World According to Washington," *Diplomatic History*, vol. 11 (Summer 1987), pp. 265–82. The quotation is from p. 265. See also Christopher Thorne, "After the Europeans: American Designs for the Remaking of Southeast Asia," ibid. vol. 12 (Spring 1988), pp. 201–8, esp. pp. 206–7.

3 Schlesinger, *Cycles of American History*, p. 215.

4 I have argued that the three most meaningful criteria in establishing a historiographic picture on the origins of the Cold War are the following: whether a historian places greater blame on the Soviet Union or on the United States for initiating the Cold War; what the historian in question sees as the main motive powers of American foreign policy; and the degree of foreign policy activity the historian attributes to the United States, particularly in Europe, during the years 1945 to 1947. For this see my *The American Non-Policy towards Eastern Europe, 1943–1947* (1975; reprint ed., New York, 1978), pp. 17–29.

5 Arthur M. Schlesinger, Jr., "The Origins of the Cold War," originally published in *Foreign Affairs*, vol. 46 (October 1967), pp. 22–52, here quoted from, *The Crisis of Confidence: Ideas, Power and Violence in America Today* (New York, 1969), pp. 110.

6 Lundestad, *The American Non-Policy*, pp. 18–19.

7 Joyce and Gabriel Kolko, *The Limits of Power: The World and United States Foreign Policy, 1945–1954* (New York, 1972), pp. 6–7.

8 Lloyd Gardner, *Architects of Illusion: Men and Ideas in American Foreign Policy, 1941–1949* (Chicago, 1970), p. 317; William Appleman Williams, *The Tragedy of American Diplomacy* (New York, 1962), pp. 206–7.

9 John Lewis Gaddis, *The United States and the Origins of the Cold War, 1941–1947* (New York, 1972), pp. 360–1.

10 Daniel Yergin, *Shattered Peace: The Origins of the Cold War and the National Security State* (Boston 1977), pp. 11, 408–10.

11 Louis J. Halle, *The Cold War as History* (New York, 1967), p. 30 (emphasis added).

12 D.C. Watt, "Rethinking the Cold War: A Letter to a British Historian," *Political Quarterly*, vol. 49 (October–December 1978), pp. 446–56. The quotation is from p. 447.

13 Martin F. Herz, *Beginnings of the Cold War* (New York, 1966); Joseph Marion

Jones, *The Fifteen Weeks: An Inside Account of the Genesis of the Marshall Plan* (New York, 1955).

14 Schlesinger, "The Origins of the Cold War," p. 78.

15 William Appleman Williams, *American-Russian Relations, 1781–1947* (New York, 1952); idem, *The Tragedy of American Diplomacy.*

16 Barton J. Bernstein, ed. *Politics and Policies of the Truman Administration* (Chicago, 1972), pp. 4–5.

17 Walter LaFeber, "War: Cold," in *America and the Origins of the Cold War,* ed. by James V. Compton (Boston 1972), pp. 185–6.

18 Yergin, *Shattered Peace, pp.* 13,409.

19 Diane Shaver Clemens, *Yalta* (Oxford, 1970). For an indication of how Barton Bernstein's position on the atomic bomb, as an example, changed from one considerably influenced by revisionist Gar Alperovitz to one more like that of postrevisionist Martin Sherwin, compare his introduction in *Politics and Policies of the Truman Administration* with his "The Uneasy Alliance: Roosevelt, Churchill, and the Atomic Bomb, 1940–1945," *Western Political Quarterly,* vol. 29 (June 1976), pp. 202–31.

20 Thomas G. Paterson, "The Economic Cold War: American Business and Economic Foreign Policy, 1945–1950" (PhD diss., University of California at Berkeley, 1968), p. 259.

21 Thomas G. Paterson, *Soviet-American Confrontation: Postwar Reconstruction and the Origins of the Cold War* (Baltimore, 1973); idem, *On Every Front: The Making of the Cold War* (New York, 1979).

22 Schlesinger, "The Origins of the Cold War," particularly p. 77; idem, *The Cycles of American History,* pp. 215–16.

23 Gaddis Smith, *Dean Acheson* (New York, 1972).

24 Lisle A. Rose, *After Yalta: America and the Origins of the Cold War* (New York, 1973); idem, *Dubious Victory: The United States and the End of World War II* (Kent, OH, 1973). The emphasis is less traditionalist in Rose's third book, *Roots of Tragedy: The United States and the Struggle for Asia, 1945–1953* (Westport, CT, 1976). See also Lynn Etheridge Davis, *The Cold War Begins: Soviet-American Conflict over Eastern Europe* (Princeton, 1974); and Robert James Maddox, *The New Left and the Origins of the Cold War* (Princeton, 1973).

25 David Horowitz, "Nicaragua: A Speech to My Former Comrades on the Left," originally published in *Commentary* vol. 81 (June 1986), pp. 27–31, also found in *At Issue: Politics in the World Arena,* ed. Steven L. Spiegel (New York, 1988), pp. 140–8.

26 For Vietnam see Robert A. Divine, "Vietnam Reconsidered," *Diplomatic History* vol. 12 (Winter 1988), pp. 79–93. The quotation is from p. 80. For examples of the Eisenhower reappraisal see, for instance, George C. Quester, "Was Eisenhower a Genius?" *International Security* vol. 3 (Spring 1979), pp. 159–79; Robert A. Divine, *Eisenhower and the Cold War* (New York, 1981); Fred I. Greenstein, *The Hidden-Hand Presidency: Eisenhower as Leader* (New York, 1982); and Stephen E. Ambrose, *Eisenhower,* vol. 2, *The President* (New York, 1984).

27 Quoted from Schlesinger, *Cycles of American History,* p. 16.

28 Warren F. Kuehl, "Webs of Common Interests Revisited: Nationalism, Internationalism, and Historians of American Foreign Relations", *Diplomatic History,* vol. 10 (Spring 1986), pp. 107–20. The quotation is from p. 119.

29 Herbert Feis, *Churchill, Roosevelt, Stalin: The War They Waged and the Peace They Sought* (Princeton, 1967), p. 655. See also his *Between War and Peace: The Potsdam Conference* (Princeton, 1960), pp. 78–9.

30 William Hardy McNeill, *America, Britain & Russia: Their Cooperation and Conflict 1941–1946* (1953; reprint ed., London, 1970), p. 614.
31 George F. Kennan, *American Diplomacy, 1900–1950* (New York, 1952), pp. 82–3.
32 Gabriel Kolko, *The Politics of War: The World and United States Foreign Policy, 1943–1945* (New York, 1968), p. 626.
33 Denna Frank Fleming, *The Cold War and Its Origins, 1917–1960*, 2 vols. (Garden City, NY, 1961); Gar Alperovitz, *Atomic Diplomacy: Hiroshima and Potsdam*, rev. ed. (New York, 1985).
34 Richard J. Barnet, *Roots of War: The Men and Institutions behind U.S. Foreign Policy* (New York, 1973).
35 Williams, *The Tragedy of American Diplomacy*, pp. 13–16.
36 Gaddis, *The United States and the Origins of the Cold War*, pp. vii, 360.
37 Yergin, *Shattered Peace*, p. 13.
38 Kuehl, "Webs of Common Interests Revisited," pp. 117–18.
39 Thorne, "After the Europeans," pp. 206–7.
40 John Gimbel, *The Origins of the Marshall Plan* (Stanford, 1976). For some further comments on Gimbel's book see my "Der Marshall-Plan und Osteuropa" [The Marshall Plan and Eastern Europe], in *Der Marshall-Plan und die europaische Linke* [The Marshall Plan and the European Left], ed. by Othmar Nikola Haberl and Lutz Niethammer (Frankfurt, 1986), pp. 59–74.
41 Fraser J. Harbutt, *The Iron Curtain: Churchill, America, and the Origins of the Cold War* (Oxford, 1986), p. 284.
42 D. W. Brogan, *American Aspects* (London, 1964), p. 9. See also Dirk Verheyen, "Beyond Cowboys and Eurowimps: European-American Imagery in Historical Context," *Orbis*, vol. 31 (Spring 1987), pp. 55–73.
43 Warren J. Cohen, *America's Response to China: An Interpretative History of Sino-American Relations* (New York, 1980); Nancy Bernkopf Tucker, *Patterns in the Dust: Chinese-American Relations and the Recognition Controversy, 1949–1950* (New York, 1983). The quotation is from William H. Chafe, *Unfinished Journey: America since World War II* (Oxford, 1986), p. 248.
44 Marks, "The World According to Washington," p. 265.
45 Jones, *The Fifteen Weeks*, pp. 263–5.
46 Harry Bayard Price, *The Marshall Plan and Its Meaning* (Ithaca, 1955); Herbert Feis, *From Trust to Terror: The Onset of the Cold War, 1945–1950* (New York, 1970), particularly parts 8 and 11; Halle, *The Cold War as History*, chs. 13 and 18.
47 Walter LaFeber, *America, Russia, and the Cold War, 1945–1966* (New York, 1968), p. 78. See also pp. 64–65, 67–68.
48 Joyce and Gabriel Kolko, *The Limits of Power*, pp. 499, 715.
49 Stephen E. Ambrose, *Rise to Globalism: American Foreign Policy since 1938* (Baltimore, 1971), p. 177. See also pp. 165–6, 169–71, 173–4, 180–2.
50 Yergin, *Shattered Peace*, p. 409.
51 Gaddis, *The United States and the Origins of the Cold War*, 357.
52 Geir Lundestad, *America, Scandinavia, and the Cold War, 1945–1949* (New York, 1980), pp. 352–8.
53 Walter LaFeber, *Inevitable Revolutions: The United States in Central America* (New York, 1983).
54 In this respect Gabriel Kolko, *Anatomy of a War: Vietnam, the United States, and the Modern Historical Experience* (New York, 1985), represents a step forward, although in other respects the book would seem to have serious flaws. For a good review of some of the new literature on Vietnam see George C.

Herring, "America and Vietnam: The Debate Continues," *American Historical Review*, vol. 92 (April 1987), pp. 350–62.

55 André Fontaine, *History of the Cold War: From the October Revolution to the Korean War, 1917–1950* (New York, 1968); Raymond Aron, *The Imperial Republic: The United States and the World, 1945–1973* (Englewood Cliffs, NJ, 1974); Desmond Donnelly, *Struggle for the World: The Cold War from Its Origins in 1917* (London, 1965); Wilfrid Knapp, *A History of War and Peace, 1939–1965* (Oxford, 1967); John Wheeler-Bennett and Anthony Nicholls, *The Semblance of Peace: The Political Settlement after the Second World War* (London, 1972); Roy Douglas, *From War to Cold War, 1942–48* (London, 1981); Victor Rothwell, *Britain and the Cold War, 1941–47* (London, 1982); Alan Bullock, *Ernest Bevin, Foreign Secretary, 1945–1951* (London, 1983).

56 Hugh Thomas, *Armed Truce: The Beginnings of the Cold War, 1945–46* (London, 1986), p. 548.

57 Claude Julien, *L'empire américain* [The American Empire] (Paris, 1968).

58 Wilfried Loth, *Die Teilung der Welt: Geschichte des Kalten Krieges 1941–1955* [The division of the world: a history of the Cold War] (Munich, 1980); Ernst Nolte, *Deutschland und der Kalte Krieg* [Germany and the Cold War] (Munich, 1974); Lundestad, *The American Non-Policy;* idem, *America, Scandinavia, and the Cold War;* idem, *East, West, North, South: Major Developments in International Politics, 1945–1986* (Oslo-Oxford, 1986).

59 Hans Wattrang, *Det kalla kriget* [The Cold War], rev. ed. (Stockholm, 1965); Torsten Thuren, *Kallt krig och fredlig samexistens: Stormaktspolitiken 1945–72* [Cold War and Peaceful Coexistence: Great Power Politics 1945–72] (Stockholm, 1971); Göran Rystad, ed., *Det kalla kriget: Atombomben* [The Cold War: the atomic bomb] (Malmö, 1970). The impact of postrevisionism can be seen in comparing this edition with the revised edition of the same book from 1979. For an early attempt to appraise traditionalism and revisionism see Helge Pharo, ed., *USA og den kalde krigen* [The USA and the Cold War] (Oslo, 1972).

60 Quoted from Christopher Thorne, *Allies of a Kind: The United States, Britain and the War against Japan, 1941–1945* (Oxford, 1978), p. 515.

61 Alan S. Milward, *The Reconstruction of Western Europe, 1945–51* (London, 1984).

62 Michael J. Hogan, *The Marshall Plan: America, Britain, and the Reconstruction of Western Europe, 1947–1952* (Cambridge, England, 1987), pp. 430–2. Both Charles S. Maier and I also commented upon Milward's views in papers at a conference on "The Marshall Plan Legacy," sponsored by the German Marshall Fund of the United States, West Berlin, 25–27 June 1987. The papers are still unpublished.

63 There are certainly traces of such an attitude both in D. Cameron Watt, *Succeeding John Bull: America in Britain's Place, 1900–1975* (Cambridge, England, 1984), and in some of the special-relationship literature Watt is so critical of.

64 McNeill, *America, Britain & Russia*, rev. ed. (New York, 1970), pp. 3–4.

65 Schlesinger, *The Cycles of American History*, p. 373.

66 McNeill, *America, Britain & Russia*, p. 4.

67 Ernest R. May, "Emergence to World Power," in *The Reconstruction of American History*, ed. by John Highman (New York, 1962), p. 195. See also Göran Rystad, "In Quest of a Usable Past: Foreign Policy and the Politics of American Historiography in the 1960s," *Scandia* vol. 48 (1982), pp. 217–30.

68 Jean-Jacques Servan-Schreiber, "Idea for 1988: A Natural U.S.–Soviet Partnership," *International Herald Tribune*, 1 September 1987, p. 4; Richard E.

Neustadt and Ernest R. May, *Thinking in Time: The Uses of History for Decision Makers* (New York, 1986), p. 86.

69 Charles S. Maier, "The Two Postwar Eras and the Conditions for Stability in Twentieth-Century Western Europe, *"American Historical Review,* vol. 86 (April 1981), pp. 333–4.

70 Hogan, *The Marshall Plan.* His conclusion is that "in the beginning, the Marshall Plan had aimed to remake Europe in an American mode. In the end, America was made the European way" (p. 445). Again, this may well be too much of a good thing. See also idem, "Corporatism: A Positive Appraisal,' and Gaddis, "The Corporatist Synthesis: A Skeptical View," *Diplomatic History,* vol. 10 (Fall 1986), pp. 363–72, 357–62. I commented upon this debate also in the unpublished paper mentioned in note 62.

71 Bruce R, Kuniholm, *The Origins of the Cold War in the Near East: Great Power Conflict and Diplomacy in Iran, Turkey, and Greece* (Princeton, 1980); James Edward Miller, *The United States and Italy, 1940–1950: The Politics and Diplomacy of Stabilization* (Chapel Hill, 1986).

72 Thorne, *Allies of a Kind;* William Roger Louis, *Imperialism at Bay: The United States and the Decolonization of the British Empire, 1941–1945* (Oxford, 1978); D. C. Watt, *Succeeding John Bull;* Tony Smith, *The Pattern of Imperialism: The United States, Great Britain, and the Late-industrializing World since 1815* (Cambridge, England, 1981). See also Philip Darby, *Three Faces of Imperialism: British and American Approaches to Asia and Africa, 1870–1970* (New Haven, 1987).

73 Lundestad, "Uniqueness and Pendulum Swings"; idem, "Empire by Invitation? The United States and Western Europe, 1945–1952," *Journal of Peace Research,* vol. 23 (September 1986), pp. 263–77. An earlier version of the latter essay was printed in *SHAFR Newsletter* no. 15 (September 1984), pp. 1–21.

74 For a similar appeal see Carl N. Degler, "In Pursuit of an American History," *American Historical Review,* vol. 92 (February 1987), pp. 1–12.

Notes to Chapter 2

1 Geir Lundestad, "Empire by Invitation? The United States and Western Europe, 1945–1952," *The Society for Historians of American Foreign Relations Newsletter,* vol. 15, no. 3, pp. 1–21; revised version with same title published in *Journal of Peace Research,* Vol. 23 (September 1986), pp. 263–77.

2 Geir Lundestad, "Moralism, Presentism, Exceptionalism, Provincialism and Other Extravagances in American Writings on the Early Cold War Years," chapter 1 of this book.

3 For examples of this, see, among the historians, for instance, Arthur M. Schlesinger, Jr., "The Origins of the Cold War," originally published in *Foreign Affairs* (October 1967), where he mentions as point 3b among the six factors that supported American "universalism" that "Hull also feared that spheres of interest would lead to closed trade areas or discriminatory systems and thus defeat his cherished dream of a low-tariff, freely trading world". The essay is also found in Schlesinger's *The Crisis of Confidence. Ideas, Power and Violence in America Today* (Bantam Books, 1969), pp. 92–6. The quotation is from p. 94. Among the political economists, see for instance Robert O. Keohane, *After Hegemony. Cooperation and Discord in the World Political Economy* (Princeton, 1984), where the only mention of NATO is the following: "American leadership in the world political economy did not exist in iso-

lation from NATO, and in these years each was reinforced by the other" (p. 137).

4 Herbert Feis, *Churchill, Roosevelt and Stalin. The War They Waged and the Peace They Sought* (Princeton, 1967), p. 655; Harry Bayard Price, *The Marshall Plan and Its Meaning* (Ithaca, 1955), pp. 315–16.

5 Lloyd Gardner, *Architects of Illusion. Men and Ideas in American Foreign Policy, 1941–1949* (Chicago, 1970), p. 317; Gabriel Kolko, *The Politics of War. The World and United States Foreign Policy 1943–1945* (New York, 1968), p. 170.

6 John Lewis Gaddis, *The United States and the Origins of the Cold War, 1941–1947* (New York, 1972).

7 Robert Gilpin, *The Political Economy of International Relations* (Princeton, 1987), particularly pp. 127, 343.

8 Michael J. Hogan, *The Marshall Plan. America, Britain, and the Reconstruction of Western Europe, 1947–1952* (Cambridge, England, 1987); Charles S. Maier, "Analog of Empire: Constitutive Moments of United States Ascendancy After World War II," unpublished paper, Woodrow Wilson Center, Washington, DC, 30 May 1989.

9 Paul Kennedy, *The Rise and Fall of the Great Powers. Economic Change and Military Conflict from 1500 to 2000* (New York, 1987), particularly ch. 7.

10 For stimulating discussions of the relationship between wars and changes in international leadership, see Robert Gilpin, *War and Change in World Politics* (Cambridge, England, 1981); Jack S. Levy, "Theories of General War," *World Politics*, Vol. 37 (April 1985), pp. 344–74; Karen A. Rasler and William R. Thompson, "Global Wars, Public Debts, and the Long Cycle," *World Politics*, Vol. 35 (July 1983), pp. 489–516.

11 The vacuum concept was developed by Louis J. Halle in his *The Cold War as History* (New York, 1967). See particularly ch. IV.

12 *Department of State Bulletin*, 12 April 1965, p. 535.

13 For a most stimulating discussion of decolonization, particularly in Africa, see Prosser Gifford and William Roger Louis, eds., *The Transfer of Power in Africa. Decolonization 1940–1960* (New Haven, 1982), particularly the chapter by Wm. Roger Louis and Ronald Robinson, "The United States and the Liquidation of the British Empire in Tropical Africa, 1941–1951," pp. 31–55.

14 For the discussion of terms, see for instance Wolfgang J. Mommsen and Jurgen Osterhammel, *Imperialism and After. Continuities* (London, 1986), particularly H. L. Wesseling's chapter "Imperialism and Empire: An Introduction," pp. 1–10; Eric Hobsbawn, *The Age of Empire 1875–1914* (London, 1987). Hobsbawn argues that in the 1890s "Emperors and empires were old, but imperialism was quite new" (p. 60). For the broader definition, see also Zbigniew Brzezinski, *Game Plan. How to Conduct the U.S.–Soviet Contest* (New York, 1986), p. 16. For a most useful discussion, see in addition Michael W. Doyle, *Empires* (Ithaca, 1986), particularly pp. 44, 130. Doyle sees empire as one state's *effective* control over another's foreign and domestic policies.

15 For a good survey of British imperialism, see Bernard Porter, *The Lion's Share. A Short History of British Imperialism 1850–1983* (London, 1984). The quotation is from pp. 267–8.

16 R. Robinson, J. Gallagher, and A. Denny, *Africa and the Victorians: The Official Mind of Imperialism* (London, 1982); Robinson and Gallagher, "The Partition of Africa," in F. H. Hinsley, ed., *The New Cambridge Modern History. Volume XI: Material Progress and World-Wide Problems, 1870–1898* (Cambridge, England, 1970), pp. 593–640. See also Winfried Baumgart, *Imperialism. The Idea and Reality of British and French Colonial Expansion,*

1880–1914 (Oxford, 1982); Robin W. Winks, "On Decolonization and Informal Empire," *American Historical Review*, June 1976, pp. 540–56; For the Athenian and Roman cases, see Doyle, *Empires*, pp. 55–6, 83–5.

17 Robinson's model IV: "Imperialism is conceived in terms of the play of international economic and political markets in which degrees of monopoly and competition in relations at world, metropolitan and local levels decide its necessity and profitability." This definition is found in Robinson's "The Excentric Idea of Imperialism, With or Without Empire" in Mommsen and Osterhammel, *Imperialism and After*, pp. 267–359, particularly p. 286.

18 Maier, "Analog of Empire," pp. 3–6. I see two main advantages in using the term empire. First, it projects an image of strength which was certainly part of the American role after the Second World War. Second, it encourages comparisons between the American "empire" and other empires. As I have argued elsewhere, there is a strong need to get away from often unquestioned assumptions of American uniqueness (see note 2).

The alternatives to "empire" also have their problems. "Hegemony" has become closely identified with its usage among political economists, then defined as a situation in which "one state is powerful enough to maintain the essential rules governing interstate relations, and willing to do so" (Robert O. Keohane and Joseph S. Nye, *Power and Interdependence: World Politics in Transition* (Boston, 1977), p. 44). Thus, the term's association with "international regimes" is much too particular for my purposes. "Sphere of influence" denotes a specific geographic area and is thus unsuitable because it downplays wider structural elements.

Dependency theorists focus on the relationship between the "center" and the "periphery." In the way they use these terms, this kind of unequal relationship is bound to be rather widespread. Virtually any relationship is unequal in some way or other. Empire is a "higher" form of influence than that denoted by simple dependence. Thus, my hierarchical system with one power clearly much stronger than any other should be seen as different from dependency theory. For interesting comments on this, see also Doyle, *Empires*, pp. 43–5. Yet, I find that Doyle's definition of empire as "effective" control over another state's foreign and *domestic* policy is too narrow and it too leaves many questions unanswered. For instance, what is "effective"?

Perhaps, needless to say, this study is based on the assumption that two international systems existed alongside each other, one dominated by the United States and one by the Soviet Union.

19 *Foreign Relations of the United States* (hereafter *FRUS*), 1947: III, Gallman to the Secretary of State, 16 June 1947, pp. 254–5.

20 The parallel is perhaps first and most explicitly made in his "A Historian of Imperial Decline Looks at America," *International Herald Tribune*, 3 November 1982, p. 6.

21 Laski is quoted in Norman Graebner, *America as a World Power. A Realist Appraisal from Wilson to Reagan* (Wilmington, 1984), p. 275.

22 US Department of Commerce, *Historical Statistics of the United States. Colonial Times to 1970* (Washington, DC, 1975), pp. 228, 464; Adam B. Ulam, *The Rivals. America and Russia Since World War II* (New York, 1971), pp. 4–6. See also Harold G. Vatter, *The U.S. Economy in World War II* (New York, 1985), pp. 15–16, 159–69.

23 Kennedy, *The Rise and Fall of the Great Powers*, pp. 149, 171; Bruce M. Russett, "The Mysterious Case of Vanishing Hegemony; or, Is Mark Twain Really Dead?", *International Organization*, vol. 39, pp. 207–231, particularly p. 212; Thomas G. Paterson, *Soviet–American Confrontation. Postwar Reconstruction*

and the Origins of the Cold War (Baltimore, 1973), pp. 11–12; Paterson, *On Every Front. The Making of the Cold War* (New York, 1979), pp. 15–16, 72, 84, 152; John Agnew, *The United States in the World-Economy* (Cambridge, England, 1987), p. 70; Eric J. Hobsbawn, *Industry and Empire. From 1750 to the Present Day* (Penguin, 1969), pp. 134–153; Alan Wolfe, *America's Impasse. The Rise and Fall of the Politics of Growth* (New York, 1981), pp. 153–5.

24 David A. Lake, "International Economic Structures and American Foreign Economic Policy, 1887–1934," *World Politics*, July 1983, pp. 517–43, particularly pp. 525, 541.

25 This point is further discussed in Kenneth N. Waltz, *Theory of International Politics* (Reading, MA, 1979), pp. 129–60; Clark A. Murdoch, "Economic Factors as Objects of Security: Economics, Security and Vulnerability," in Klaus Knorr and Frank N. Trager, eds., *Economic Issues and National Security* (Kansas, 1977), pp. 67–98.

26 For GNP figures, see Appendix of this book. For investments, see Gabriel Kolko, *Confronting the Third World. United States Foreign Policy, 1945–1980* (New York, 1988), p. 237; Hobsbawn, *The Age of Empire, 1875–1914*, p. 51. For development aid, see Michael H. Armacost, "U.S. National Interest and the Budget Crisis," Department of State, *Current Policy*, No. 972, p. 1.

27 The best treatments of the role of the atomic bomb are McGeorge Bundy, *Danger and Survival. Choices about the Bomb in the First Fifty Years* (New York, 1988) and Martin J. Sherwin, *A World Destroyed. The Atomic Bomb and the Grand Alliance* (New York, 1973). The quotation is from *FRUS*, 1948: III, Memorandum of conversation by the Secretary of State, 20 November 1948, p. 281.

28 Paterson,*On Every Front*, pp. 15–16, 72, 84, 152; Brian McKercher, "Wealth, Power, and the New International Order: Britain and the American Challenge in the 1920s," *Diplomatic History*, vol. 12 (Fall 1988), pp. 411–41; Geoffrey Till, ed., *Maritime Strategy and the Nuclear Age* (London, 1984), p. 56; *Historical Statistics of the United States*, p. 1141; Ulam, *The Rivals*, pp. 4–6. The 51 percent estimate is from Kenneth A. Oye, "Constrained Confidence and the Evolution of Reagan's Foreign Policy" in Kenneth A. Oye, Robert J. Lieber, and Donald Rothchild, eds., *Eagle Resurgent? The Reagan Era in American Foreign Policy* (Boston, 1987), p. 11.

29 Franz Schurman, *The Logic of World Power. An Inquiry into the Origins, Currents, and Contradictions of World Power* (New York, 1974), pp. 46–68. For substantial studies of isolationism, see in particular Selig Adler, *The Isolationist Impulse: Its Twentieth-Century Reaction* (London, 1957); Manfred Jonas, *Isolationism in America, 1935–1941* (Ithaca, 1966); Wayne S. Cole, *Roosevelt and the Isolationists 1932–45* (Lincoln, 1983).

30 Stephen E. Ambrose, *Eisenhower. The President* (New York, 1984), pp. 151–5. See also Anna Kasten Nelson, "John Foster Dulles and the Bipartisan Congress", *Political Science Quarterly*, vol. 102 (Spring 1987), pp. 43–64.

31 Michael Howard, "The Military Factor in European Expansion" in Hedley Bull and Adam Watson, eds., *The Expansion of International Society* (Oxford, 1985), p. 33; V. G. Kiernan, *European Empires from Conquest to Collapse 1815–1960* (London, 1982); V. G. Kiernan, *The Lords of Human Kind. Black Man, Yellow Man, and White Man in an Age of Empire* (New York, 1986), esp. pp. 23–27, 311–312, 321; John M. MacKenzie, *Propaganda and Empire. The Manipulation of British Public Opinion, 1880–1960* (Manchester, 1984), particularly pp. 1–12, 97–99, 174–176; Stuart Anderson, *Race and Rapprochement. Anglo-Saxonism and Anglo-American Relations, 1895–1904* (Rutherford, 1981), pp. 23–5.

32 Michael H. Hunt, *Ideology and U.S. Foreign Policy* (New Haven, 1987). For a review of Hunt's book, see James A. Field, "Novus Ordo Seclorum," *Diplomatic History*, vol. 13 (Winter 1989), pp. 113–22.

33 Bull and Watson, *The Expansion of International Society*, p. 240; A. P. Thornton, *Imperialism in the Twentieth Century* (Minneapolis, 1977), p. 238; Thomas J. Schoenbaum, *Waging Peace and War. Dean Rusk in the Truman, Kennedy and Johnson Years* (New York, 1988), p. 193. For portraits of some of the leading policymakers, see Walter Isaacson and Evan Thomas, *The Wise Men. Six Friends and the World They Made.* (New York, 1986).

34 Walter Millis, ed., *The Forrestal Diaries* (New York, 1951), p. 281.

35 Thomas G. Paterson, ed., *Kennedy's Quest for Victory. American Foreign Policy, 1961–1963* (Oxford, 1989), p. 15.

36 Quoted from Christopher Thorne, *Allies of a Kind. The United States, Britain, and the War Against Japan, 1941–1945* (Oxford, 1978), p. 515.

37 *Penguin Atlas of World History. From the French Revolution to the Present* (Penguin, 1978), p. 102; Correlli Barnett, *The Collapse of British Power* (London, 1972), pp. 71–4; Anderson, *Race and Rapprochement*, p. 21.

38 Hinsley, ed., *The New Cambridge Modern History*, XI, chapters XV (India) and XXII (Africa); Watson, "European International Society and its Expansion," in Bull and Watson, *The Expansion of International Society*, pp. 13–32.

39 Aaron L. Friedberg, *The Weary Titan. Britain and the Experience of Relative Decline, 1895–1905* (Princeton, 1988), pp. 218–20.

40 Walter LaFeber, "The Evolution of the Monroe Doctrine from Monroe to Reagan," in Lloyd C. Gardner, ed., *Redefining the Past. Essays in Diplomatic History in Honor of William Appleman Williams* (Corvallis, 1986), pp. 121–41.

41 *Historical Statistics of the United States*, pp. 872–5.

42 *FRUS*, 1945: II, Record of conversation Byrnes-Bevin, 17 December 1945, p. 629.

43 Thorne, *Allies of a Kind*, pp. 687–8.

44 *FRUS*, 1945: IV, Memorandum of conversation Truman–de Gaulle, 22 August 1945, p. 710.

45 William Roger Louis, *The British Empire in the Middle East 1945–1951* (Oxford, 1984), esp. pp. 183–93, 594–8, 733–46. The Lend-Lease quotation is from p. 191. See also Aaron David Miller, *Search for Security: Saudi Arabian Oil and American Foreign Policy, 1939–1949* (Chapel Hill, 1980); Michael B. Stoff, *Oil, War and American Security: The Search for a National Policy in Foreign Oil, 1941–1947* (New Haven, 1980); David S. Painter, *Oil and the American Century. The Political Economy of U.S. Foreign Oil Policy, 1941–1954* (Baltimore, 1986); James L. Gormly, "Keeping the Door Open in Saudi Arabia: The United States and the Dhahran Airfield, 1945–1946," *Diplomatic History*, vol. 4 (Spring 1980), pp. 189–205. The Eden quotation is from David Carlton, *Anthony Eden* (London, 1981), p. 348.

46 Thomas G. Paterson, *Meeting the Communist Threat. Truman to Reagan* (Oxford, 1988), pp. 159–70, 178–80; Ayesha Jalal, "Towards the Baghdad Pact: South Asia and Middle East Defence in the Cold War, 1947–1955," *International History Review*, vol. 11 (1989), pp. 409–33.

47 Douglas Little, "The New Frontier on the Nile: JFK, Nasser, and Arab Nationalism," *Journal of American History*, vol. 75 (September 1988), pp. 501–27. The quotation is from Dwight D. Eisenhower, *Waging Peace* (New York, 1965), p. 178.

48 Robert J. McMahon, "United States Cold War Strategy in South Asia: Making a Military Commitment to Pakistan," *Journal of American History*, vol. 75 (December 1988), pp. 812–40; McMahon, "Choosing Sides in South Asia," in

Paterson, *Kennedy's Quest for Victory*, pp. 198–222; Gary R. Hess, "Global Expansion and Regional Balances: The Emerging Scholarship on United States Relations with India and Pakistan," *Pacific Historical Review*, May 1987, pp. 259–95.

49 Gary R. Hess, *The United States' Emergence as a Southeast Asian Power, 1940–1950* (New York, 1987); Lloyd C. Gardner, *Approaching Vietnam. From World War II through Dienbienphu* (New York, 1988).

50 Geir Lundestad, *America, Scandinavia, and the Cold War 1945–1949* (New York, 1980), pp. 23–4.

51 John Lewis Gaddis, "Was the Truman Doctrine a Real Turning Point?", *Foreign Affairs*, vol. 52, pp. 388–402; Friedberg, *The Weary Titan*, pp. 220, 277.

52 *Historical Statistics of the United States*, pp. 884, 887; Walt W. Rostow, *The World Economy: History and Prospect* (Austin, 1978), p. 79.

53 *Historical Statistics of the United States*, pp. 868–72.

54 For a good recent treatment of the Soviet role not only in Hungary, despite the title, but in all of Eastern Europe, see Charles Gati, *Hungary and the Soviet Bloc* (Durham, 1986), particularly pp. 82, 88–90, 94–5.

55 For examples of invitations within the British and even earlier empires, see Doyle, *Empires*, pp. 162–3.

56 Watson and Bull, *The Expansion of International Society*, pp. 111–14; Prosser Gifford and William Roger Louis, eds., *France and Britain in Africa. Imperial Rivalry and Colonial Rule* (New Haven, 1971), particularly pp. 409–11, 571–92. For the African opposition, see David Levering Lewis, *The Race to Fashoda. European Colonialism and African Resistance in the Scramble for Africa* (New York, 1987).

57 *The Penguin Atlas of World History*, p. 102; Gifford and Louis, *France and Britain in Africa*, p. 576.

58 Porter, *The Lion's Share*, pp. XI, 27, 74–5.

59 For a short earlier discussion of motive powers in US foreign policy, see my *East, West, North, South. Major Developments in International Politics 1945–1986* (Oslo, 1986), pp. 55–9. For a compilation of writings on 19th century imperialism, see Harrison M. Wright, ed., *Analysis of Late Nineteenth Century Expansion* (Lexington, 1976).

60 My argument has frequently been taken to mean that the invitations *determined* American actions. I have never suggested this. Thus, in my "Empire by Invitation?" article in *Journal of Peace Research* I explicitly wrote that ". . . I just take it for granted that the United States had important strategic, political and economic motives of its own for taking on such a comprehensive world role" (p. 268). In a discussion of the relationship between the United States and the rest of the world, the outside response is a most significant factor in and by itself. But on many occasions the foreign attitude influenced at least the timing and scope of the American decision to expand its role.

61 Robert M. Hathaway, *Ambiguous Partnership. Britain and America, 1944–1947* (New York, 1981); Henry Butterfield Ryan, *The Vision of Anglo-America: The US–UK Alliance and the Emerging Cold War, 1943–1946* (Cambridge, England, 1987).

62 Geir Lundestad, *The American Non-Policy Towards Eastern Europe 1943–1947* (Oslo, 1976), pp. 393–4.

63 *FRUS*, 1948: III, Inverchapel to Lovett, 27 January 1948, pp. 14–16. The quotation is from p. 14; Lundestad, *America, Scandinavia, and the Cold War*, pp. 167–77; Cees Weibes and Bert Zeeman, "The Pentagon Negotiations March 1948: The Launching of the North Atlantic Treaty," *International Affairs*, vol. 59, pp. 351–63.

64 Lundestad, *America, Scandinavia, and the Cold War*, pp. 178–97.
65 See for instance the collection of articles in Olav Riste, ed., *Western Security: The Formative Years. European and Atlantic Defence 1947–1953* (Oslo, 1985), particularly the articles by Wells (pp. 181–97), Wiggershaus (pp. 198–214), Warner (pp. 247–65), and Melandri (pp. 266–82).
66 Lundestad, "Empire by Invitation?", *Journal of Peace Research*, pp. 272–73, in turn based on Gallup polls, particularly from Britain and France.
67 George H. Gallup, ed., *The Gallup International Public Opinion Polls. France 1939, 1944–1975.* Vol. 1: *1939, 1944–1967* (New York, 1977), pp. 27, 51, 55, 77, 88, 92–3, 113, 114, 119, 126, 133, 137–8, 139, 145, 147.
68 Gene M. Lyons and Michael O'Leary, eds., *European Views of America: Problems of Communication in the Atlantic World* (Hanover, NH, 1965), pp. 82–97; Gallup, *The Gallup International Public Opinion Polls. France, 1939, 1944–1967*, particularly pp. 269, 280, 459, 521, 669, 712.
69 Thomas M. Campbell, *Masquerade Peace: America's UN Policy, 1944–1945* (Tallahasee, 1973), p. 168.
70 Richard M. Immerman, *The CIA in Guatemala: The Foreign Policy of Intervention* (Austin, 1982), pp. 168–72.
71 For the US–Brazilian relationship, see Stanley E. Hilton, "The United States, Brazil, and the Cold War, 1945–1960: End of the Special Relationship," *Journal of American History*, vol. 68, pp. 599–624; The OAS charter is found in for instance Senate Committee on Foreign Relations, *A Decade of American Foreign Policy. Basic Documents, 1941–49* (Washington, 1950), pp. 427–45. The quotation is from p. 430; For the Johnson Doctrine, see for instance Walter LaFeber, *Inevitable Revolutions. The United States in Central America* (New York, 1983), pp. 157–8.
72 See the references under note 48.
73 For the most far-reaching interpretations, see Warren J. Cohen, *America's Response to China: An Interpretative History of Sino-American Relations* (New York, 1980); Nancy Bernkopf Tucker, *Patterns in the Dust: Chinese-American Relations and the Recognition Controversy, 1949–1950* (New York, 1983). For the more tactical angle, see Robert M. Blum, *Drawing the Line. The Origin of the American Containment Policy in East Asia* (New York, 1982); Michael Schaller, *The United States and China in the Twentieth Century* (New York, 1979); William Whitney Stueck, Jr., *The Road to Confrontation: American Policy Toward China and Korea, 1947–1950* (Chapel Hill, 1981).
74 Harold Mueller and Thomas Risse-Kappen, "Origins of Estrangement. The Peace Movement and the Changed Image of America in West Germany," *International Security*, vol. 12 (Summer 1987), esp. pp. 73–6.
75 Akio Watanabe, "Japanese Public Opinion and Foreign Affairs: 1964–1973," in Robert A. Scalapino, ed., *The Foreign Policy of Modern Japan* (Berkeley, 1971), pp. 105–45, particularly pp. 125–6.
76 Robert E. Ward and Sakamoto Yoshikazu, eds., *Democratizing Japan. The Allied Occupation* (Honolulu, 1987), particularly Ward's introduction and conclusion.
77 Anna J. Merritt and Richard L. Merritt, eds., *Public Opinion in Occupied Germany* (Urbana, 1970), pp. 9–29, 43–58, 180–1. The quotation is from p. 51.
78 Charles P. Kindleberger, *The World in Depression, 1929–1939* (Berkeley, 1973).
79 These characteristics are largely derived from Charles P. Kindleberger, "Hierarchy versus Inertial Cooperation," *International Organization*, vol. 40 (Autumn 1986), p. 841.

80 For a good survey of these developments, see Gilpin, *The Political Economy of International Relations*, pp. 123–42.

81 *Historical Statistics of the United States*, pp. 872–5; Edward S. Mason and Robert E. Asher, *The World Bank Since Bretton Woods* (Washington, DC, 1973), pp. 63–5.

82 Theodore H. White, *Fire in the Ashes* (New York, 1953), p. 359. See also White's *In Search of History. A Personal Adventure* (New York, 1978), pp. 273–318.

83 Henry R. Linden, "World Oil—An Essay on its Spectacular 120-Year Rise (1859–1979), Recent Decline, and Uncertain Future," *Energy Systems and Policy*, 1987/88, vol. 11, pp. 255–7; Robert O. Keohane, *After Hegemony. Cooperation and Discord in the World Political Economy* (Princeton, 1984), pp. 169–74, 202–6.

84 Arthur A. Stein, "The Hegemon's Dilemma: Great Britain, the United States, and the International Economic Order," *International Organization*, vol. 38 (Spring 1984), pp. 355–86; Gilpin, *The Political Economy of International Relations*, pp. 190–5.

85 For two fine accounts of the international property regime, see Charles Lipson, *Standing Guard. Protecting Foreign Capital in the Nineteenth and Twentieth Centuries* (Berkeley, 1985); Kenneth A. Rodman, *Sanctity versus Sovereignty. The United States and the Nationalization of Natural Resource Investments* (New York, 1988). The quotation is from Rodman, pp. 325–6.

86 Ward and Yoshikazu, *Democratizing Japan*, pp. 221–52, 420–3; Michael Schaller, *The American Occupation in Japan. The Origins of the Cold War in Asia* (Oxford, 1985), pp. 30–51; Hogan, *The Marshall Plan*, pp. 432–45.

87 Barry M. Blechman and Stephen S. Kaplan, *Force Without War. U.S. Armed Forces as a Political Instrument* (Washington, DC, 1978), pp. 14, 23–8, 547–53; Stephen S. Kaplan, *Diplomacy of Power. Soviet Armed Forces as a Political Instrument* (Washington, DC, 1981), p. 42.

88 Lundestad, *The American Non-Policy Towards Eastern Europe*, pp. 167–73.

89 Dwight D. Eisenhower, *Mandate for Change* (New York, 1965), pp. 409, 449. The quotation is from p. 449.

90 Lawrence S. Wittner, *American Intervention in Greece, 1943–1949* (New York, 1982), pp. 73–4, 100–1, 121–8, 171–91; Hadley Arkes, *Bureaucracy, the Marshall Plan, and the National Interest* (Princeton, 1972), pp. 293–4.

91 James Edwards Miller, *The United States and Italy, 1940–1950. The Politics and Diplomacy of Stabilization* (Chapel Hill, 1986), pp. 228–30, 244–9.

92 For good general accounts of these operations, see John Ranelagh, *The Agency. The Rise and Decline of the CIA* (New York, 1986); John Prados, *Presidents' Secret Wars. CIA and Pentagon Covert Operations from World War II Through Transcam* (New York, 1986).

93 Louis and Robinson, "The United States and the Liquidation of the British Empire," in Gifford and Louis, *The Transfer of Power in Africa*, pp. 31–55. The quotation is from p. 49.

94 For an analysis of these strategic changes, particularly the one noted in the title, see Jane Stromseth, *The Origins of Flexible Response. NATO's Debate over Strategy in the 1960s* (New York, 1988).

95 Akio Watanabe, "A New Look at Japan Policy: 1951–54," unpublished paper; Jonathan Haslam, "Moscow Talks to Tokyo 1955–56," unpublished paper.

96 Frank Trommler and Joseph McVeigh, eds., *America and the Germans. An Assessment of a Three-hundred-year History*, II: *The Relationship in the Twentieth Century* (Philadelphia, 1985), particularly the essay by Wolfram F. Hanrieder, "German–American Relations in the Postwar Decades," pp. 92–116;

Frank Ninkovich, *Germany and the United States. The Transformation of the German Question since 1945* (Boston, 1988); Alan P. Dobson, "The Kennedy Administration and Economic Warfare Against Communism," *International Affairs*, vol. 4 (1988), pp. 607–10.

97 Peter Boyle, "The Special Relationship with Washington," in John Young, ed., *The Foreign Policy of Churchill's Peacetime Administration 1951–1955* (Leicester, 1988), p. 43.

98 Teddy Brett, Steve Gilliat, and Andrew Pople, "Planned Trade, Labour Party Policy and US Intervention: The Successes and Failures of Post-War Reconstruction," *History Workshop*, Spring 1982, pp. 130–42.

99 See, for instance, Hugh Thomas, *The Suez Affair* (rev. ed., London, 1986); Carlton, *Anthony Eden*, pp. 451–65; Robert Rhodes James, *Anthony Eden. A Biography* (New York, 1986), pp. 567–78; Geoffrey Warner, "The Anglo-American Special Relationship," *Diplomatic History*, vol. 13 (Fall 1989), pp. 486–7. The quotation is from p. 487.

100 Alan S.Milward, *The Reconstruction of Western Europe 1945–51* (Berkeley, 1984); G. John Ikenberry, "Rethinking the Origins of American Hegemony," *Political Science Quarterly*, vol. 104 (Fall 1989), pp. 375–400.

101 Hogan, *The Marshall Plan*, particularly ch. 6; On trade with Eastern Europe, see Michael Mastanduno, "Trade as a Strategic Weapon: American and Alliance Export Control in the Early Postwar Period," *International Organization*, vol. 42 (Winter 1988), pp. 121–50.

102 Ambrose, *Eisenhower. The President*, pp. 143–5; The quotation is from Brzezinski, *Game Plan*, p. 176; Ernest R. May, "The American Commitment to Germany, 1949–1955", *Diplomatic History*, vol. 13 (Fall 1989), pp. 431–60; Paterson, *Kennedy's Quest for Victory*, pp. 24–85.

103 Ambrose, *Eisenhower. The President*, pp. 143–4.

104 Murray Weidenbaum, *Military Spending and the Myth of Global Overstretch* (Center for Strategic and International Studies, Washington, DC, 1989), p. 18; Friedman, *The Weary Titan*, pp. 36–9.

105 Stein, "The Hegemon's Dilemma", pp. 376–81.

106 For capital formation, see Charles S. Maier, "Two Postwar Eras and the Conditions of Stability in Twentieth-Century Western Europe," *American Historical Review*, vol. 86 (1981), p. 342; For unity as opposed to divide and rule, see Armin Rappaport, "The United States and European Integration: The First Phase," *Diplomatic History*, Spring 1981, pp. 121–49, esp. p. 121.

107 William S. Borden, *The Pacific Alliance. United States Foreign Economic Policy and Japanese Trade Recovery, 1947–1955* (Madison, 1984), pp. 143–7. The quotations are from *FRUS*, 1952–54, XIV: 2, Minutes of Cabinet meeting, 6 August 1954, pp. 1693–5, Memorandum of discussion NSC Council, 12 September 1954, pp. 1724–5.

108 Borden, *The Pacific Alliance*, pp. 168–88.

109 Borden, *The Pacific Alliance*, pp. 190, 227–8.

110 Paul A. Tiffany, *The Decline of American Steel. How Management, Labor, and Government Went Wrong* (Oxford, 1988), pp. 117, 169–76; the quotation is from *FRUS*, 1952–54, VI: 1, Secretary of the Treasury (Humphrey) to the Secretary of State, 8 December 1953, pp. 333–4.

111 Tiffany, *The Decline of American Steel*, pp. 117, 169–70.

112 Tiffany, *The Decline of American Steel*, pp. 169–70; Barry Bluestone and Bennett Harrison, *The Deindustrialization of America. Plant Closings, Community Abandonment, and the Dismantling of Basic Industry* (New York, 1982), pp. 143–5.

113 *FRUS*, 1952–54, VI: 1, Minutes of meeting Truman–Churchill, 7 January 1952, p. 755.

114 Borden, *The Pacific Alliance*, p. 5.

115 Ambrose, *Eisenhower. The President*, pp. 70–1, 86–91, 143–5, 454–6, 517–19, 625–6; John Lewis Gaddis, *Strategies of Containment. A Critical Appraisal of Postwar American National Security Policy* (Oxford, 1982), p. 359.

116 Paterson, *Kennedy's Quest for Victory*, pp. 3–85.

117 Lundestad, *America, Scandinavia, and the Cold War*, pp. 112–18. The quotation is from p. 114.

118 Paterson, *Kennedy's Quest for Victory*, pp. 33–5, 48–56.

119 May, "The American Commitment to Germany," pp. 436–58; Robert O. Keohane, "The Big Influence of Small Allies," *Foreign Policy*, Spring 1971, pp. 161–82.

120 Hogan, *The Marshall Plan*, pp. 161–74; Milward, *The Reconstruction of Western Europe*, pp. 113–25, 180–95.

121 *FRUS*, 1952–54, VI: 1, Ambassador Dillon to the Department of State, 26 April 1954, p. 385.

122 *FRUS*, 1952–54, VI: 1, Memorandum by Assistant Secretary Merchant to the Secretary of State, 11 June 1954, p. 691.

123 *FRUS*, 1952–54, VI: 1, Memorandum of conversation by MacArthur, p. 1072; ibid., VI: 2, National Intelligence Estimate, 24 November 1953, p. 1395.

124 The pioneering article was Mancur Olson, Jr. and Richard Zeckhauser, "An Economic Theory of Alliances," *Review of Economics and Statistics*, vol. 48, pp. 266–79. For the empirical data on defense spending, see David N. Nelson and Joseph Legvold, "Alliances and Burden-sharing: A NATO–Warsaw Pact Comparison," *Defense Analysis*, vol. (1986), pp. 205–24.

125 Hogan, *The Marshall Plan*, particularly pp. 238–92; Lundestad, *America, Scandinavia, and the Cold War*, particularly pp. 132–66.

126 The quotation is from Mastanduno, "Trade as a Strategic Weapon," p. 145; Hogan, *The Marshall Plan*, pp. 443–5; Lundestad, *America, Scandinavia, and the Cold War*, pp. 151–4.

127 *FRUS*, 1952–54, VI:1, Churchill to Eisenhower, 7 December 1954, p. 1057; ibid., Eisenhower to Churchill, 14 December 1954, p. 1060.

128 The quotation is from *FRUS*, 1951, III: 2, Hillenbrand to the Director of the Office of German Political Affairs, 1 October 1951, p. 1539; On Germany I am most grateful to Thomas A. Schwartz for having let me read his substantial manuscript "America's Germany: John J. McCloy, the Federal Republic of Germany, and the Creation of the American Empire, 1949–1955."

129 *FRUS*, 1952–54, XIV: 2, Allison to the Department of State, 7 December 1953, pp. 1556–9. I owe this point to Akio Watanabe.

130 On Dulles and the tyranny of the weak, see *Executive Sessions of the Senate Foreign Relations Committee (Historical Series)* (Washington, DC, 1977), vol. 5, p. 387. I owe this quotation to Ronald Preussen; Arthur M. Schlesinger, Jr., *A Thousand Days. John F. Kennedy in the White House* (Boston, 1965), pp. 769–71. The quotation is from p. 769.

131 Stuart Schram, ed., *Mao Tse-Tung Unrehearsed. Talks and Letters: 1965–71* (Penguin, 1974), p. 102.

132 Rupert Emerson, *Africa and United States Policy* (Englewood Cliffs, 1967), particularly pp. 25–7; Thomas J. Noer, *Black Liberation. The United States and White Rule in Africa, 1948–1968* (Columbia, 1985), particularly pp. 48–9. The first *Foreign Relations of the United States* volume devoted to Africa is 1955–1957, XVIII: Africa.

133 Nohr, *Black Liberation*, pp. 58–95; Schoenbaum, *Waging Peace and War*, pp.

374–81; Richard D. Mahoney, *JFK: Ordeal in Africa* (Oxford, 1983). The quotation is from *Department of State Bulletin*, 2 November 1973, p. 789.

134 Lundestad, *The American Non-Policy Towards Eastern Europe*.

135 Paterson, *Meeting the Communist Threat*, pp. 54–75. The quotation is from p. 58.

136 For a discussion of the recent literature on the Korean War, see Philip West, "Interpreting the Korean War," *American Historical Review*, vol. 94 (February 1989), pp. 80–96. The numbers are from *Historical Statistics of the United States*, p. 1140.

137 For a good survey of the American role, also in the early phase, see George C. Herring, *America's Longest War: The United States and Vietnam, 1950–1975* (New York, 1979).

138 Kindleberger, *The World in Depression*; Robert Gilpin, *U.S. Power and the Multinational Corporation: The Political Economy of Foreign Direct Investment* (New York, 1975), *War and Change in World Politics,* and *The Political Economy of International Relations*; David Calleo, *The Imperious Economy* (Cambridge, MA, 1982), and *Beyond American Hegemony. The Future of the Western Alliance* (New York, 1987); Stephen D. Krasner, ed., *International Regimes* (Ithaca, 1983); Keohane, *After Hegemony*; Russett, "The Mysterious Case of Vanishing Hegemony;" Susan Strange, "Cave! Hic Dragones: A Critique of Regime Analysis," *International Organization*, vol. 36 (1982), pp. 479–96.

139 Kennedy, *The Rise and Fall of the Great Powers*; Gilpin, *War and Change in World Politics*, particularly ch. 4.

140 Kennedy, *The Rise and Fall of the Great Powers*, p. 532.

141 Joseph S. Nye, "Understating U.S. Strength," *Foreign Policy*, Fall 1988, pp. 105–29; Samuel P. Huntingdon, "The U.S.—Decline or Renewal?," *Foreign Affairs*, Winter 1988/89, pp. 76–96; Walt W. Rostow, "Beware of Historians Bearing False Analogies," *Foreign Affairs*, Spring 1988, pp. 863–8 (review of Kennedy's book) and also *Foreign Affairs*, Summer 1988, pp. 1108, 1113 (Kennedy's answer and Rostow's reply); Henry Kissinger and Cyrus Vance, "Bipartisan Objectives for American Foreign Policy," *Foreign Affairs*, Summer 1988, pp. 899–921; "Dukakis and the World," *Washington Post*, 23 September 1988, p. A21 (articles by Stephen S. Rosenfeld and Charles Krauthammer).

142 Russett, "The Mysterious Case of Vanishing Hegemony," pp. 210–11; Nye, "Understating U.S. Strength," p. 106; Huntingdon, "The U.S.—Decline or Renewal?," pp. 81–2.

143 Walt W. Rostow, *Rich Countries and Poor Countries. Reflections on the Past, Lessons for the Future* (Boulder, 1987), p. 175; Rostow, "Beware of Historians Bearing False Analogies," p. 863.

144 Kennedy, *The Rise and Fall of the Great Powers*, p. 514.

145 See for instance Adam B. Ulam, *Dangerous Relations. The Soviet Union in World Politics, 1970–1982* (Oxford, 1983); David Holloway, *The Soviet Union and the Arms Race* (New Haven, 1983); Seweryn Bialer, *The Soviet Paradox. External Expansion, Internal Decline* (New York, 1986); Raymond L. Garthoff, *Detente and Confrontation. American–Soviet Relations from Nixon to Reagan* (Washington, DC, 1985).

146 Garthoff, *Detente and Confrontation*, pp. 795–6; Geir Lundestad, "Uniqueness and Pendulum Swings in US Foreign Policy," chapter 3 of this book; Gaddis, *Strategies of Containment*; Holloway, *The Soviet Union and the Arms Race*.

147 US Department of Commerce, *Statistical Abstract, 1981* (Washington, DC, 1982), p. 880.
148 Armacost, "U.S. National Interest and the Budget Crisis," p. 1.
149 See Appendix.
150 For the monetary reserves, see Wolfe, *America's Impasse*, p. 153; for the 10 largest banks, see *International Herald Tribune*, 27 July 1989, p. 15; For the investment deficits, see *The World Almanac and Book of Facts, 1989* (New York, 1988), p. 132; *New York Times*, 6 October 1988, p. D1; *The Economist*, 22 December 1989, pp. 65–6; See also Daniel Burstin, *Yen! Japan's New Financial Empire and its Threat to America* (New York, 1988); for the patent balance, see Agnew, *The United States in the World-Economy*, pp. 138–41; for the semi-conductor market, see Charles H. Ferguson, "America's High-Tech Decline," *Foreign Policy*, Spring 1989, pp. 132–5; Clyde V. Prestowitz, Jr., *Trading Places. How We Are Giving Our Future to Japan and How to Reclaim It* (New York, 1988); for technology dependence, see Aaron L. Friedberg, "The Strategic Implications of Relative Economic Decline," *Political Science Quarterly*, vol. 104 (Fall 1989), pp. 415–23.
151 The trade percentages are my own calculations based on the numbers in *Statistical Abstract, 1988* (Washington, DC); for the creditor to debtor development, see Martin and Susan Tolchin, *Buying Into America. How Foreign Money is Changing the Face of Our Nation* (New York, 1988), pp. 194–5.
152 Benjamin Friedman, *Day of Reckoning. The Consequences of American Economic Policy Under Reagan and After* (New York, 1988), pp. 223–32.
153 Daniel Yergin, "Energy Security in the 1990s," *Foreign Affairs*, Fall 1988, pp. 110–32, particularly p. 125; *US Statistical Abstract, 1978*, p. 608; Andrew Boyd, *An Atlas of World Affairs* (London, 1987), pp. 10–11; Ian Sheet, *OPEC: Twenty-Five Years of Price and Politics* (Cambridge, England, 1988).
154 Robert D. Putnam and Nicholas Bayne, *Hanging Together. Cooperation and Conflict in the Seven-Power Summits* (Cambridge, MA, 1987), p. 14.
155 Arthur M. Schlesinger,Jr., *The Imperial Presidency* (Boston, 1973); Ole N. Holsti and James N. Rosenau, *American Leadership in World Affairs. Vietnam and the Breakdown of Consensus* (Boston, 1984).
156 *The Public Papers of the Presidents of the United States. Richard Nixon, 1971* (Washington, DC, 1972), p. 804.
157 Terry L. Deibel, "Reagan's Mixed Legacy," *Foreign Policy*, Summer 1989, p. 52.
158 Lundestad, "Moralism, Presentism, Exceptionalism, Provincialism," pp. 16–17; Porter, *The Lion's Share*, pp. 282–95.
159 *The Public Papers of the Presidents of the United States. Ronald Reagan, 1982* (Washington, DC, 1983), p. 79 and *1983* (Washington, DC, 1984), pp. 265, 271. The 25 January 1988 State of the Union address is quoted from the full text as distributed by the American Embassy, Oslo.
160 Deibel, "Reagan's Mixed Legacy," p. 52.
161 For defense spending, see U.S. Arms Control and Disarmament Agency, *World Military Expenditures and Arms Transfers 1986* (Washington, DC, 1987), pp. 1–3. For the British role, see MacKenzie, *Propaganga and Empire*, pp. 1–12, 97–9, 174–6. For the economic side, see Friedman, *Day of Reckoning*, pp. 19, 31–2. See also Robert W. Tucker, "Reagan's Foreign Policy," *Foreign Affairs*, 1988/89, pp. 1–27.
162 Joanna Gowa, *Closing the Gold Window. Domestic Politics and the End of Bretton Woods* (Ithaca, 1983).
163 Helen Milner, "Trading Places: Industries for Free Trade," *World Politics*, vol. 40 (April 1988), pp. 350–76.

164 Lipson, *Standing Guard*, particularly pp. 134–5, 142–3, 148–66, 213–19; Rodman, *Sanctity versus Sovereignty*, particularly pp. 232–69, 325–40.
165 *Historical Statistics of the United States*, p. 1140; Herring, *America's Longest War*.
166 For a fine study of the Nixon Doctrine, see Robert S. Litwak, *Detente and the Nixon Doctrine. American Foreign Policy and the Pursuit of Stability, 1969– 1976* (Cambridge, England, 1984).
167 In addition to the memoirs by Carter, Brzezinski, and Vance, see Gaddis Smith, *Morality, Reason, and Power. American Diplomacy in the Carter Years* (New York, 1986), particularly pp. 111–15; Lundestad, *East, West, North, South*, pp. 133–8; Garthoff, *Detente and Confrontation*, particularly chs. 17– 27; Mike Bowker and Phil Williams, *Superpower Detente: A Reappraisal* (London, 1988), chs. 7, 9–10.
168 Garthoff, *Detente and Confrontation*, pp. 580–1; Noer, *Black Liberation*, pp. 238–52; the quotation is from *Department of State Bulletin*, 14 April 1977, p. 319, statement by Under Secretary Philip C. Habib.
169 Garthoff, *Detente and Confrontation*, p. 247; Littwak, *Detente and the Nixon Doctrine*, p. 123.
170 Garthoff, *Detente and Confrontation*, pp. 950, 971–82.
171 For analyses of Reagan's foreign policy, see David Kyvig, ed., *Reagan and the World*, (Westport, 1990).
172 David B. Ottoway, "New Realism: U.S. Seeks Local Answers to Regional Conflicts," *International Herald Tribune*, 19 September 1989, p. 2.
173 Geir Lundestad, "The United States and Western Europe under Ronald Reagan" in Kyvig, *Reagan and the World*, pp. 39–66; Stromseth, *The Origins of Flexible Response*; Garthoff, *Detente and Confrontation*, pp. 977–82, 1033–5.
174 Putnam and Bayne, *Hanging Together*, pp. 14–20, 249–50, 271–3.
175 Michael Howard, "Reassurance and Deterrence: Western Defense in the 1980s," *Foreign Affairs*, vol. 61 (1982/83), pp. 309–24. The quotation is from p. 319.
176 Lundestad, "The United States and Western Europe," in Kyvig, *Reagan and the World*, pp. 57–9; Richard C. Eichenberg, *Public Opinion and National Security in Western Europe* (Ithaca, 1989).
177 Alfred Grosser, *The Western Alliance. European–American Relations Since 1945* (London, 1980), p. 222; *The World Almanac, 1989*, p. 132.
178 Speech by Deputy Secretary of the Treasury Peter McPherson to the Institute for International Economics, 4 August 1988, *USIS Economics*, US Embassy Oslo, 4 August 1988, p. 1; US Department of State, Bureau of Public Affairs, *Western Europe. Regional Brief*, November 1988, pp. 1–6; Stuart Auerbach, "Europe 1992: Land of Opportunity Beckons," *Washington Post*, 20 March 1989, pp. 1, 24.
179 Senate Select Committee to Study Governmental Operations, *Alleged Assassination Plots Involving Foreign Leaders* (New York, 1976).
180 Ranelagh, *The Agency*; Prados, *Presidents' Secret Wars*.
181 Few attempts have apparently been made to study the rise of local power in any detail. This is certainly a subject where we need more work. For the diffusion of weapons technology, see Friedberg, "The Strategic Implications of Relative Economic Decline," pp. 423–8; the Ho quotation is from John T. McAlister, Jr., *Viet Nam: The Origins of Revolution* (New York, 1969), p. 296. See also Andrew Mack, "Why Big Nations Lose Small Wars: The Politics of Asymmetric Conflict," *World Politics*, vol. 27 (January 1975), pp. 175–200; Stephen M. Walt, *The Origins of Alliances* (Ithaca, 1987), pp. 244–51.
182 See the references under note 141. The Kissinger–Vance quotation is from

Kissinger and Vance, "Bipartisan Objectives for American Foreign Policy," p. 902; a copy of Eagleburger's speech has been provided me by the American Embassy, Oslo.

183 The quotations are from Huntingdon, "The U.S.—Decline or Renewal?," p. 77; Rostow, "Beware of Historians Bearing False Analogies," p. 867; Nye, "Understating U.S. Strength", p. 129.

184 Kennedy, *The Rise and Fall of the Great Powers*, p. 533; Kennedy, "Can the US Remain Number One?," *New York Review of Books*, 16 March 1989, pp. 36–42, particularly p. 38.

185 Gilpin, *War and Change*, particularly pp. 53–88, 231–42.

186 Kennedy, *The Rise and Fall of the Great Powers*, pp. 514–15.

187 Lance E. Davis and Robert A. Huttenbach, *Mammon and the Pursuit of Empire. The Political Economy of British Imperialism, 1860–1912* (Cambridge, England, 1986), particularly pp. 304–5, 315–16; Patrick K. O'Brien, "The Costs and Benefits of British Imperialism 1864–1914," *Past and Present*, August 1988, particularly pp. 191–3.

188 Friedberg, *The Weary Titan*, pp. 90, 131.

189 Friedberg, *The Weary Titan*, pp. 297–8.

190 Henry S. Rowen and Charles Wolf, Jr., eds., *The Future of the Soviet Empire* (New York, 1987), esp. pp. 129–40, 283; Michael Marrese and Jan Vanous, *Soviet Subsidization of Trade with Eastern Europe: A Soviet Perspective* (University of California Institute of International Studies, Berkeley, 1983); Paul Marer, "The Political Economy of Soviet Relations with Eastern Europe," in Sarah Meiklejohn Terry, ed., *Soviet Policy in Eastern Europe* (New Haven, 1984), pp. 155–88, particularly pp. 171–80; Josef C. Brada, "Interpreting the Soviet Subsidization of Eastern Europe," *International Organization*, vol. 42 (Autumn 1988), pp. 639–58; David Holloway and Jane M. O. Sharp, eds., *The Warsaw Pact. Alliance in Transition* (Ithaca, 1984), pp. 60–5 (Condoleezza Rice's article), 216–17, 220–30 (Paul Marer); Nelson and Lepgold, "Alliances and Burden-sharing;" *The Economist*, 22 December 1989, p. 74.

191 Hugh S. Mosley, *The Arms Race. Economic and Social Consequences* (Lexington, 1985); Nicole Ball, *Security and Economy in the Third World* (Princeton, 1988); Charles A. Kupchan, "Defence Spending and Economic Performance," *Survival*, vol. 31 (1989), pp. 447–61; Miles Kahler, "External Ambition and Economic Performance," *World Politics*, vol. 40 (1987/88), pp. 419–51; Seymour Melman, "Limits of Military Power. Economic and Other," *International Security*, vol. 11 (Summer 1986), pp. 72–87; Richard Cohen and Peter A. Wilson, "Superpowers in Decline? Economic Performance and National Security," *Comparative Strategy*, vol. 7, pp. 99–132; Charles A. Kupchan, "Empire, Military Power, and Economic Decline," *International Security*, vol. 13 (Spring 1989), pp. 40–7.

192 Dan Oberdorfer, "Snags Hit Gorbachev Economics," *Washington Post*, 23 April 1989, pp. 1, 38; Michael Dobbs, "Soviets Admit Massive Deficit, Call for Defense Spending Cuts," *Washington Post*, 8 June 1989, pp. 25, 27; Myron Rush, "Guns Over Growth in Soviet Policy," *International Security*, vol. 7 (1982/83), esp. p. 177; Bialer, *The Soviet Paradox*, pp. 272–92.

193 Rowen and Wolf, *The Future of the Soviet Empire*, pp. 135–8, 283.

194 Kupchan, "Defence Spending and Economic Performance," pp. 452, 460, note 30; Melman, "Limits of Military Power," pp. 75–85.

195 Rostow, "Beware of Historians Bearing False Analogies," pp. 864–65. See also Michael Mandelbaum, *The Fate of Nations. The Search for National Security in the Nineteenth and Twentieth Centuries* (Cambridge, England, 1989), chs. 1 (Britain) and 3 (the U.S.); Tony Smith, *The Pattern of Imperialism. The*

United States, Great Britain, and the Late-Industrializing World Since 1815
(Cambridge, England, 1981).
196 For a fine study of a complex topic, see Stephen D. Krasner, *Defending the
National Interest: Raw Materials Investments and U.S. Foreign Policy* (Princeton, 1978).
197 Kupchan, "Empire, Military Power, and Economic Decline," pp. 47–52;
Friedberg, *The Weary Titan*, pp. 130–1, 232–4.
198 Huntingdon, "The U.S.—Decline or Renewal?," p. 92.
199 Kennedy, *The Rise and Fall of the Great Powers*, p. 514; Walter Lippmann,
U.S. Foreign Policy: Shield of the Republic (Boston, 1943), p. 9; Samuel P.
Huntingdon, "Coping with the Lippmann Gap," *Foreign Affairs*, vol. 66
(1987/88), pp. 453–77.
200 See for instance Francis M. Bator, "Must We Retrench?," *Foreign Affairs*,
Spring 1989, pp. 93–123.
201 Huntingdon, "The U.S.—Decline or Renewal?," pp. 79, 81; Kennedy, *The
Rise and Fall of the Great Powers*, p. 534. See also Kennedy's "The Tradition
of Appeasement in British Foreign Policy, 1865–1939" in his *Strategy and Diplomacy 1870–1945* (Fontana, 1983), pp. 13–39.

Notes to Chapter 3

1 For a fairly recent treatment of the theme of American uniqueness, see Loren
Baritz, *Backfire: A History of How American Culture Led us into Vietnam and
Made us Fight the Way We Did* (New York, 1985), pp. 19–54.
2 Ronald Reagan in his speech to the American Legion, 22 February 1983, as
quoted in US Department of State, *Realism, Strength, Negotiation: Key Foreign
Policy Statements of the Reagan Administration* (Washington, DC, May 1984),
p. 6.
3 Frances FitzGerald, *America Revised: What History Textbooks Have Taught
our Children about their Country, and How and Why These Textbooks Have
Changed in Different Decades* (New York, 1980), pp. 128–45. The quotation is
from p. 137.
4 Arthur M. Schlesinger, Jr., "The Origins of the Cold War," *Foreign Affairs,*
vol. 46, (Fall 1967), p. 23.
5 William Appleman Williams, *The Tragedy of American Diplomacy* (New York,
1959; revised and enlarged ed., 1962).
6 Winston S. Churchill, *The Second World War* (London, 1948), Vol. 1: *The
Gathering Storm*, p. 162.
7 Quoted from Richard J. Barnet, *The Alliance: America-Europe-Japan: Makers
of the Postwar World* (New York, 1983), p. 248.
8 See, for instance, Adam B. Ulam, *Expansion and Coexistence: Soviet Foreign
Policy, 1917–1973.* (New York, 1974), pp. 3–30, esp. p. 12. For the Western
observer, see Schlesinger, "The Origins of the Cold War," p. 52.
9 These three factors have been taken from Seyom Brown, *The Faces of Power,
Constancy and Change in United States Foreign Policy from Truman to Reagan*
(New York, 1983), pp. 7–9.
10 Dexter Perkins, *The American Approach to Foreign Policy* (New York, 1973),
pp. 136–55. The book was originally published in 1951.
11 Frank L. Klingberg, "The Historical Alternation of Moods in American Foreign Policy," *World Politics*, vol. 2 (January 1952), pp. 239–73.
12 Henry F. Kissinger, *White House Years* (Boston, 1979), p. 12.
13 George P. Shultz, "New Realities and New Ways of Thinking," *Foreign*

Affairs, vol. 63 (Spring 1985), pp. 705–21, particularly p. 706. See also James Schlesinger, "The Eagle and the Bear," *Foreign Affairs*, vol. 63 (Summer 1985), pp. 937–961.

14 For an early version of this argument, see my "Empire by Invitation? The United States and Western Europe, 1945–1952," *Society for Historians of American Foreign Relations Newsletter*, vol. 15 (September 1984), pp. 1–21; rev. version in *Journal of Peace Research*, vol. 23 (Summer 1986), pp. 263–77.

15 This brief survey of Soviet-American relations is based primarily on my *East, West, North, South. Major Developments in International Politics 1945–1986* (Oslo-Oxford, 1985). See also Joseph S. Nye, ed., *The Making of America's Soviet Policy* (New Haven, 1984).

16 Warren F. Kimball, ed., *Churchill and Roosevelt: The Complete Correspondence*, Vol. 1: *Alliance Emerging* (Princeton, 1984), p. 421.

17 John Lewis Gaddis, *The United States and the Origins of the Cold War, 1941–1947* (New York, 1972), p. 38.

18 Hadley Cantril and Mildred Strunk, eds., *Public Opinion 1935–1946* (Princeton, 1951), pp. 370–1.

19 Harry S. Truman, *Years of Trial and Hope* (New York, 1965), pp. 378–9.

20 Quoted from Les K. Adler and Thomas G. Paterson, "Red Fascism: The Merger of Nazi Germany and Soviet Russia in the American Image of Totalitarianism, 1930's–1950's," *American Historical Review*, vol. 75 (April 1970), p. 1054, note 50.

21 George H. Gallup, *The Gallup Poll: Public Opinion 1935–1971* (New York, 1972), vol. 2: *1949–1958*, p. 1464. See also p. 1266.

22 Gerard Smith, *Doubletalk: The Story of the First Strategic Arms Limitation Talks* (New York, 1980), p. 451.

23 George H. Gallup, *The Gallup Poll: Public Opinion 1972–1977* (Wilmington, 1978), vol. 1: *1972–1975*, pp. 39, 129; vol. 2, *1976–1977*, pp. 918–19.

24 US Department of State, *Realism, Strength, Negotation*, p. 80.

25 William P. Bundy, "A Portentous Year," *Foreign Affairs*, vol. 62 (Supplement 1983), p. 496, note 15.

26 *Newsweek*, 14 December 1987, "Gorbachev in America: How the Soviets View the United States," particularly p. 16; Henry Allen, "The Great American Hero '87: Gorbachev," *International Herald Tribune*, 1 December 1987, pp. 1–2.

27 A superior account of American defense policy since 1945 is found in John Lewis Gaddis, *Strategies of Containment: A Critical Appraisal of Postwar American National Security Policy* (Oxford, 1982). For the defense budget figures, see p. 359.

28 *Public Papers of the Presidents of the United States: John F. Kennedy, 1961* (Washington, DC, 1962), p. 1.

29 Gaddis, *Strategies of Containment*, p. 359. See also Samuel P. Huntington, "The Defense Policy of the Reagan Administration, 1981–1982," in Fred I. Greenstein, ed., *The Reagan Presidency: An Early Assessment* (Baltimore, 1983), pp. 82–8.

30 Bill Keller, "As Military Buildup Eases, US Evaluates Spending," *International Herald Tribune*, 22 May 1985, p. 1.

31 US Department of State, *Realism, Strength, Negotiation*, p. 3.

32 *International Herald Tribune*, 22 May 1985, p. 5.

33 *SIPRI Yearbook 1989: World Armaments and Disarmament* (London, 1989), pp. 139–40; Kathy Sawyer, "Cheney Sees Arms Cuts as East Relaxes," *International Herald Tribune*, 20 November 1989, pp. 1, 4.

34 Churchill, *The Second World War*, vol. 3: *The Grand Alliance*, p. 331.

35 For a brief analysis of the British public's attitude to the Soviet Union during the Second World War, see Paul Addison, *The Road to 1945* (London, 1977), pp. 134–41. For the elite level, see also D. Cameron Watt, "Britain, the United States and the Opening of the Cold War," in Ritchie Ovendale, ed., *The Foreign Policy of the British Labour Governments, 1945–1951* (Leicester, 1984), pp. 43–60.

36 See, for instance, Alan Bullock, *Ernest Bevin: Foreign Secretary, 1945–1951* (London, 1983), pp. 820–5.

37 For a summary of British policy toward the Soviet Union see Joseph Frankel, *British Foreign Policy 1945–1973* (London, 1975), pp. 193–203.

38 George H. Gallup, *The Gallup International Public Opinion Polls: Great Britain 1937–1975* (New York, 1977), Vol. 1: *1937–1964*, pp. 241, 325.

39 Frankel, *British Foreign Policy 1945–1973*, p. 202. See also F. S. Northedge, *Descent from Power: British Foreign Policy 1945–1973* (London, 1974), pp. 265–70.

40 Gallup, *The Gallup International Public Opinion Polls*, Vol. 2: *1965–1975*, pp. 1220, 1321.

41 Geir Lundestad, "The United States and Western Europe under Ronald Reagan," in David Kyvig, ed., *Reagan and the World* (Westport, 1990), pp. 47–51.

42 *Economist*, 28 February 1988, p. 38; Geoffrey Warner, "The Anglo-American Special Realtionship," *Diplomatic History*, vol. 3, (Fall 1989), pp. 497–9.

43 *SIPRI Yearbook 1989*, pp. 134–49, 183.

44 Schlesinger, "The Eagle and the Bear," p. 952.

45 Vojtech Mastny, *Russia's Road to the Cold War: Diplomacy, Warfare, and the Politics of Communism, 1941–1945* (New York, 1979), pp. 162–5.

46 Adam B. Ulam, *Dangerous Relations: The Soviet Union in World Politics, 1970–1982* (Oxford, 1982), pp. 86–8.

47 Quoted from Robert H. Donaldson, "Soviet Policy in South Asia," in W. Raymond Duncan, *Soviet Policy in the Third World* (New York, 1980), p. 234.

48 Strobe Talbott, *The Russians and Reagan* (New York, 1984), p. 81.

49 Bill Keller, "In Soviet Media, It's Now America the Nice," *International Herald Tribune*, 10 December 1987, p. 1; *Newsweek*, 10 December 1987, particularly p. 16.

50 *SIPRI Yearbook 1985* (London, 1985), p. 251, note b.

51 *International Herald Tribune*, 22 May 1985, pp. 1, 5.

52 *SIPRI Yearbook 1989*, pp. 150–1; Patrick E. Tyler and R. Jeffrey Smith, "Bush Knew in May of Soviet Arms Shift," *International Herald Tribune*, 12 December 1989, p. 12.

53 For a brief review of some such factors, see Nye, *The Making of America's Soviet Policy*, pp. 4–8.

54 Lundestad, "Empire by Invitation?" pp. 1–3.

55 John Lukacs, *A New History of the Cold War* (Garden City, 1966), pp. 367–73.

56 John Gaddis, "Strategies of Containment," *The Society for Historians of American Foreign Relations Newsletter*, June 1980, Vol. 11, No. 2, pp. 1–14. The quotation is from p. 11.

57 Arthur Schlesinger, Jr., "Congress and the Making of American Foreign Policy," *Foreign Affairs*, Fall 1972, Vol. 51, No. 1, pp. 78–113. The quotation is from p. 94. See also Arthur M. Schlesinger, Jr., *The Imperial Presidency* (Boston, 1973), esp. ch. 9.

58 Nye, *The Making of America's Soviet Policy*, pp. 6–7.

59 William Schneider, "Public Opinion," in Nye, *The Making of America's Soviet Policy*, pp. 11–35. See also Daniel Yankelovich and John Doble, "The Public Mood: Nuclear Weapons and the USSR," *Foreign Affairs*, vol. 63 (Fall 1984),

pp. 33–46; Joseph Fitchett, "Soviets Upgrading Weapon," *International Herald Tribune,* 12 January 1990, p. 1.

60 Sir Harold Nicolson, *Diplomacy* (Oxford, 1969), p. 120. See also Kenneth N. Waltz, *Foreign Policy and Democratic Politics: The American and British Experience* (Boston, 1967), pp. 133–9.

61 Nye, *The Making of America's Soviet Policy,* pp. 329–54, esp. pp. 348–54; George F. Kennan, *American Diplomacy, 1900–1950* (Chicago, 1963), p. 82.

62 Klingberg, "The Historical Alternation of Moods in American Foreign Policy," pp. 260–8, particularly pp. 262–3.

63 John Spanier, *Games Nations Play: Analyzing International Politics* (New York, 1972), pp. 325, 327–8.

64 George F. Kennan, "The Sources of Soviet Conduct," *Foreign Affairs,* vol. 29 (Summer 1947), pp. 581–2.

65 For interesting comments on some of these pairs, see Knud Krakau, "American Foreign Relations: A National Style?," *Diplomatic History,* vol. 8 (Summer 1984), pp. 253–72; Stanley Hoffmann, *Gulliver's Troubles: or, the Setting of American Foreign Policy* (New York, 1968), part 2, esp. pp. 177–8.

66 Kissinger, *White House Years,* p. 61.

67 Quoted from Robert Dallek, *Ronald Reagan: The Politics of Symbolism* Cambridge, MA, 1984), p. 141.

Notes to Chapter 4

1 *Department of State Bulletin,* 4 March 1945, p. 361.

2 Quoted from Martin Gilbert, *Winston S. Churchill,* vol. VII: *Road to Victory, 1941–1945* (London, 1986), pp. 1233–4.

3 *Foreign Relations of the United States* (hereafter *FRUS),* 1944, I, Hull to Winant, 18 April 1944, p. 33; Lundestad, *The American Non-Policy,* pp. 83–4.

4 The texts of the armistices are found in Senate Committee on Foreign Relations, *A Decade of American Foreign Policy. Basic Documents, 1941–1949,* (Washington DC, 1950,) pp. 455–9 (Italy), 482–5 (Bulgaria), pp 487–91 (Rumania), pp. 494–9 (Hungary). See also Lundestad, *The American Non-Policy,* pp. 81–3.

5 The best study on the events in Warsaw is Jan M. Ciechanowski, *The Warsaw Rising of 1944,* (Cambridge, England, 1974). See also Lundestad, *The American Non-Policy,* pp. 83–4, 189–90.

6 *FRUS, The Conferences at Malta and Yalta, 1945* (Washington, 1955), Briefing Book Paper, Reconstruction of Poland and the Balkans: American Interests and Soviet Attitude, undated, p. 234.

7 The most important books on the British attitude are Sir Llewellyn Woodward, *British Foreign Policy in the Second World War* (single volume), (London, 1962); Woodward, *British Foreign Policy in the Second World War* (five volumes), (London 1970–1976); Gilbert, *Winston S. Churchill;* Elisabeth Barker, *British Policy in South-East Europe in the Second World War,* (London, 1976); Graham Ross (ed.), *The Foreign Office and the Kremlin. British Documents on Anglo-Soviet Relations, 1941–45* (Cambridge, England, 1984); Victor Rothwell, *Britain and the Cold War, 1941–47* (London, 1982). See also Roy Douglas, *From War to Cold War, 1942–48* (London, 1981).

8 Gilbert, *Winston S. Churchill,* p. 756; Woodward, *British Foreign Policy* (single volume), pp. 295–6.

9 For good accounts of the percentage agreements, see Albert Resis, "The Churchill-Stalin Secret "Percentages' Agreement on the Balkans, October 1944," *American Historical Review* (April 1978), pp. 368–87; Joseph M. Siracusa, "The Night Stalin and Churchill Divided Europe: The View from Washington," *The Review of Politics* (July 1981), pp. 381–409; Bruce R. Kuniholm, *The Origins of the Cold War in the Near East. Great Power Conflict and Diplomacy in Iran, Turkey, and Greece* (Princeton, 1980), pp. 100–29. For a Soviet account denying that there was any such understanding between Churchill and Stalin, see Valentin Berezhkov, *History in the Making. Memoirs of World War II Diplomacy* (Moscow, 1983), pp. 370–2.

10 Lundestad, *The American Non-Policy*, pp. 88–92.

11 Thomas M. Campbell and George C. Herring eds, *The Diaries of Edward R. Stettinius, Jr., 1943–1946* (New York, 1975), 11 January 1945, p. 214; Robert L. Messer, *The End of an Alliance. James F. Byrnes, Roosevelt, Truman, and the Origins of the Cold War* (Chapel Hill, 1982), p. 42.

12 David Dilks ed., *The Diaries of Sir Alexander Cadogan, 1938–1945* (New York, 1972, p. 671.

13 Diane S. Clemens, *Yalta* (Oxford, 1970), p. 287. See also Vojtech Mastny, *Russia's Road to the Cold War. Diplomacy, Warfare, and the Politics of Communism, 1941–1945* (New York, 1979), pp. 242–53.

14 Fraser J. Harbutt, *The Iron Curtain. Churchill, America, and the Origins of the Cold War* (Oxford, 1986), pp. 57–8.

15 *FRUS, The Conferences at Malta and Yalta*, pp. 677-8, 711-15, 789-90; Clemens, *Yalta*, pp. 198–9; Mastny, *Russia's Road to the Cold War*, pp. 245–7.

16 Warren F. Kimball, ed., *Churchill & Roosevelt. The Complete Correspondence*, vol. III: *Alliance Declining, February 1944-April 1945* (Princeton, 1984), Roosevelt to Churchill, 29 March 1945, p. 593; Lundestad, *The American Non-Policy*, p. 195.

17 *FRUS, The Conferences at Malta and Yalta*, pp. 238–9; Ross, *The Foreign Office and the Kremlin*, pp. 53–4.

19 *FRUS, The Conferences at Malta and Yalta*, pp. 513, 738, 882, 981; Lundestad, *The American Non-Policy*, p. 263.

20 *FRUS, The Conferences at Malta and Yalta*, pp. 848, 863, 873.

21 Lynn Etheridge Davis, *The Cold War Begins. Soviet-American Conflict over Eastern Europe* (Princeton, 1974), pp. 173–6, 184–7; Messer, *The End of an Alliance*, pp. 46–7.

22 *FRUS, The Conferences at Malta and Yalta*, pp. 873, 899; Clements, *Yalta*, pp. 262–4.

23 National Archives (NA), State Department Decimal File No. 501. BC/1-945, Bohlen to Hickerson, 9 January 1945; For a study of the attitudes of State Department officials toward the Soviet Union, see Hugh De Santis, *The Diplomacy of Silence. The American Foreign Service, the Soviet Union, and the Cold War, 1933–1947* (Chicago, 1980).

24 Lundestad, *The American Non-Policy*, p. 196.

25 Gilbert, *Winston S. Churchill*, pp. 1228–9; Ross, *The Foreign Office and the Kremlin*, pp. 55–6; Dilks, *The Diaries of Sir Alexander Cadogan*, pp. 709 (11 February), 711 (13 February), 717 (20 February, 1945).

26 Gilbert, *Winston S. Churchill*, pp. 1230–1.

27 *FRUS, 1945*, V, Harriman to the Secretary of State, 7 March 1945, p. 145.

28 Kimball, *Churchill & Roosevelt Correspondence*, Roosevelt to Churchill, 15 March 1945, pp. 568–9.

29 Jaime Reynolds, "Lublin versus London. The Party and the Underground Movement in Poland, 1944–1945," *Journal of Contemporary History*, vol. 16

(1981), pp. 617–48. The quotation is from p. 644. See also Ito Takayuki, "The Genesis of the Cold War: Confrontation over Poland, 1941–44", in Yonosuke Nagai and Akira Iriye, *The Origins of the Cold War in Asia,* (New York, 1977), pp. 147–202; Anthony Polonsky and Boleslaw Drukier, *The Beginnings of Communist Rule in Poland* (London, 1980). For two Polish accounts of Western diplomacy, see Longin Pastusiak, *Roosevelt a sprawa polska 1939–1945* (Warszawa, 1980) (brief English summary); Lubomir Zyblikiewicz, *Polityka Stanow Zjednoczonych I Wielkiej Brytanii Wobec Polski 1944–1949* (Warszawa, 1984), (no English summary).

30 Lundestad, *The American Non-Policy,* p. 197.

31 Harbutt, *The Iron Curtain,* pp. 202–54, particularly pp. 234–9.

32 Harbutt, *The Iron Curtain,* pp. 105–7, particularly p. 106. See also John Lewis Gaddis, *The United States and the Origins of the Cold War, 1941–1947* (New York, 1972), pp. 230–5; Daniel Yergin, *Shattered Peace. The Origins of the Cold War and the National Security State* (Boston, 1977), pp. 100–5; Mastny, *Russia's Road to the Cold War,* pp. 284-7; Herbert Feis, *Between War and Peace. The Potsdam Conference,* (Princeton, 1960), pp. 82–5, 102–10; Melvyn P. Leffler, "Adherence to Agreements. Yalta and the Experience of the Early Cold War," *International Security,* (Summer 1986), pp. 88–123, particularly pp. 94–9.

33 Most of the rest of part IV is based on Lundestad, *The American Non-Policy,* pp. 197–205.

34 *FRUS, 1945,* V, Harriman to the Secretary of State, 7 March 1945, pp. 145–7. The quotation is from p. 146. See also *ibid.,* Grew to Harriman, 9 March 1945; NA, 860C.01/3–945, Grew to Stettinius.

35 Ministry of Foreign Affairs of the USSR, *Stalin's Correspondence with Roosevelt and Truman, 1941–1945* (New York, 1965), Roosevelt to Stalin, 1 April 1945, pp. 201–4. The quotations is from pp. 202–3.

36 Lundestad, *The American Non-Policy,* pp. 199–200; Robert J. Maddox, "Roosevelt and Stalin: The Final Days," *Continuity: A Journal of History,* (Spring 1983), pp. 113–22. Robert Dallek even argues that "had he lived, Roosevelt would probably have moved more quickly than Truman to confront the Russians." For this, see Dallek, *Franklin D. Roosevelt and American Foreign Policy, 1932-1945.* (Oxford, 1979), p. 534.

37 Harbutt, *The Iron Curtain,* p. 99.

38 *FRUS, 1945,* V, Truman to Churchill, 13 April 1945, pp. 211–12.

39 Lundestad, *The American Non-Policy,* p. 200; Woodward, *British Foreign Policy in the Second World War,* vol. III, pp. 519–39.

40 Lundestad, *The American Non-Policy,* pp. 200–1.

41 Gilbert, *Winston S. Churchill,* p. 1315.

42 *FRUS, 1945,* V, Memorandum of Conversation by Charles E. Bohlen, 9 May 1945, p. 291. See also Woodward, *British Foreign Policy in the Second World War,* vol. III, pp. 536–42; Lundestad, *The American Non-Policy,* pp. 201–3.

43 Gilbert, *Winston S. Churchill,* pp. 1329–30.

44 *FRUS, 1945,* V, Churchill to Truman, 9 June 1945, p. 334; Woodward, *British Foreign Policy in the Second World War,* vol. III, pp. 548–52. For Truman''s attitude to Hopkins's mission, see also Robert H. Ferrel ed., *Off the Record. The Private Papers of Harry S. Truman* (New York, 1980), 19 May (p. 31) and 22 May (p. 35).

46 Harbutt, *The Iron Curtain,* p. 106. Others have noted the UN-Poland connection as well. For this, see for instance Lundestad, *The American Non-Policy,* p. 204.

47 *FRUS, The Conference of Berlin (Potsdam) 1945,* (2 vol), (Washington, DC,

1960), I, Harriman to the Secretary of State, 28 June 1945, p. 278; Lundestad, *The American Non-Policy*, p. 204. For some interesting comments from the Soviet side, see Berezhkov, *History in the Making*, pp. 441–2.

48 Gilbert, *Winston S. Churchill*, pp. 1238, 1240–1; Kimball, *Churchill & Roosevelt Correspondence*, Churchill to Roosevelt, 8 March 1945, pp. 547–8.

49 Woodward, *British Foreign Policy in the Second World War*, vol. V, pp. 482–91.

50 Kimball, *Churchill & Roosevelt Correspondence*, Roosevelt to Churchill, 11 March 1945, pp. 561–2.

51 Davis, *The Cold War Begins*, pp. 257–61.

52 *FRUS, 1945*, V, Harriman to the Secretary of State, 14 March 1945, pp. 511–12; Lundestad, *The American Non-Policy*, pp. 233–34.

53 Lundestad, *The American Non-Policy*, p. 231. For a short review of developments in Rumania, see Bela Vago, "Romania" in Martin McCauley, ed., *Communist Power in Europe 1944–1949* (London, 1977) pp. 111–30. Vago writes that "most observers agree that at least a two-thirds majority opposed the [Groza] takeover" (p. 121)

54 Harbutt, *The Iron Curtain*, p. 94.

55 *FRUS, 1945*, V, Secretary of State to the Ambassador in the United Kingdom, 16 March 1945, pp. 515–16.

56 *FRUS, 1945*, V, Harriman to the Secretary of State, 24 March 1945, pp. 520–1.

57 Harbutt, *The Iron Curtain*, p. 94.

58 Kimball, *Churchill & Roosevelt Correspondence*, Roosevelt to Churchill, 21 March 1945, pp. 579–80; Churchill to Roosevelt, 3 April, pp. 606–7; Roosevelt to Churchill, 8 April, pp. 618–19.

59 Lundestad, *The American Non-Policy*, pp. 85–7; Cortland V.R. Scuyler, "The View from Romania", in Thomas T. Hammond, ed., *Winesses to the Origins of the Cold War* (Seattle, 1982), pp. 138–9.

60 Lundestad, *The American Non-Policy*, pp. 86–7; Michael M. Boll, *Cold War in the Balkans. American Foreign Policy and the Emergence of Communist Bulgaria, 1943–1947*, (Lexington, Kentucky, 1984), pp. 113–20.

61 Kimball, *Churchill & Roosevelt Correspondence*, Churchill to Roosevelt, 11 April 1945, pp. 625–6. See also Churchill to Roosevelt, 8 March, p. 547.

62 Paul D. Quinlan, *Clash over Romania. British and American Policies towards Romania: 1938–1947* (Los Angeles, 1977) pp. 105–30; Boll, *Cold War in the Balkans*, pp. 96–7, 112–13; Cyril E. Black "The Start of the Cold War in Bulgaria: A Personal View", *Review of Politics*, 2 (1979), pp. 182–3; Hammond, *Witnesses to the Origins of the Cold War*, pp. 74–9, 133–42; Davis, *The Cold War Begins*, pp. 262–3; Lundestad, *The American Non-Policy*, pp. 231–3.

63 Woodward, *British Foreign Policy in the Second World War*, vol. III, pp. 587–95; *Stalin's Correspondence with Roosevelt and Truman, 1941–1945*, Stalin to Truman, 27 May 1945, p. 239; Lundestad, *The American Non-Policy*, pp. 122–3.

64 See the references under note 63. See also Davis, *The Cold War Begins*, pp. 282–7.

65 *FRUS, The Conference of Berlin*, Briefing Book Paper: Recommended Policy on the Question of Establishing Diplomatic Relations and Concluding Peace Treaties with the Former Axis Satellite States, 29 June 1945, p. 362.

66 Woodward, *British Foreign Policy in the Second World War*, vol. V, pp. 471, 473–4, 477, 478–9, 499; Lundestad, *The American Non-Policy*, pp. 124–5.

67 Lundestad, *The American Non-Policy*, pp. 101–2, 245, 329–46, particularly pp. 342–3. For an interesting personal book on Hungary and the peace treaties, see

Stephen D. Kertesz, *Between Russia and the West. Hungary and the Illusions of Peacemaking, 1945–1947* (Notre Dame, 1984).

68 Davis, *The Cold War Begins*, pp. 288–9, 297; Lundestad, *The American Non-Policy*, p. 125.

69 Lundestad, *The American Non-Policy*, pp. 99–100.

70 By far the best study of the role of the atomic bombs is Martin J. Sherwin, *A World Destroyed. The Atomic Bomb and the Grand Alliance* (New York, 1975). See also Gregg Herken, *The Winning Weapon. The Atomic Bomb in the Cold War*. (New York, 1980); Messer, *The End of an Alliance*, pp. 84–94, 102–7, 111–14; Thomas T. Hammond, "Atomic Diplomacy Revisited," *Orbis*, vol. 4 (1975/76), pp. 1403–28. For indications of how an important scholar in the field changed his view, compare Barton Bernstein's Alperovitz-inspired presentation in his *Politics & Policies of the Truman Administration* (Chicago, 1970), pp. 15–77 with his more Sherwin-inspired article "The Uneasy Alliance: Roosevelt, Churchill, and the Atomic Bomb, 1940–1945," *The Western Political Quarterly*, vol 2 (1976), pp. 202–30. See even Gar Alperovitz's new introduction to his *Atomic Diplomacy. Hiroshima and Nagasaki. The Use of the Atomic Bomb & the American Confrontation with Soviet Power* (Penguin Books, 1985), pp. 1–60. For a good summing up of the debate on the origins of the Cold War, including the role of the atomic bomb, see Thomas G. Paterson, *On Every Front. The Making of the Cold War* (New York, 1979), particularly pp. 88–90. See also Lundestad, *The American Non-Policy*, pp. 359–69.

71 Herbert Feis, *The Atomic Bomb and the End of World War II* (Princeton, 1966), p. 36.

72 Lundestad, *The American Non-Policy*, p. 362; Hammond, *Witness to the Origins of the Cold War*, pp. 143–5; Alperovitz, *Atomic Diplomacy* (1985), notes 136 and 140, pp. 390–3.

73 Kimball, *Churchill & Roosevelt Correspondence*, Churchill to Roosevelt, 1 April 1945, pp. 603–5. For a recent summing up of the debate from the American point of view, see Theodore Draper's articles "Eisenhower: At War, 1943–1945," *The New York Review of Books*, 25 September 1986, pp. 30–42; 9 October, pp. 34–40; 23 October, pp. 61–7.

74 The preceding and the next two paragraphs are based on Lundestad, *The American Non-Policy*, pp. 372–5; Draper, "Eisenhower: At War, 1943–1945," 23 October 1986, pp. 61–4.

75 Gilbert, *Winston S. Churchill*, p. 1330; Lundestad, *The American Non-Policy*, p. 373.

76 Lundestad, *The American Non-Policy*, pp. 374–6.

77 Lundestad, ibid, pp. 379–97.

78 The quotations are from *FRUS, 1945*, V, Harriman to the Secretary of State, 12 June 1945, p. 1022; *FRUS, The Conference of Berlin*, I, Harriman to the Secretary of State, 18 June 1945, p. 728. See also Lundestad, *The American Non-Policy*, pp. 120, 205, 379–94.

79 The best study of economic leverage in US policies is still George C. Herring, Jr., *Aid to Russia, 1941–1946: Strategy, Diplomacy, and the Origins of the Cold War* (New York, 1973). See also Leon Martel, *Lend-Lease, Loans, and the Coming of the Cold War: A Study of the Implementation of Foreign Policy* (Boulder, 1979).

80 *FRUS, 1946*, VI, Byrnes to Soviet Charge, Orekhov, 12 February 1946, pp. 828–9; Lundestad, *The American Non-Policy*, pp. 384–94.

81 *FRUS, 1945*, I, Minutes of the 16th Meeting of the US Delegation, 25 April 1945, p. 390; Davis, *The Cold War Begins*, pp. 227–8.

82 *Stalin's Correspondence with Roosevelt and Truman*, Stalin to Truman, 7 June

1945, pp. 241–42); Lundestad, *The American Non-Policy*, pp. 289–91. For a superior study of Finland's role, see Tuomo Polvinen, *Between East and West. Finland in International Politics, 1944–1947*, (Minneapolis, 1986), particularly pp. 111–14, 136–8.

83 *FRUS, 1945*, IV, Memorandum prepared in the Department of State, June 23, 1945, p. 463; Lundestad, *The American Non-Policy*, pp. 154–9; Woodward, *British Foreign Policy in the Second World War*, vol. III, pp. 585–7.

84 Eduard M. Mark, "American Policy Toward Eastern Europe and the Origins of the Cold War, 1941–1946: An Alternative Interpretation," *Journal of American History*, September 1981, pp. 313–36. See also his "Charles E. Bohlen and the Acceptable Limits of Soviet Hegemony in Eastern Europe: A Memorandum of 18 October 1945," *Diplomatic History* (Spring 1979), pp. 201–13; Lundestad, *The American Non-Policy*, particularly pp. 104–6. In 1979 Eduard Mark and I had a considerable correspondence to clarify our points of agreement and disagreement.

85 Lundestad, *The American Non-Policy*, pp. 167–73. The best analysis of Soviet policies is found in Mastny, *Russia's Road to the Cold War*. I have tried to analyse Soviet policies in *The American Non-Policy*, pp. 435–65.

86 Vojtech Mastny, "The Cassandra in the Foreign Commmissariat. Maxim Litvinov and the Cold War," *Foreign Affairs*, January 1976, pp. 366–76. The quotation is from p. 373.

87 Mastny, *Russia's Road to the Cold War*, pp. 299–300.

88 *Stalin's Correspondence with Churchill and Attlee, 1941–1945*, Stalin to Churchill, 24 April 1945, pp. 330–1.

89 Churchill to Stalin, 28 April pp. 338–44, particularly pp. 340, 342.

90 Ross, *The Foreign Office and the Kremlin*, pp. 199–203. The quotation is from p. 202.

91 Charles E. Bohlen, *Witness to History, 1929–1969* (New York, 1973) pp. 175–6. For a recent study of Kennan's attitude, see David Myers "Soviet War Aims and the Grant [sic] Alliance: George Kennan's Views, 1944–1946," *Journal of Contemporary History*, 1 (1986) pp. 57–79, particularly pp. 67–71, 76–7. For interesting studies on the state of American public opinion, see Paterson, *On Every Front*, pp. 113–37; Walter LaFeber, "American Policy-Makers, Public Opinion, and the Outbreak of the Cold War, 1945–50," in Nagai and Iriye, *The Origins of the Cold War in Asia*, pp. 66–8.

92 For a discussion of the inevitability of the Cold War, see the articles by Detlef Junker, Andreas Hillgruber, Alexander Fischer, Wernker Link, and Geir Lundestad "War der Kalte Krieg unvermeidlich", *Beilage zur Wochenzeitung das Palament*, 25 June 1983, pp. 3–36. See also Robert L. Messer, "Paths Not Taken: The United States Department of State and Alternatives to Containment, 1945–46," *Diplomatic History*, Fall 1977, pp. 297–319.

93 Lundestad, *The American Non-Policy*, particularly pp. 98–104.

Appendix
US Share of World Gross National Product

	1950 %	1960 %	1970 %	1980 %	1987 %
(1)	39.3	33.9	30.2	Not available	Not available
(2)	Not available	25.9	23.0	21.5	Not available
(3)	34.2	29.7	26.5	24.4[6]	Not available
(4)	45	33	29	27	26
(5)	Not available	Not available	25	23	23

(1) Council on International Economic Policy Series; from Kenneth A. Oye, Robert J. Lieber, and Donald Rothchild, eds., *Eagle Resurgent? The Reagan Era in American Foreign Policy* (Boston, 1987), p. 10.

(2) Central Intelligence Agency Series; from Oye, Lieber, and Rothchild, *Eagle Resurgent,* p. 10.

(3) State Department, *The Planetary Product;* from Alan Wolfe, *America's Impasse. The Rise and Fall of the Politics of Growth* (New York, 1981), p. 164.

(4) Weidenbaum's estimates based on various sources; from Murray Weidenbaum, *Military Spending and the Myth of Global Overstretch* (The Center for Strategic and International Studies, Washington, DC, 1989), p. 16.

(5) Council on Competitiveness, *Competitiveness Index. Trends, Background Data and Methodology* (Washington, DC, 1988), Appendix I, no pagination.

(6) Herbert Block, *The Planetary Product in 1980: A Creative Pause* (Washington, DC, 1981), p. 31.

Index

Cooperation and Conflict

Nordic Journal of International Studies

The only journal in English devoted to studies of the foreign policies of the Scandinavian countries and to studies of international politics by Scandinavian scholars. Quarterly.

EDITOR:
Christian Thune, Institute of Political Studies, Rosenborgsgade 15, DK-1130 Copenhagen, Denmark.

ISSN: 0010-8367

Subscription can be ordered from:
Universitetsforlaget
(Norwegian University Press)
Subscription Dept.
P.O. Box 2959 Toeyen
N-0608 Oslo 6, Norway